Anonymous

Selections from the Satires of Juvenal to which is Added the fifth Satire of Persius

Vol. 1

Anonymous

Selections from the Satires of Juvenal to which is Added the fifth Satire of Persius
Vol. 1

ISBN/EAN: 9783337320775

Printed in Europe, USA, Canada, Australia, Japan

Cover: Foto ©Thomas Meinert / pixelio.de

More available books at **www.hansebooks.com**

CHASE AND STUART'S CLASSICAL SERIES.

SELECTIONS

FROM THE

SATIRES OF JUVENAL.

TO WHICH IS ADDED THE

FIFTH SATIRE OF PERSIUS.

With Notes.

BY

THOMAS CHASE,

M. A. OF HARVARD COLLEGE,
PRESIDENT OF HAVERFORD COLLEGE.

PHILADELPHIA:
ELDREDGE & BROTHER,
No. 17 North Seventh Street.
1876.

J. FAGAN & SON,
ELECTROTYPERS, PHILAD'A.

CAXTON PRESS OF SHERMAN & CO.

PREFACE.

THE text in these selections is based upon that of Jahn; but in doubtful or disputed places I have used an independent judgment, the grounds of which will be found stated in the Notes.

Few ancient authors impose a heavier task upon the commentator than Juvenal, both on account of occasional obscurities of meaning and corruptions of the text, and from the large number of antiquarian and historical allusions which require explanation. I submit my labors to the judgment of competent scholars, hoping that they will contribute to the successful and interested study of a writer in whose terse and sententious diction the Latin language shows some of its highest capabilities.

Room has been made to insert one of the satires of Persius, to give a taste of the peculiar quality of an author, who, if dainty and bookish, is attractive for his moral elevation and earnestness.

T. C.

INTRODUCTION.

IN various manuscripts of Juvenal short lives of the satirist are to be found, one of which is not uncommonly supposed to have been written by the grammarian Probus, although it is published among the memoirs attributed to Suetonius. There are but few references to the personal history of their author in the Satires themselves; for the reticent Juvenal is very unlike the confiding Horace, who wears his heart upon his sleeve. Putting together such scanty indications of the facts as we have from these two sources, an imperfect sketch may be made of a biography, which I will give nearly in the words of Macleane:

"DECIMUS JUNIUS JUVENALIS was born, possibly at Aquinum in Latium, about the beginning of Nero's reign, that is soon after A. D. 54, of respectable parents, his father being a rich libertinus, and he himself therefore ingenuus. He received the usual education of a Roman boy and youth, attending a school of rhetoric after the grammar-school. He took the toga virilis about the beginning of Vespasian's reign, A. D. 70, and having learnt rhetoric, continued to practise it as a man, not professionally, but for his own amusement. Soon after the year 100, in the early part of the reign of Trajan, Juvenal first published a volume of Satires (of which the first in our collection was one), having already recited them to large audiences. It is not unlikely that some of these, or parts of them, had been composed in the reign of Domitian (A. D. 81–96), or even earlier, but that the poet had not ventúred to make them public. He continued to write freely during Trajan's reign, which ended A. D. 117, when Juvenal was about sixty, and during the early years of Hadrian's reign, that is, till about A. D. 120. In this reign he may have lived in comfort through the liberality of the emperor, though his household was on a frugal scale, as he tells us in Sat. xi., from which (verse 65) we learn that he had property at Tibur. It is not impossible he may have lived till the accession of Antoninus Pius, who succeeded Hadrian A. D. 138, when Juvenal was eighty or a little more."

I have omitted in this sketch any allusion to Juvenal's banishment, on account of the great uncertainty which attends the whole subject. The pseudo-Suetonius says of Juvenal, "Having written a clever satire of a few verses on Paris the pantomimus, and a poet of his who was puffed up with his paltry six months' military rank, he took pains to perfect himself in this kind of writing. And yet for a very long time he did not venture to trust anything even to a small audience. But after a while he was heard by great crowds, and with great success, several times; so that he was led to insert in his new writings those verses which he had written first:

> quod non dant proceres, dabit histrio : tu Camerinos
> et Bareas, tu nobilium magna atria curas?
> praefectos Pelopea facit, Philomela tribunos. — (vii. 90 sqq.)

"The player was at that time one of the favorites at court, and many of his supporters were daily promoted. Juvenal, therefore, fell under suspicion as one who had covertly censured the times; and forthwith, under color of military promotion, though he was eighty years of age, he was removed from the city, and sent to be praefectus of a cohort which was stationed in the farthest part of Egypt. That sort of punishment was determined upon as being suited to a light and jocular offence. Within a very short time he died of vexation and disgust."

There are things intrinsically difficult of credence in this story, and it is told with great variations in the different manuscript lives. The part of the offended emperor is played by Nero and Trajan, as well as Domitian, and three of the lives make Scotland the scene of the exile, whither Juvenal is sent as praefectus militum in the hope that he would be killed in battle. Of recent scholars who accept the banishment, Hermann makes Domitian send the satirist to Scotland, Friedländer dates the event under Trajan, with whom the actor Pylades had great influence, Ribbeck under Hadrian. Macleane discredits the whole story, although allowing that, if placed in the reign of Domitian, it is not chronologically impossible. It is thought that Sidonius Apollinaris refers to Juvenal in the lines, where, after mentioning the banishment of Ovid, he adds:

> nec qui consimili deinde casu
> ad vulgi tenuem strepentis auram
> *irati fuit histriónis exsul.* — Carm. ix. 270.

From the Satires themselves, it would appear that Juvenal was most certainly writing after Domitian had perished in A. D. 96, for he speaks of the death of that emperor (iv. 153); and after the conviction of Marius Priscus (i. 47), which we know to have taken place in A. D. 100. The thirteenth satire was probably written as late as A. D. 127 (see verse 17); the fifteenth soon after that date (see verse 27).

There are three epigrams in Martial containing allusions to a Juvenal who is probably our satirist: one (vii. 24) against a slanderer who tried to bring about a quarrel between the two poets; another (vii. 91), sent with a Saturnalian present of nuts, in which the recipient is addressed as " facunde Juvenalis;" and a third (xii. 18), which begins with the following lines:

> Dum tu forsitan inquietus erras
> clamosa, Juvenalis, in Subura,
> aut collem dominae teris Dianae,
> dum per limina te potentiorum
> sudatrix toga ventilat, vagumque
> major Caelius et minor fatigant,
> me multos repetita post Decembres
> accepit mea rusticumque fecit
> auro Bilbilis et superba ferro.

One other witness has come down to us from the times of our poet. There is an inscription (Mommsen *Inscr. Neapol.* 4312) at Aquinum, which (with the omissions supplied in small letters) runs thus:

> cereRI · SACRVM
> d.iuNIVS · IVVENALIS
> tRIb · COH · i. DELMATARVM
> II · VIR · QVINQ · FLAMEN
> DIVI · VESPASIANI
> VOVIT · DEDICAVitqVE
> SVA   PEC

The inscription marks an altar dedicated by Juvenal to the Helvina Ceres mentioned in Sat. iii. 320.

The most interesting speculation of recent times in regard to our author was originated by Ribbeck, in his treatise *Der echte und der unechte Juvenal,* which appeared in Berlin in 1865. According to this acute scholar, the first nine satires, — with the exception of verses 1–36 in the fourth, — the eleventh satire, — with the exception of verses 1–55, — and possibly the sixteenth, are the only genuine productions of Juvenal preserved to us, and they themselves are disfigured with interpolations, corruptions, and transpositions of verses. The remaining satires, together with the introductions to the fourth and eleventh, are the tasteless forgeries of some unknown *declamator*, a hungry commonplace poet, to whose combination with a speculating bookseller they owe their origin.

That there is a marked difference between the two divisions of the reputed works of Juvenal which Ribbeck has made, cannot be denied. The satires admitted to be genuine, deal directly with men, manners, vices, follies, and are a rich storehouse of information in regard to the condition of Roman society in the time when they were written. They are the indignant voice of a live man lashing real vices of real men. The satires of the other class are declamations on stock themes, illustrated by stock characters, — Alexander, Hannibal, Priam, gods and goddesses. They could have been written by a recluse pedant; the others could only have come from a man of vigorous sense and keen observation, who knew the world. In literary execution, the satires of the second class are inferior to those of the first; it has been charged against them, not without truth, that they are spun out, their style is sometimes turgid, the illustrations sometimes inapt. These differences Ribbeck undoubtedly exaggerates. He speaks of the *declamator* with a contempt quite unwarranted. There are great beauties in the disputed satires, — whatever their defects,— to which the world will never refuse its admiration.

Ribbeck has probably succeeded in opening a question which will never be fully settled. The vital defect, however, of his argument lies in the impossibility of fixing the precise limits of possible variation in quality between different productions of the same mind. It would not be difficult to cite among the acknowledged works of other authors, ancient and modern, instances of as great difference as exists between these two divisions of Juvenal's satires. Nor is a satisfactory explanation of the variance impossible. The lively, vigorous, burning satires wrote themselves. *Fecit indignatio versum.* The others were written in cold blood, either (as I think it most probable) by a man whose reputation was already established, so that he had a market for his wares, and at an advanced age when calm reflection and even commonplace generalization are more natural than keen observation and impetuous sallies of temper, or by a young rhetorician whose fiery zeal is yet to be excited when he leaves his books and reads in actual life the stern lessons of which the seething mass of Roman society in the imperial times was full.

We have more reason to doubt whether all the satires as we have them received their author's final touches and editorial revision. Carelessness may account for some of the faults which have been charged to forgery.

It is generally safe to leave a reader to discover and observe for himself the characteristics of the author who engages his attention; but I can hardly refrain from inserting here some lively remarks of Lewis upon the great Roman satirist:

"In depicting character, in drawing scenes, even in turns of expression, Juvenal is, of all ancient authors, the most distinctly *modern.* His scenes are manipulated with a few broad touches, in which the salient points are always brought into the foreground; and it has been well observed that a painter of kindred genius would have small difficulty in transferring them to canvas. If we believed in the metempsychosis doctrine, we might almost suppose that the soul of Juvenal reappeared in Hogarth. The crowd hurrying to the sportula or ' dole ; ' the streets of Rome by day and night ; the court of Domitian, his worthless parasites and their trumpery subjects of discussion ; the poor dependent dining with the rich patron, and the insults he is exposed to ; the senator's wife eloping with a gladiator ; the interior of fashionable ladies' boudoirs, and the frivolous pursuits and superstitions of ladies of rank ; the arts and shifts of starveling poets ; the nobleman addicted to the turf ; the aspect of the city on the fall of a great minister ; a *tête-à-tête* supper of two friends : these and many other scenes of Roman life are brought before us with the vivid touches of a Defoe or a Swift. They are ' sketches ' in the modern sense ; and I know of nothing exactly resembling them in any other ancient author. The modes of expression, again, the turns of thought, the humor, are often distinctly modern, and such as we should look for in the pages of Fielding or Thackeray. The upstart coming on in his litter, which is ' filled up by himself ; ' the poor man who had nothing, it is true, ' but who lost all that nothing ' in the fire ; the sycophant who, when his patron complains of the heat, immediately ' sweats ; ' ' the rustic infant in his mother's lap, gazing with horror at the frightful mask of the actor ' when taken to the play ; the chaff, as we style it, of the fast young Roman noble directed against the plebeian whom he is going to pommel, ' Whose vinegar and beans are you distended with ? What cobbler have you been supping off sheep's-head with, you beggar ? ' the description of the fight, ' if fight it may be called, where one man does the pommelling and the

other man's part is limited to being pommelled;' the
prayer of the poor wretch that he may be allowed to return home 'with a *few* teeth left him;' the compliment
of the fisherman on presenting an enormous turbot to
Domitian, 'Depend upon it, sire, the fish got himself
caught on purpose!' the school-master whose class pro-
ceeds to 'destroy wicked tyrants,' and whose head is
made to ache by that 'dreadful Hannibal;' Hannibal
himself stalking across the Alps 'in order to amuse
school-boys, and be turned into the theme for an exercise;'
the exclamations of the Romans on hearing of the
fall of Sejanus, 'Believe me, there was something about
that man which I never liked. What a repulsive
countenance he had, to be sure!' the picture of the old
ex-Dictator, in the primitive times, trudging off with
a spade over his shoulder to a supper party, where
bacon and perhaps a trifle of fresh meat were to be the
fare, 'with a dash of haste' so as to be sure to be
in time; the advice to the civilian in a dispute with
soldiers never to commence an action, with only two legs
to plead against a thousand hobnails; such turns of expression as 'the fires, the falling in of roofs, the thousand
perils of cruel Rome, last of all, *the poets reciting in the
dog-days;*' or again, in a comparison of Orestes and
Nero, 'At any rate, Orestes did not murder his sister and
his wife, he did not poison his relations, *he did not write
rubbishy poems about Troy;*' the remark about Horace,
'Horace has had enough to eat when he cries out 'Euoe!'—
examples of this kind might be multiplied in support of my
assertion that there is in Juvenal a humor quite distinct
from the quaint humor of Plautus and the delicate banter
of Horace, of which no example existed previous to his
time in Roman literature, while modern literature fur-
nishes much that is akin to it."

D. IVNII IVVENALIS

SATVRAE.

—∘∘⦂∘⦂∘∘—

I.

SEMPER ego auditor tantum? numquamne reponam,
vexatus totiens rauci Theseide Cordi?
impune ergo mihi recitaverit ille togatas,
hic elegos? impune diem consumpserit ingens
Telephus, aut summi plena jam margine libri   5
scriptus et in tergo nec dum finitus Orestes?
nota magis nulli domus est sua, quam mihi lucus
Martis et Aeoliis vicinum rupibus antrum
Vulcani.   quid agant venti, quas torqueat umbras
Aeacus, unde alius furtivae devehat aurum   10
pelliculae, quantas jaculetur Monychus ornos,
Frontonis platani convulsaque marmora clamant
semper et adsiduo ruptae lectore columnae:
exspectes eadem a summo minimoque poeta.
et nos ergo manum ferulae subduximus, et nos   15
consilium dedimus Sullae, privatus ut altum
dormiret; stulta est clementia, cum tot ubique
vatibus occurras, periturae parcere chartae.
cur tamen hoc potius libeat decurrere campo,

B   13

per quem magnus equos Auruncae flexit alumnus,   20
si vacat ac placidi rationem admittitis, edam.

    Cum tener uxorem ducat spado, Mevia Tuscum
figat aprum et nuda teneat venabula mamma,
patricios omnis opibus cum provocet unus
quo tondente gravis juveni mihi barba sonabat,   25
cum pars Niliacae plebis, cum verna Canopi
Crispinus, Tyrias umero revocante lacernas,
ventilet aestivum digitis sudantibus aurum,
nec sufferre queat majoris pondera gemmae,
difficile est saturam non scribere. nam quis iniquae 30
tam patiens urbis, tam ferreus, ut teneat se,
causidici nova cum veniat lectica Mathonis
plena ipso, post hunc magni delator amici
et cito rapturus de nobilitate comesa
quod superest, quem Massa timet, quem munere palpat
Carus et a trepido Thymele summissa Latino?   36
quid referam quanta siccum jecur ardeat ira,   45
cum populum gregibus comitum premit hic spoliator
pupilli prostantis? et hic damnatus inani
judicio (quid enim salvis infamia nummis?)
exul ab octava Marius bibit et fruitur dis
iratis, at tu victrix provincia ploras?   50

    Haec ego non credam Venusina digna lucerna?
haec ego non agitem? sed quid magis? Heracleas
aut Diomedeas aut mugitum labyrinthi
et mare percussum puero fabrumque volantem?
cum leno accipiat moechi bona, si capiendi   55

jus nullum uxori, doctus spectare lacunar,
doctus et ad calicem vigilanti stertere naso ;
cum fas esse putet curam sperare cohortis,
qui bona donavit praesepibus et caret omni
majorum censu, dum pervolat axe citato   60
Flaminiam puer Automedon ; nam lora tenebat
ipse, lacernatae cum se jactaret amicae !
nonne libet medio ceras implere capaces
quadrivio, cum jam sexta cervice feratur,
hinc atque inde patens ac nuda paene cathedra   65
et multum referens de Maecenate supino,
signator falso, qui se lautum atque beatum
exiguis tabulis et gemma fecerat uda ?
occurrit matrona potens, quae molle Calenum
porrectura viro miscet sitiente rubetam,   70
instituitque rudes melior Lucusta propinquas
per famam et populum nigros efferre maritos.
aude aliquid brevibus Gyaris et carcere dignum,
si vis esse aliquid.   probitas laudatur et alget.
criminibus debent hortos, praetoria, mensas,   75
argentum vetus, et stantem extra pocula caprum.
quem patitur dormire nurus corruptor avarae,
quem sponsae turpes et praetextatus adulter ?
si natura negat, facit indignatio versum,
qualemcunque potest, quales ego vel Cluvienus.   80
    Ex quo Deucalion, nimbis tollentibus aequor,
navigio montem ascendit sortesque poposcit,
paulatimque anima caluerunt mollia saxa,

et maribus nudas ostendit Pyrra puellas,
quidquid agunt homines, votum, timor, ira, voluptas,   85
gaudia, discursus, nostri farrago libelli est.
et quando uberior vitiorum copia? quando
major avaritiae patuit sinus? alea quando
hos animos? neque enim loculis comitantibus itur
ad casum tabulae, posita sed luditur arca.   90
proelia quanta illic dispensatore videbis
armigero! simplexne furor sestertia centum
perdere, et horrenti tunicam non reddere servo?
quis totidem erexit villas, quis fercula septem
secreto cenavit avus? nunc sportula primo   95
limine parva sedet, turbae rapienda togatae:
ille tamen faciem prius inspicit et trepidat, ne
suppositus venias ac falso nomine poscas.
agnitus accipies.   jubet a praecone vocari
ipsos Trojugenas (nam vexant limen et ipsi   100
nobiscum): 'da praetori, da deinde tribuno.'
sed libertinus prior est. 'prior,' inquit, 'ego adsum.
cur timeam dubitemve locum defendere, quamvis
natus ad Euphraten, molles quod in aure fenestrae
arguerint, licet ipse negem? sed quinque tabernae   105
quadringenta parant.   quid confert purpura major
optandum, si Laurenti custodit in agro
conductas Corvinus oves, ego possideo plus
Pallante et Licinis?' exspectent ergo tribuni,
vincant divitiae, sacro ne cedat honori   110
nuper in hanc urbem pedibus qui venerat albis;

quandoquidem inter nos sanctissima divitiarum
majestas, etsi, funesta Pecunia, templo
nondum habitas, nullas nummorum ereximus aras,
ut colitur Pax atque Fides, Victoria, Virtus,   115
quaeque salutato crepitat Concordia nido.

    Sed cum summus honor finito computet anno
sportula quid referat, quantum rationibus addat,
quid facient comites, quibus hinc toga, calceus hinc est
et panis fumusque domi? densissima centum   120
quadrantes lectica petit, sequiturque maritum
languida vel praegnas et circumducitur uxor.
hic petit absenti, nota jam callidus arte,
ostendens vacuam et clausam pró conjuge sellam.
'Galla mea est,' inquit, 'citius dimitte.   moraris?   125
profer, Galla, caput! noli vexare, quiescet.'

    Ipse dies pulchro distinguitur ordine rerum :
sportula, deinde forum jurisque peritus Apollo,
atque triumphales, inter quas ausus habere
nescio quis titulos Aegyptius atque Arabarches,   130
cujus ad effigiem non tantum meiere fas est.
vestibulis abeunt veteres lassique clientes
votaque deponunt, quamquam longissima cenae
spes homini : caulis miseris atque ignis emendus.
optima silvarum interea pelagique vorabit   135
rex horum, vacuisque toris tantum ipse jacebit.
nam de tot pulchris et latis orbibus et tam
antiquis una comedunt patrimonia mensa.
nullus jam parasitus erit.   sed quis ferat istas

luxuriae sordes? quanta est gula, quae sibi totos   140
ponit apros, animal propter convivia natum!
poena tamen praesens, cum tu deponis amictus   .
turgidus et crudum pavonem in balnea portas.
hinc subitae mortes atque intestata senectus,
et, nova nec tristis per cunctas fabula cenas,   145
ducitur iratis plaudendum funus amicis.

   Nil erit ulterius, quod nostris moribus addat
posteritas; eadem facient cupientque minores;
omne in praecipiti vitium stetit; utere velis,
totos pande sinus! dicas hic forsitan: 'unde   150
ingenium par materiae? unde illa priorum
scribendi quodcumque animo flagrante liberet
simplicitas, "cujus non audeo dicere nomen?
quid refert dictis ignoscat Mucius an non?"
pone Tigellinum, taeda lucebis in illa,   155
qua stantes ardent, qui fixo pectore fumant,
et latum media sulcum deducis harena.'
qui dedit ergo tribus patruis aconita, vehatur
pensilibus plumis, atque illinc despiciat nos?
'cum veniet contra, digito compesce labellum.   160
accusator erit qui verbum dixerit "hic est."
securus licet Aenean Rutulumque ferocem
committas, nulli gravis est percussus Achilles
aut multum quaesitus Hylas urnamque secutus:
ense velut stricto quotiens Lucilius ardens   165
infremuit, rubet auditor, cui frigida mens est
criminibus, tacita sudant praecordia culpa:

inde irae et lacrimae.   tecum prius ergo voluta
haec animo ante tubas.   galeatum sero duelli
paenitet.' — experiar, quid concedatur in illos,   170
quorum Flaminia tegitur cinis atque Latina.

III. .

Quamvis digressu veteris confusus amici,
laudo tamen, vacuis quod sedem figere Cumis
destinet atque unum civem donare Sibyllae.
janua Baiarum est et gratum litus amoeni
secessus.   ego vel Prochytam praepono Suburae.   5
nam quid tam miserum, tam solum vidimus, ut non
deterius credas horrere incendia, lapsus
tectorum adsiduos, ac mille pericula saevae
urbis, et Augusto recitantes mense poetas ?
Sed dum tota domus reda componitur una,   10
substitit ad veteres arcus madidamque Capenam.
hic, ubi nocturnae Numa constituebat amicae,
nunc sacri fontis nemus et delubra locantur
Judaeis, quorum cophinus faenumque supellex ;
(omnis enim populo mercedem pendere jussa est   15
arbor, et ejectis mendicat silva Camenis) ;
in vallem Egeriae descendimus et speluncas
dissimiles veris.   quanto praesentius esset
numen aquae, viridi si margine cluderet undas
herba nec ingenuum violarent marmora tofum !   20
hic tunc Umbricius, 'quando artibus,' inquit, ' honestis
nullus in urbe locus, nulla emolumenta laborum,

res hodie minor est here quam fuit, atque eadem cras
deteret exiguis aliquid, proponimus illuc
ire, fatigatas ubi Daedalus exuit alas,   25
dum nova canities, dum prima et recta senectus,
dum superest Lachesi quod torqueat, et pedibus me
porto meis nullo dextram-subeunte bacillo.
cedamus patria.   vivant Artorius istic
et Catulus, maneant qui nigrum in candida vertunt, 30
quîs facile est aedem conducere, flumina, portus,
siccandam eluviem, portandum ad busta cadaver,
et praebere caput domina venale sub hasta.
quondam hi cornicines et municipalis harenae
perpetui comites notaeque per oppida buccae   35
munera nunc edunt, et verso pollice vulgus
quem jubet occidunt populariter; inde reversi
conducunt foricas, et cur non omnia? cum sint
quales ex humili magna ad fastigia rerum
extollit quotiens voluit Fortuna jocari.   40
quid Romae faciam? mentiri nescio, librum,
si malus est, nequeo laudare et poscere, motus
astrorum ignoro, funus promittere patris
nec volo nec possum, ranarum viscera numquam
inspexi; ferre ad nuptam quae mittit adulter,   45
quae mandat, norunt alii; me nemo ministro
fur erit, atque ideo nulli comes exeo, tamquam
mancus et exstinctae corpus non utile dextrae.
quis nunc diligitur, nisi conscius, et cui fervens
aestuat occultis animus semperque tacendis?   50

nil tibi se debere putat, nil conferet umquam,
participem qui te secreti fecit honesti;
carus erit Verri, qui Verrem tempore quo vult
accusare potest.   tanti tibi non sit opaci
omnis harena Tagi quodque in mare volvitur aurum, 55
ut somno careas ponendaque praemia sumas
tristis et a magno semper timearis amico.

   Quae nunc divitibus gens acceptissima nostris
et quos praecipue fugiam, properabo fateri,
nec pudor obstabit.   non possum ferre, Quirites,   60
Graecam urbem. quamvis quota portio faecis Achaei?
jam pridem Syrus in Tiberim defluxit Orontes,
et linguam et mores et cum tibicine chordas
obliquas nec non gentilia tympana secum
vexit et ad circum jussas prostare puellas: 65
ite quibus grata est picta lupa barbara mitra!
rusticus ille tuus sumit trechedipna, Quirine,
et ceromatico fert niceteria collo!
hic alta Sicyone, ast hic Amydone relicta,
hic Andro, ille Samo, hic Trallibus aut Alabandis,   70
Esquilias dictumque petunt a vimine collem,
viscera magnarum domuum dominique futuri.
ingenium velox, audacia perdita, sermo
promptus et Isaeo torrentior.   ede, quid illum
esse putes? quem vis hominem secum attulit ad nos: 75
grammaticus, rhetor, geometres, pictor, aliptes,
augur, schoenobates, medicus, magus, omnia novit
Graeculus esuriens: in caelum, jusseris, ibit.

in summa, non Maurus erat neque Sarmata nec Thrax
qui sumpsit pinnas, mediis sed natus Athenis.   80
horum ego non fugiam conchylia? me prior ille
signabit fultusque toro meliore recumbet,
advectus Romam quo pruna et cottona vento?
usque adeo nihil est, quod nostra infantia caelum
hausit Aventini, baca nutrita Sabina?   85
quid quod adulandi gens prudentissima laudat
sermonem indocti, faciem deformis amici,
et longum invalidi collum cervicibus aequat
Herculis Antaeum procul a tellure tenentis,
miratur vocem angustam, qua deterius nec   90
ille sonat quo mordetur gallina marito?
haec eadem licet et nobis laudare; sed illis
creditur.   an melior, cum Thaida sustinet aut cum
uxorem comoedus agit vel Dorida nullo
cultam palliolo? mulier nempe ipsa videtur,   95
non persona loqui; vacua et plana omnia dicas
infra ventriculum et tenui distantia rima.
nec tamen Antiochus, nec erit mirabilis illic
aut Stratocles aut cum molli Demetrius Haemo:
natio comoeda est.   rides, majore cachinno   100
concutitur; flet, si lacrimas conspexit amici,
nec dolet; igniculum brumae si tempore poscas,
accipit endromidem; si dixeris " aestuo," sudat.
[non sumus ergo pares: melior, qui semper et omni]
nocte dieque potest aliena sumere vultum   105
a facie, jactare manus, laudare paratus,

si bene ructavit, si rectum minxit amicus,
si trulla inverso crepitum dedit aurea fundo.   108
et quoniam coepit Graecorum mentio, transi   114
gymnasia atque audi facinus majoris abollae.
stoicus occidit Baream delator, amicum
discipulumque senex, ripa nutritus in illa,
ad quam Gorgonei delapsa est pinna caballi.
non est Romano cuiquam locus hic, ubi regnat
Protogenes aliquis vel Diphilus aut Hermarchus,   120
qui gentis vitio numquam partitur amicum,
solus habet; nam cum facilem stillavit in aurem
exiguum de naturae patriaeque veneno,
limine summoveor, perierunt tempora longi
servitii; nusquam minor est jactura clientis.   125
    Quod porro officium, ne nobis blandiar, aut quod
pauperis hic meritum, si curet nocte togatus
currere, cum praetor lictorem impellat et ire
praecipitem jubeat, dudum vigilantibus orbis,
ne prior Albinam et Modiam collega salutet?   130
da testem Romae tam sanctum, quam fuit hospes   137
numinis Idaei, procedat vel Numa vel qui
servavit trepidam flagranti ex aede Minervam:
protinus ad censum, de moribus ultima fiet   140
quaestio. "quot pascit servos? quot possidet agri
jugera? quam multa magnaque paropside cenat?"
quantum quisque sua nummorum servat in arca,
tantum habet et fidei.   jures licet et Samothracum
et nostrorum aras, contemnere fulmina pauper   145

creditur atque deos, dis ignoscentibus ipsis.
quid quod materiam praebet causasque jocorum
omnibus hic idem, si foeda et scissa lacerna,
si toga sordidula est et rupta calceus alter
pelle patet, vel si consuto vulnere crassum   150
atque recens linum ostendit non una cicatrix?
uil habet infelix paupertas durius in se,
quam quod ridiculos homines facit. "exeat," inquit,
"si pudor est, et de pulvino surgat equestri,
cujus res legi non sufficit, et sedeant hic   155
lenonum pueri quocumque e fornice nati;
hic plaudat nitidi praeconis filius inter
pinnirapi cultos juvenes juvenesque lanistae;
sic libitum vano, qui nos distinxit, Othoni."
quis gener hic placuit censu minor atque puellae   160
sarcinulis impar? quis pauper scribitur heres?
quando in consilio est aedilibus? agmine facto
debuerant olim tenues migrasse Quirites.
haut facile emergunt, quorum virtutibus obstat
res angusta domi; sed Romae durior illis   165
conatus: magno hospitium miserabile, magno
servorum ventres, et frugi cenula magno.
fictilibus cenare pudet, quod turpe negabis
translatus subito ad Marsos mensamque Sabellam
contentusque illic veneto duroque cucullo.   170
pars magna Italiae est, si verum admittimus, in qua
nemo togam sumit nisi mortuus. ipsa dierum
festorum herboso colitur si quando theatro

majestas, tandemque redit ad pulpita notum
exodium, cum personae pallentis hiatum 175
in gremio matris formidat rusticus infans,
aequales habitus illic similesque videbis
orchestram et populum; clari velamen honoris
sufficiunt tunicae summis aedilibus albae.
hic ultra vires habitus nitor, hic aliquid plus 180
quam satis est interdum aliena sumitur arca.
commune id vitium est, hic vivimus ambitiosa
paupertate omnes. quid te moror? omnia Romae
cum pretio. quid das, ut Cossum aliquando salutes?
ut te respiciat clauso Veiento labello? 185
ille metit barbam, crinem hic deponit amati,
plena domus libis venalibus. accipe et istud
fermentum tibi habe, praestare tributa clientes
cogimur et cultis augere peculia servis.

  Quis timet aut timuit gelida Praeneste ruinam, 190
aut positis nemorosa inter juga Volsiniis, aut
simplicibus Gabiis, aut proni Tiburis arce?
nos urbem colimus tenui tibicine fultam
magna parte sui: nam sic labentibus obstat
vilicus, et, veteris rimae cum texit hiatum, 195
securos pendente jubet dormire ruina.
vivendum est illic, ubi nulla incendia, nulli
nocte metus. jam poscit aquam, jam frivola transfert
Ucalegon, tabulata tibi jam tertia fumant,
tu nescis: nam si gradibus trepidatur ab imis, 200
ultimus ardebit, quem tegula sola tuetur
                      C

a pluvia, molles ubi reddunt ova columbae.
lectus erat Codro Procula minor, urceoli sex,
ornamentum abaci, nec non et parvulus infra
cantharus et recubans sub eodem marmore Chiron,　205
jamque vetus Graecos servabat cista libellos,
et divina opici rodebant carmina mures.
nil habuit Codrus, quis enim negat? et tamen illud
perdidit infelix totum nihil; ultimus autem
aerumnae est cumulus, quod nudum et frusta rogantem　210
nemo cibo, nemo hospitio tectoque juvabit.
si magna Asturici cecidit domus, horrida mater,
pullati proceres, differt vadimonia praetor
tunc gemimus casus urbis, tunc odimus ignem.
ardet adhuc, et jam accurrit qui marmora donet,　215
conferat impensas: hic nuda et candida signa,
hic aliquid praeclarum Euphranoris et Polycliti,
phaecasiatorum vetera ornamenta deorum,
hic libros dabit et forulos mediamque Minervam,
hic modium argenti.　meliora ac plura reponit　220
Persicus, orborum lautissimus, et merito jam
suspectus tamquam ipse suas incenderit aedes.
si potes avelli circensibus, optima Sorae
aut Fabrateriae domus aut Frusinone paratur,
quanti nunc tenebras unum conducis in annum.　225
hortulus hic puteusque brevis nec reste movendus
in tenuis plantas facili defunditur haustu.
vive bidentis amans et culti vilicus horti,
unde epulum possis centum dare Pythagoreis.

est aliquid, **quocumque loco,** quocumque **recessu,** 230
unius sese **dominum fecisse lacertae.**

Plurimus hic **aeger moritur** vigilando; sed ipsum
languorem peperit cibus inperfectus et haerens
ardenti stomacho; nam quae meritoria somnum
admittunt? magnis opibus dormitur in urbe: 235
inde caput morbi. **redarum transitus arto**
vicorum inflexu et **stantis convicia mandrae**
eripient somnum Druso vitulisque **marinis.**

Si vocat officium, turba cedente **vehetur**
dives et ingenti curret super ora Liburno, 240
atque obiter leget aut scribet vel **dormiet intus,**
namque **facit somnum clausa lectica fenestra;**
ante tamen veniet: nobis properantibus obstat
unda prior, **magno** populus premit agmine lumbos
qui sequitur, ferit hic cubito, ferit **assere duro** 245
alter, at hic tignum capiti incutit, **ille metretam;**
pinguia crura luto; planta mox undique magna
calcor, et in digito clavus mihi militis haeret.

Nonne vides, quanto celebretur sportula fumo?
centum convivae, sequitur sua quemque culina. 250
Corbulo **vix** ferret tot vasa **ingentia, tot res**
impositas capiti, quas recto vertice portat
servulus **infelix** et cursu ventilat ignem.
scinduntur tunicae sartae modo, longa coruscat
serraco veniente abies, atque altera pinum 255
plaustra vehunt, **nutant** alte populoque minantur.
nam si procubuit qui saxa Ligustica portat

axis et eversum fudit super agmina montem,
quid superest de corporibus? quis membra, quis ossa
invenit? obtritum vulgi perit omne cadaver   260
more animae.   domus interea secura patellas
jam lavat et bucca foculum excitat et sonat unctis
striglibus et pleno componit lintea guto.
haec inter pueros varie properantur, at ille
jam sedet in ripa taetrumque novicius horret   265
porthmea, nec sperat cenosi gurgitis alnum
infelix, nec habet quem porrigat ore trientem.

 Respice nunc alia ac diversa pericula noctis,
quod spatium tectis sublimibus, unde cerebrum
testa ferit, quotiens rimosa et curta fenestris   270
vasa cadant, quanto percussum pondere signent
et laedant silicem.   possis ignavus haberi
et subiti casus inprovidus, ad cenam si
intestatus eas: adeo tot fata, quot illa
nocte patent vigiles te praetereunte fenestrae.   275
ergo optes votumque feras miserabile tecum,
ut sint contentae patulas defundere pelves.
ebrius ac petulans, qui nullum forte cecidit,
dat poenas, noctem patitur lugentis amicum
Pelidae, cubat in faciem, mox deinde supinus.   280
[ergo non aliter poterit dormire? quibusdam]
somnum rixa facit.   sed, quamvis improbus annis
atque mero fervens, cavet hunc, quem coccina laena
vitari jubet et comitum longissimus ordo,
multum praeterea flammarum et aënea lampas;   285

me, quem luna solet deducere vel breve lumen
candelae, cujus dispenso et tempero filum,
contemnit.   miserae cognosce prooemia rixae,
si rixa est, ubi tu pulsas, ego vapulo tantum.
stat contra starique jubet: parere necesse est,   290
nam quid agas, cum te furiosus cogat et idem
fortior? "unde venis?" exclamat; "cujus aceto,
cujus conche tumes? quis tecum sectile porrum
sutor et elixi vervecis labra comedit?
nil mihi respondes? aut dic, aut accipe calcem!   295
ede, ubi consistas! in qua te quaero proseucha?"
dicere si temptes aliquid tacitusve recedas,
tantumdem est, feriunt pariter, vadimonia deinde
irati faciunt; libertas pauperis haec est:
pulsatus rogat et pugnis concisus adorat,   300
ut liceat paucis cum dentibus inde reverti.
nec tamen haec tantum metuas; nam qui spoliet te
non derit, clausis domibus postquam omnis ubique
fixa catenatae siluit compago tabernae.
interdum et ferro subitus grassator agit rem: 305
armato quotiens tutae custode tenentur
et Pomptina palus et Gallinaria pinus,
sic inde huc omnes tamquam ad vivaria currunt.
qua fornace graves, qua non incude, catenae?
maximus in vinclis ferri modus, ut timeas ne   310
vomer deficiat, ne marrae et sarcula desint.
felices proavorum atavos, felicia dicas
saecula, quae quondam sub regibus atque tribunis

C 2

viderunt uno contentam carcere Romam.

His alias poteram et pluris subnectere causas,   315
sed jumenta vocant, et sol inclinat, eundum est;
nam mihi commota jandudum mulio virga
annuit. — ergo vale nostri memor, et quotiens te
Roma tuo refici properantem reddet Aquino,
me quoque ad Helvinam Cererem vestramque Dianam 320
converte a Cumis: saturarum ego, ni pudet illas,
adjutor gelidos veniam caligatus in agros.'

IV.

Ecce iterum Crispinus, et est mihi saepe vocandus
ad partes, monstrum nulla virtute redemptum
a vitiis, aegrae solaque libidine fortes
deliciae: viduas tantum spernatur adulter.
quid refert igitur, quantis jumenta fatiget   5
porticibus, quanta nemorum vectetur in umbra,
jugera quot vicina foro, quas emerit aedes?
nemo malus felix, minime corruptor et idem
incestus, cum quo nuper vitiata jacebat
sanguine adhuc vivo terram subitura sacerdos.   10
sed nunc de factis levioribus — et tamen alter
si fecisset idem, caderet sub judice morum;
nam quod turpe bonis, Titio Seioque, decebat
Crispinum — quid agas, cum dira et foedior omni
crimine persona est? mullum sex milibus emit,   15
aequantem sane paribus sestertia libris,
ut perhibent qui de magnis majora loquuntur.

consilium laudo artificis, si munere tanto
praecipuam in tabulis ceram senis abstulit orbi;
est ratio ulterior, magnae si misit amicae,   20
quae vehitur cluso latis specularibus antro.
nil tale exspectes, emit sibi. multa videmus,
quae miser et frugi non fecit Apicius. hoc tu,
succinctus patria quondam, Crispine, papyro,
hoc pretio squamam? potuit fortasse minoris   25
piscator quam piscis emi; provincia tanti
vendit agros, sed majores Apulia vendit.
quales tunc epulas ipsum gluttisse putamus
induperatorem, cum tot sestertia, partem
exiguam et modicae sumptam de margine cenae,   30
purpureus magni ructarit scurra Palati,
jam princeps equitum, magna qui voce solebat
vendere municipes fracta de merce siluros?
incipe, Calliope! licet et considere: non est
cantandum, res vera agitur. narrate, puellae   35
Pierides! prosit mihi vos dixisse puellas.

Cum jam semianimum laceraret Flavius orbem
ultimus et calvo serviret Roma Neroni,
incidit Adriaci spatium admirabile rhombi
ante domum Veneris, quam Dorica sustinet Ancon,   40
implevitque sinus; nec enim minor haeserat illis,
quos operit glacies Maeotica ruptaque tandem
solibus effundit torrentis ad ostia Ponti,
desidia tardos et longo frigore pingues.

destinat hoc monstrum cumbae linique magister   45
pontifici summo. quis enim proponere talem
aut emere auderet, cum plena et litora multo
delatore forent? dispersi protinus algae
inquisitores agerent cum remige nudo,
non dubitaturi fugitivum dicere piscem   50
depastumque diu vivaria Caesaris, inde
elapsum veterem ad dominum debere reverti.
si quid Palfurio, si credimus Armillato,
quidquid conspicuum pulchrumque est aequore toto,
res fisci est, ubicumque natat: donabitur ergo,   55
ne pereat. jam letifero cedente pruinis
autumno, jam quartanam sperantibus aegris,
stridebat deformis hiems praedamque recentem
servabat; tamen hic properat, velut urgueat auster.
utque lacus suberant, ubi quamquam diruta servat   60
ignem Trojanum et Vestam colit Alba minorem,
obstitit intranti miratrix turba parumper;
ut cessit, facili patuerunt cardine valvae;
exclusi spectant admissa obsonia patres.
itur ad Atriden. tum Picens 'accipe,' dixit,   65
'privatis majora focis; genialis agatur
iste dies; propera stomachum laxare saginans,
et tua servatum consume in saecula rhombum;
ipse capi voluit.' quid apertius? et tamen illi
surgebant cristae: nihil est quod credere de se   70
non possit, cum laudatur dis aequa potestas.
sed derat pisci patinae mensura. vocantur

ergo in consilium proceres, quos oderat ille,
in quorum facie miserae magnaeque sedebat
pallor amicitiae.   primus, clamante Liburno   75
'currite, jam sedit!' rapta properabat abolla
Pegasus, attonitae positus modo vilicus urbi;
anne aliud tunc praefecti? quorum optimus atque
interpres legum sanctissimus, omnia, quamquam
temporibus diris, tractanda putabat inermi   80
justitia.   venit et Crispi jucunda senectus,
cujus erant mores qualis facundia, mite
ingenium.   maria ac terras populosque regenti
quis comes utilior, si clade et peste sub illa
saevitiam damnare et honestum adferre liceret   85
consilium? sed 'quid violentius aure tyranni,
cum quo de pluviis aut aestibus aut nimboso
vere locuturi fatum pendebat amici?
ille igitur numquam direxit bracchia contra
torrentem, nec civis erat qui libera posset   90
verba animi proferre et vitam inpendere vero
sic multas hiemes atque octogensima vidit
solstitia, his armis illa quoque tutus in aula.
proximus ejusdem properabat Acilius aevi,
cum juvene indigno quem mors tam saeva maneret   95
et domini gladiis tam festinata : sed olim
prodigio par est in nobilitate senectus,   .
unde fit ut malim fraterculus esse gigantis.
profuit ergo nihil misero, quod comminus ursos
figebat Numidas Albana nudus harena   100
  3 — Juv.

venator. quis enim jam non intellegat artes
patricias? quis priscum illud miratur acumen,
Brute, tuum? facile est barbato inponere regi.
nec melior vultu, quamvis ignobilis, ibat
Rubrius, offensae veteris reus atque tacendae,   105
et tamen inprobior saturam scribente cinaedo.
Montani quoque venter adest abdomine tardus,
et matutino sudans Crispinus amomo,
quantum vix redolent duo funera; saevior illo
Pompeius tenui jugulos aperire susurro,   110
et qui vulturibus servabat viscera Dacis
Fuscus, marmorea meditatus proelia villa,
et cum mortifero prudens Veiento Catullo,
qui numquam visae flagrabat amore puellae,
grande et conspicuum nostro quoque tempore mon-
    strum,   115
caecus adulator dirusque a ponte satelles,
dignus Aricinos qui mendicaret ad axes
blandaque devexae jactaret basia redae.
nemo magis rhombum stupuit: nam plurima dixit
in laevum conversus; at illi dextra jacebat   120
belua. sic pugnas Cilicis laudabat et ictus
et pegma et pueros inde ad velaria raptos.
non cedit Veiento, set ut fanaticus oestro
percussus, Bellona, tuo divinat et 'ingens
omen habes,' inquit, 'magni clarique triumphi: 125
regem aliquem capies, aut de temone Britanno
excidet Arviragus: peregrina est belua; cernis

erectas in terga sudes?' hoc defuit unum
Fabricio, patriam ut rhombi memoraret et annos.
"quidnam igitur censes? conciditur?" 'absit ab illo 130
dedecus hoc!' Montanus ait; 'testa alta paretur,
quae tenui muro spatiosum colligat orbem:
debetur magnus patinae subitusque Prometheus;
argillam atque rotam citius properate! sed ex hoc
tempore jam, Caesar, figuli tua castra sequantur.'   135
vicit digna viro sententia: noverat ille
luxuriam inperii veterem noctesque Neronis
jam medias aliamque famem, cum pulmo Falerno
arderet.   nulli major fuit usus edendi
tempestate mea: Circeis nata forent an   140
Lucrinum ad saxum Rutupinove edita fundo
ostrea, callebat primo depraendere morsu;
et semel aspecti litus dicebat echini.
surgitur, et misso proceres exire jubentur
consilio, quos Albanam dux magnus in arcem   145
traxerat attonitos et festinare coactos,
tamquam de Cattis aliquid torvisque Sycambris
dicturus, tamquam e diversis partibus orbis
anxia praecipiti venisset epistula pinna.

  atque utinam his potius nugis tota illa dedisset 150
tempora saevitiae, claras quibus abstulit urbi
inlustresque animas impune et vindice nullo!
sed periit, postquam cerdonibus esse timendus
coeperat: hoc nocuit Lamiarum caede madenti.

V.

Si te propositi nondum pudet atque eadem est mens,
ut bona summa putes aliena vivere quadra,
si potes illa pati, quae nec Sarmentus iniquas
Caesaris ad mensas nec vilis Gabba tulisset,
quamvis jurato metuam tibi credere testi.   5
ventre nihil novi frugalius; hoc tamen ipsum
defecisse puta, quod inani sufficit alvo:
nulla crepido vacat? nusquam pons et tegetis pars
dimidia brevior? tantine injuria cenae?
tam jejuna fames, cum possit honestius illic   10
et tremere et sordes farris mordere canini?

   Primo fige loco, quod tu discumbere jussus
mercedem solidam veterum capis officiorum.
fructus amicitiae magnae cibus; inputat hunc rex,
et quamvis rarum tamen inputat. ergo duos post   15
si libuit menses neglectum adhibere clientem,
tertia ne vacuo cessaret culcita lecto,
'una simus' ait. votorum summa! quid ultra
quaeris? habet Trebius, propter quod rumpere somnum
debeat et ligulas dimittere, sollicitus ne   20
tota salutatrix jam turba peregerit orbem,
sideribus dubiis, aut illo tempore quo se
frigida circumagunt pigri serraca Bootae.

   Qualis cena tamen? vinum, quod sucida nolit
lana pati: de conviva Corybanta videbis.   25
jurgia proludunt; sed mox et pocula torques

saucius et rubra deterges vulnera mappa,
inter vos quotiens libertorumque cohortem
pugna Saguntina fervet commissa lagona.
ipse capillato diffusum consule potat   30
calcatamque tenet bellis socialibus uvam,
cardiaco numquam cyathum missurus amico;
cras bibet Albanis aliquid de montibus aut de
Setinis, cujus patriam titulumque senectus
delevit multa veteris fuligine testae,   35
quale coronati Thrasea Helvidiusque bibebant
Brutorum et Cassi natalibus.   ipse capaces
Heliadum crustas et inaequales berullo
Virro tenet phialas: tibi non committitur aurum,
vel, si quando datur, custos adfixus ibidem,   40
qui numeret gemmas, ungues observet acutos.
da veniam: praeclara illi laudatur iaspis.
nam Virro, ut multi, gemmas ad pocula transfert
a digitis, quas in vaginae fronte solebat
ponere zelotypo juvenis praelatus Iarbae: 45
tu Beneventani sutoris nomen habentem
siccabis calicem nasorum quattuor ac jam
quassatum et rupto poscentem sulpura vitro.
si stomachus domini fervet vinoque ciboque,
frigidior Geticis petitur decocta pruinis: 50
non eadem vobis poni modo vina querebar?
vos aliam potatis aquam.   tibi pocula cursor
Gaetulus dabit aut nigri manus ossea Mauri,
et cui per mediam nolis occurrere noctem,

clivosae veheris dum per monumenta Latinae: 55
flos Asiae ante ipsum, pretio majore paratus
quam fuit et Tulli census pugnacis et Anci
et, ne te teneam, Romanorum omnia regum
frivola.   quod cum ita sit, tu Gaetulum Ganymedem
respice, cum sities.   nescit tot milibus emptus   60
pauperibus miscere puer: sed forma, sed aetas
digna supercilio.   quando ad te pervenit ille?
quando rogatus adest calidae gelidaeque minister?
quippe indignatur veteri parere clienti,
quodque aliquid poscas, et quod se stante recumbas.   65
maxima quaeque domus servis est plena superbis.
ecce alius quanto porrexit murmure panem
vix fractum, solidae jam mucida frusta farinae,
quae genuinum agitent, non admittentia morsum:
sed tener et niveus mollique siligine factus   70
servatur domino.   dextram cohibere memento,
salva sit artoptae reverentia!   finge tamen te
inprobulum, superest illic qui ponere cogat:
'vis tu consuetis audax conviva canistris
impleri panisque tui novisse colorem?'   75
"scilicet hoc fuerat, propter quod saepe relicta
conjuge per montem adversum gelidasque cucurri
Esquilias, fremeret saeva cum grandine vernus
Juppiter et multo stillaret paenula nimbo!"
aspice, quam longo distinguat pectore lancem,   80
quae fertur domino squilla, et quibus undique saepta
asparagis qua despiciat convivia cauda,

dum venit excelsi manibus sublata ministri :
sed tibi dimidio constrictus cammarus ovo
ponitur, exigua feralis cena patella.   85
ipse Venafrano piscem perfundit ; at hic qui
pallidus affertur misero tibi caulis olebit
lanternam : illud enim vestris datur alveolis, quod
canna Micipsarum prora subvexit acuta,
propter quod Romae cum Boccare nemo lavatur,   90
[quod tutos etiam facit a serpentibus atris.]
mullus erit domini, quem misit Corsica vel quem
Tauromenitanae rupes, quando omne peractum est
et jam defecit nostrum mare, dum gula saevit,
retibus assiduis penitus scrutante macello   95
proxima, nec patimur Tyrrhenum crescere piscem.
instruit ergo focum provincia, sumitur illinc
quod captator emat Laenas, Aurelia vendat.
Virroni muraena datur, quae maxima venit
gurgite de Siculo ; nam dum se continet Auster,   100
dum sedet et siccat madidas in carcere pinnas,
contemnunt mediam temeraria lina Charybdim :
vos anguilla manet, longae cognata colubrae,
aut glacie aspersus maculis Tiberinus, et ipse
vernula riparum, pinguis torrente cloaca,   105
et solitus mediae cryptam penetrare Suburae.
    Ipsi pauca velim, facilem si praebeat aurem.
'nemo petit, modicis quae mittebantur amicis
a Seneca, quae Piso bonus, quae Cotta solebat
largiri ; (namque et titulis et fascibus olim   110

major habebatur donandi gloria :) solum
poscimus, ut cenes civiliter; hoc face et esto,
esto, ut nunc multi, dives tibi, pauper amicis.'

    Anseris ante ipsum magni jecur, anseribus par
altilis, et flavi dignus ferro Meleagri   115
fumat aper; post hunc tradentur tubera, si ver
tunc erit et facient optata tonitrua cenas
majores. 'tibi habe frumentum,' Alledius inquit,
'o Libye, disjunge boves, dum tubera mittas.'
structorem interea, ne qua indignatio desit,   120
saltantem spectes et chironomunta volanti
cultello, donec peragat dictata magistri
omnia; nec minimo sane discrimine refert,
quo gestu lepores et quo gallina secetur.

    Duceris planta, velut ictus ab Hercule Cacus,   125
et ponere foris, si quid temptaveris umquam
hiscere, tamquam habeas tria nomina. quando propinat
Virro tibi sumitve tuis contacta labellis
pocula? quis vestrum temerarius usque adeo, quis
perditus, ut dicat regi 'bibe?' plurima sunt, quae   130
non audent homines pertusa dicere laena;
quadringenta tibi si quis deus aut similis dîs
et melior fatis donaret homuncio, quantus
ex nihilo, quantus fieres Virronis amicus!
'da Trebio! pone ad Trebium! vis, frater, ab ipsis   135
ilibus?' o nummi, vobis hunc praestat honorem,
vos estis fratres! dominus tamen et domini rex
si vis tu fieri, nullus tibi parvolus aula

luserit Aeneas nec filia dulcior illo :
jucundum et carum sterilis facit uxor amicum.   140
set tua nunc Mygale pariat licet et pueros tres
in gremium patris fundat simul, ipse loquaci
gaudebit nido, viridem thoraca jubebit
adferri minimasque nuces assemque rogatum,
ad mensam quotiens parasitus venerit infans.   145
  Vilibus ancipites fungi ponentur amicis,
boletus domino, set quales Claudius edit
ante illum uxoris, post quem nil amplius edit.
Virro sibi et reliquis Virronibus illa jubebit
poma dari, quorum solo pascaris odore,   150
qualia perpetuus Phaeacum autumnus habebat,
credere quae possis subrepta sororibus Afris ;
tu scabie frueris mali, quod in aggere rodit
qui tegitur parma et galea metuensque flagelli
discit ab hirsuta jaculum torquere capella.   155
  Forsitan impensae Virronem parcere credas ;
hoc agit, ut doleas ; nam quae comoedia, mimus
quis melior plorante gula? ergo omnia fiunt,
si nescis, ut per lacrimas effundere bilem
cogaris pressoque diu stridere molari.   160
tu tibi liber homo et regis conviva videris :
captum te nidore suae putat ille culinae,
nec male conjectat ; quis enim tam nudus, ut illum
bis ferat, Etruscum puero si contigit aurum
vel nodus tantum et signum de paupere loro?   165
spes bene cenandi vos decipit : 'ecce dabit jam

semesum leporem atque aliquid de clunibus apri,
ad nos jam veniet minor altilis;' inde parato
intactoque omnes et stricto pane tacetis.
ille sapit, qui te sic utitur.   omnia ferre   170
si potes, et debes: pulsandum vertice raso
praebebis quandoque caput, nec dura timebis
flagra pati, his epulis et tali dignus amico!

VII.

Et spes et ratio studiorum in Caesare tantum:
solus enim tristes hac tempestate Camenas
respexit, cum jam celebres notique poetae
balneolum Gabiis, Romae conducere furnos
temptarent, nec foedum alii nec turpe putarent   5
praecones fieri, cum desertis Aganippes
vallibus esuriens migraret in atria Clio.
nam si Pieria quadrans tibi nullus in umbra
ostendatur, ames nomen victumque Machaerae,
et vendas potius, commissa quod auctio vendit   10
stantibus, oenophorum, tripodes, armaria, cistas,
Alcithoen Pacci, Thebas et Terea Fausti.
hoc satius, quam si dicas sub judice 'vidi,'
quod non vidisti; faciant equites Asiani
quamquam et Cappadoces, faciant equites Bithyni,   15
altera quos nudo traducit Gallia talo.
nemo tamen studiis indignum ferre laborem
cogetur posthac, nectit quicumque canoris
eloquium vocale modis laurumque momordit.

hoc agite, o juvenes! circumspicit et stimulat vos 20
materiamque sibi ducis indulgentia quaerit.
si qua aliunde putas rerum exspectanda tuarum
praesidia, atque ideo crocea membrana tabella
impletur, lignorum aliquid posce ocius, et quae
componis dona Veneris, Telesine, marito ; 25
aut clude et positos tinea pertunde libellos.
frange miser calamos vigilataque proelia dele,
qui facis in parva sublimia carmina cella,
ut dignus venias hederis et imagine macra.
spes nulla ulterior : didicit jam dives avarus 30
tantum admirari, tantum laudare disertos,
ut pueri Junonis avem.   sed defluit aetas
et pelagi patiens et cassidis atque ligonis.
taedia tunc subeunt animos, tunc seque suamque
Terpsichoren odit facunda et nuda senectus. 35
    Accipe nunc artes.   ne quid tibi conferat iste,
quem colis et Musarum et Apollinis aede relicta,
ipse facit versus atque uni cedit Homero
propter mille annos ; et si dulcedine famae
succensus recites, maculosas commodat aedes : 40
haec longe ferrata domus servire jubetur,
in qua sollicitas imitatur janua portas.
scit dare libertos extrema in parte sedentis
ordinis et magnas comitum disponere voces ;
nemo dabit regum quanti subsellia constant 45
et quae conducto pendent anabathra tigillo
quaeque reportandis posita est orchestra cathedris.

nos tamen hoc agimus, tenuique in pulvere sulcos
ducimus, et litus sterili versamus aratro.
nam si discedas, laqueo tenet ambitiosi   50
consuetudo mali, tenet insanabile multos
scribendi cacoethes et aegro in corde senescit.
sed vatem egregium, cui non sit publica vena,
qui nihil expositum soleat deducere, nec qui
communi feriat carmen triviale moneta,   55
hunc, qualem nequeo monstrare et sentio tantum,
anxietate carens animus facit, omnis acerbi
impatiens, cupidus silvarum aptusque bibendis
fontibus Aonidum.   neque enim cantare sub antro
Pierio thyrsumque potest contingere maesta   60
paupertas atque aeris inops, quo nocte dieque
corpus eget.   satur est, cum dicit Horatius ‘euhoe!’
qui locus ingenio, nisi cum se carmine solo
vexant et dominis Cirrae Nysaeque feruntur
pectora vestra, duas non admittentia curas?   65
magnae mentis opus nec de lodice paranda
attonitae, currus et equos faciesque deorum
aspicere et qualis Rutulum confundat Erinys.
nam si Vergilio puer et tolerabile desset
hospitium, caderent omnes a crinibus hydri,   70
surda nihil gemeret grave bucina.   poscimus, ut sit
non minor antiquo Rubrenus Lappa cothurno,
cujus et alveolos et laenam pignerat Atreus?
non habet infelix Numitor quod mittat amico,
Quintillae quod donet habet, nec defuit illi   75

unde emeret multa pascendum carne leouem
jam domitum`: constat leviori belua sumptu
nimirum, et capiunt plus intestina poetae.
contentus fama jaceat Lucanus in hortis
marmoreis; at Serrano tenuique Saleio   80
gloria quantalibet quid erit, si gloria tantum est?
curritur ad vocem jucundam et carmen amicae
Thebaidos, laetam cum fecit Statius urbem
promisitque diem: tanta dulcedine captos
adficit ille animos, tantaque libidine volgi   85
auditur; sed cum fregit subsellia versu,
esurit, intactam Paridi nisi vendat Agaven.
ille et militiae multis largitus honorem
semenstri digitos vatum circumligat auro.
quod non dant proceres, dabit histrio. tu Camerinos 90
et Baream, tu nobilium magna atria curas?
praefectos Pelopea facit, Philomela tribunos.
haut tamen invideas vati, quem pulpita pascunt.
quis tibi Maecenas, quis nunc erit aut Proculeius
aut Fabius, quis Cotta iterum, quis Lentulus alter?   95
tunc par ingenio pretium; tunc utile multis
pallere et vinum toto nescire Decembri.

    Vester porro labor fecundior, historiarum
scriptores? petit hic plus temporis atque olei plus.
nullo quippe modo millensima pagina surgit   100
omnibus et crescit multa damnosa papyro;
sic iugens rerum numerus jubet atque operum lex.
quae tamen inde seges, terrae quis fructus apertae?

quis dabit historico, quantum daret acta legenti?

  'Sed genus ignavum, quod lecto gaudet et umbra.' 105
dic igitur, quid causidicis civilia praestent
officia et magno comites in fasce libelli?
ipsi magna sonant, sed tum cum creditor audit
praecipue, vel si tetigit latus acrior illo,
qui venit ad dubium grandi cum codice nomen.   110
tunc immensa cavi spirant mendacia folles
conspuiturque sinus: veram depraendere messem
si libet, hinc centum patrimonia causidicorum,
parte alia solum russati pone Lacernae.
consedere duces, surgis tu pallidus Ajax,   115
dicturus dubia pro libertate, bubulco
judice.   rumpe miser tensum jecur, ut tibi lasso
figantur virides, scalarum gloria, palmae.
quod vocis pretium? siccus petasunculus et vas
pelamydum, aut veteres, Maurorum epimenia, bulbi, 120
aut vinum Tiberi devectum, quinque lagonae.
si quater egisti, si contigit aureus unus,
inde cadunt partes ex foedere pragmaticorum.
Aemilio dabitur quantum licet, et melius nos
egimus; hujus enim stat currus aeneus, alti   125
quadrijuges in vestibulis, atque ipse feroci
bellatore sedens curvatum hastile minatur
eminus, et statua meditatur proelia lusca.
sic Pedo conturbat, Matho deficit; exitus hic est
Tongilii, magno cum rhinocerote lavari   130
qui solet, et vexat lutulenta balnea turba,

perque forum juvenes longo premit assere Maedos,
empturus pueros, argentum, murrina, villas;
spondet enim Tyrio stlattaria purpura filo.
et tamen est illis hoc utile; purpura vendit   135
causidicum, vendunt amethystina; convenit illis
et strepitu et facie majoris vivere census.
[sed finem inpensae non servat prodiga Roma.]
fidimus eloquio? Ciceroni nemo ducentos
nunc dederit nummos, nisi fulserit anulus ingens.   140
respicit haec primum qui litigat, an tibi servi
octo, decem comites, an post te sella, togati
ante pedes. ideo conducta Paulus agebat
sardonyche, atque ideo pluris quam Gallus agebat,
quam Basilus. rara in tenui facundia panno.   145
quando licet Basilo flentem producere matrem?
quis bene dicentem Basilum ferat? accipiat te
Gallia, vel potius nutricula causidicorum
Africa, si placuit mercedem ponere linguae.

Declamare doces? o ferrea pectora Vetti,   150
cui perimit saevos classis numerosa tyrannos!
nam quaecumque sedens modo legerat, haec eadem stans
perferet atque eadem cantabit versibus isdem;
occidit miseros crambe repetita magistros.
quis color et quod sit causae genus atque ubi summa   155
quaestio, quae veniant diversae forte sagittae,
nosse velint omnes, mercedem solvere nemo.
'mercedem appellas? quid enim scio?' "culpa docentis
scilicet arguitur, quod laeva parte mamillae

nil salit Arcadico juveni, cujus mihi sexta   160
quaque die miserum dirus caput Annibal implet;
quidquid id est, de quo deliberat, an petat urbem
a Cannis, an post nimbos et fulmina cautus
circumagat madidas a tempestate cohortes.
quantum vis stipulare, et protinus accipe, quod do,   165
ut totiens illum pater audiat." haec alii sex
vel plures uno conclamant ore sophistae,
et veras agitant lites raptore relicto;
fusa venena silent, malus ingratusque maritus,
et quae jam veteres sanant mortaria caecos.   170
ergo sibi dabit ipse rudem, si nostra movebunt
consilia, et vitae diversum iter ingredietur,
ad pugnam qui rhetorica descendit ab umbra,
summula ne pereat, qua vilis tessera venit
frumenti: quippe haec merces lautissima. tempta,   175
Chrysogonus quanti doceat vel Polio quanti
lautorum pueros: artem scindes Theodori.
balnea sescentis, et pluris porticus, in qua
gestetur dominus, quotiens pluit — anne serenum
exspectet spargatque luto jumenta recenti?   180
[hic potius, namque hic mundae nitet ungula mulae.]
parte alia longis Numidarum fulta columnis
surgat et algentem rapiat cenatio solem.
quanticumque domus, veniet qui fercula docte
conponat, veniet qui plumentaria condiat.   185
hos inter sumptus sestertia Quintiliano,
ut multum, duo sufficient: res nulla minoris

constabit patri quam filius. ‘unde igitur tot
Quintilianus habet saltus?’ exempla novorum
fatorum transi: felix et pulcher et acer, 190
felix et sapiens et nobilis et generosus
adpositam nigrae lunam subtexit alutae;
felix orator quoque maximus et jaculator,
et, si perfrixit, cantat bene. distat enim, quae
sidera te excipiant modo primos incipientem 195
edere vagitus et adhuc a matre rubentem.
si Fortuna volet, fies de rhetore consul;
si volet haec eadem, fies de consule rhetor.
Ventidius quid enim? quid Tullius? anne aliud quam
sidus et occulti miranda potentia fati? 200
servis regna dabunt, captivis fata triumphum.
felix ille tamen corvo quoque rarior albo,
paenituit multos vanae sterilisque cathedrae,
sicut Tharsymachi probat exitus atque Secundi
Carrinatis: et hunc inopem vidistis, Athenae, 205
nil praeter gelidas ausae conferre cicutas.
di, majorum umbris tenuem et sine pondere terram
spirantisque crocos et in urna perpetuum ver,
qui praeceptorem sancti voluere parentis
esse loco! metuens virgae jam grandis Achilles 210
cantabat patriis in montibus et cui non tunc
eliceret risum citharoedi cauda magistri;
sed Rufum atque alios caedit sua quemque juventus,
Rufum, quem totiens Ciceronem Allobroga dixit.
    Quis gremio Celadi doctique Palaemonis adfert 215

4 — Juv.   E

quantum grammaticus meruit labor? et tamen ex hoc
quodcumque est (minus est autem quam rhetoris aera)
discipuli custos praemordet acoenonetus,
et qui dispensat, franget sibi.   cede, Palaemon,
et patere inde aliquid decrescere, non aliter quam   220
institor hibernae tegetis niveique cadurci :
dummodo non pereat, mediae quod noctis ab hora
sedisti, qua nemo faber, qua nemo sederet,
qui docet obliquo lanam deducere ferro ;
dummodo non pereat, totidem olfecisse lucernas,   225
quot stabant pueri, cum totus decolor esset
Flaccus et haereret nigro fuligo Maroni.
rara tamen merces, quae cognitione tribuni
non egeat.   sed vos saevas inponite leges,
ut praeceptori verborum regula constet,   230
ut legat historias, auctores noverit omnes
tamquam ungues digitosque suos, ut forte rogatus,
dum petit aut thermas aut Phoebi balnea, dicat
nutricem Anchisae, nomen patriamque novercae
Anchemoli, dicat quot Acestes vixerit annis,   235
quot Siculi Phrygibus vini donaverit urnas.
exigite ut mores teneros ceu pollice ducat,
ut si quis cera voltum facit ; exigite ut sit
et pater ipsius coetus, ne turpia ludant.
'haec,' inquit, 'cura ; set cum se verterit annus,   240
accipe, victori populus quod postulat, aurum.'

VIII.

Stemmata quid faciunt? quid prodest, Pontice, longo
sanguine censeri, pictos ostendere vultus
majorum, et stantis in curribus Aemilianos,
et Curios jam dimidios, umerosque minorem
Corvinum, et Galbam auriculis nasoque carentem?   5
quis fructus, generis tabula jactare capaci
[Corviuum, posthac multa contingere virga]
fumosos equitum cum dictatore magistros,
si coram Lepidis male vivitur? effigies quo
tot bellatorum, si luditur alea pernox   10
ante Numantinos, si dormire incipis ortu
luciferi, quo signa duces et castra movebant?
cur Allobrogicis et magna gaudeat ara
natus in Herculeo Fabius lare, si cupidus, si
vanus et Euganea quantumvis mollior agna,   15
si tenerum attritus Catinensi pumice lumbum
squalentis traducit avos, emptorque veneni
frangenda miseram funestat imagine gentem?
tota licet veteres exornent undique cerae
atria, nobilitas sola est atque unica virtus.   20
Paulus vel Cossus vel Drusus moribus esto;
hos ante effigies majorum pone tuorum,
praecedant ipsas illi te consule virgas.
prima mihi debes animi bona.   sanctus haberi
justitiaeque tenax factis dictisque mereris,   25
adgnosco procerem: salve, Gaetulice, seu tu

Silanus. quocumque alio de sanguine rarus
civis et egregius patriae contingis ovanti,
exclamare libet, populus quod clamat Osiri
iuvento. quis enim generosum dixerit hunc, qui   30
indignus genere et praeclaro nomine tantum
insignis? nanum cujusdam Atlanta vocamus,
Aethiopem Cycnum, parvam extortamque puellam
Europen; canibus pigris scabieque vetusta
levibus et siccae lambentibus ora lucernae   35
nomen erit pardus, tigris, leo, si quid adhuc est
quod fremat in terris violentius. ergo cavebis
et metues, ne tu sic Creticus aut Camerinus.

His ego quem monui? tecum est mihi sermo, Rubelli
Blande. tumes alto Drusorum stemmate, tamquam   40
feceris ipse aliquid, propter quod nobilis esses,
ut te conciperet quae sanguine fulget Iuli,
non quae ventoso conducta sub aggere texit.
'vos humiles,' inquis, 'vulgi pars ultima nostri,
quorum nemo queat patriam monstrare parentis: 45
ast ego Cecropides.' vivas et originis hujus
gaudia longa feras! tamen ima plebe Quiritem
facundum invenies; solet hic defendere causas
nobilis indocti; veniet de plebe togata,
qui juris nodos et legum aenigmata solvat.   50
hic petit Euphraten juvenis domitique Batavi
custodes aquilas, armis industrius: at tu
nil nisi Cecropides truncoque simillimus Hermae.
nullo quippe alio vincis discrimine, quam quod

illi marmoreum caput est, tua vivit imago.   55
dic mihi, Teucrorum proles, animalia muta
quis generosa putet, nisi fortia? nempe volucrem
sic laudamus equum, facili cui plurima palma
fervet et exultat rauco victoria circo.
nobilis hic, quocumque venit de gramine, cujus   60
clara fuga ante alios et primus in aequore pulvis ;
sed venale pecus Coryphaei posteritas et
Hirpini, si rara jugo Victoria sedit.
nil ibi majorum respectus, gratia nulla
umbrarum ; dominos pretiis mutare jubentur   65
exiguis, trito ducunt epiredia collo
segnipedes dignique molam versare Nepotis.
ergo ut miremur te, non tua, privum aliquid da,
quod possim titulis incidere praeter honores,
quos illis damus ac dedimus, quibus omnia debes.   70
    Haec satis ad juvenem, quem nobis fama superbum
tradit et inflatum plenumque Nerone propinquo.
rarus enim ferme sensus communis in illa
fortuna ; sed te censeri laude tuorum,
Pontice, noluerim sic ut nihil ipse futurae   75
laudis agas.   miserum est aliorum incumbere famae,
ne conlapsa ruant subductis tecta columnis.
stratus humi palmes viduas desiderat ulmos.
esto bonus miles, tutor bonus, arbiter idem
integer.   ambiguae si quando citabere testis   80
incertaeque rei, Phalaris licet imperet ut sis
falsus et admoto dictet perjuria tauro,

summum crede nefas animam praeferre pudori
et propter vitam vivendi perdere causas.
dignus morte perit, cenet licet ostrea centum   85
Gaurana et Cosmi toto mergatur aeno.
expectata diu tandem provincia cum te
rectorem accipiet, pone irae frena modumque,
pone et avaritiae, miserere inopum sociorum:
ossa vides regum vacuis exucta medullis.   90
respice, quid moneant leges, quid curia mandet,
praemia quanta bonos maneant, quam fulmine justo
et Capito et Numitor ruerint, damnante senatu,
piratae Cilicum.   sed quid damnatio confert?
praeconem, Chaerippe, tuis circumspice pannis,   95
cum Pansa eripiat, quidquid tibi Natta reliquit,
 jamque tace; furor est post omnia perdere naulon.
non idem gemitus olim neque vulnus erat par
damnorum sociis florentibus et modo victis.
plena domus tunc omnis, et ingens stabat acervos   100
nummorum, Spartana chlamys, conchylia Coa,
et cum Parrasii tabulis signisque Myronis
Phidiacum vivebat ebur, nec non Polycliti
multus ubique labor, rarae sine Mentore mensae.
inde Dolabellae atque hinc Antonius, inde   105
sacrilegus Verres referebant navibus altis
occulta spolia et plures de pace triumphos.
nunc sociis juga pauca boum; grex parvus equarum
et pater armenti capto eripietur agello,
ipsi deinde lares, si quod spectabile signum,   110

[si quis in aedicula deus unicus. haec etenim sunt
pro summis, nam sunt haec maxima. despicias tu]
forsitan inbellis Rhodios unctamque Corinthon,
despicias merito ; quid resinata juventus
cruraque totius facient tibi levia gentis?   115
horrida vitanda est Hispania, Gallicus axis
Illyricumque latus ; parce et messoribus illis,
qui saturant urbem circo scenaeque vacantem.
quanta autem inde feres tam dirae praemia culpae,
cum tenues nuper Marius discinxerit Afros?   120
curandum in primis, ne magna injuria fiat
fortibus et miseris. tollas licet omne quod usquam est
auri atque argenti, scutum gladiumque relinques
[et jaculum et galeam : spoliatis arma supersunt].
quod modo proposui, non est sententia, verum est;   125
credite me vobis folium recitare Sibyllae.
si tibi sancta cohors comitum, si nemo tribunal
vendit acersecomes, si nullum in conjuge crimen,
nec per conventus et cuncta per oppida curvis
unguibus ire parat nummos raptura Celaeno,   130
tu licet a Pico numeres genus, altaque si te
nomina delectant, omnem Titanida pugnam
inter majores ipsumque Promethea ponas :
de quocumque voles proavum tibi sumito libro.
quod si praecipitem rapit ambitio atque libido,   135
si frangis virgas sociorum in sanguine, si te
delectant hebetes lasso lictore secures,
incipit ipsorum contra te stare parentum

nobilitas claramque facem praeferre pudendis.
omne animi vitium tanto conspectius in se   140
crimen habet, quanto major qui peccat habetur.
quo mihi te solitum falsas signare tabellas
in templis quae fecit avus statuamque parentis
ante triumphalem? quo, si nocturnus adulter
tempora Santonico velas adoperta cucullo?   145
    Praeter majorum cineres atque ossa volucri
carpento rapitur pinguis Lateranus, et ipse,
ipse rotam astringit multo sufflamine consul,
nocte quidem, sed luna videt, sed sidera testes
intendunt oculos.   fiuitum tempus honoris   150
cum fuerit, clara Lateranus luce flagellum
sumet et occursum numquam trepidabit amici
jam senis, ac virga prior annuet atque maniplos
solvet et infundet jumentis hordea lassis.
interea, dum lanatas robumque juvencum   155
more Numae caedit Jovis ante altaria, jurat
solam Eponam et facies olida ad praesepia pictas.
sed cum pervigiles placet instaurare popinas,
obvius adsiduo Syrophoenix udus amomo
[currit, Idumaeae Syrophoenix incola portae,]   160
hospitis adfectu dominum regemque salutat,
et cum venali Cyane succincta lagona.
defensor culpae dicat mihi 'fecimus et nos
haec juvenes.' esto. desisti nempe, nec ultra
fovisti errorem. breve sit, quod turpiter audes;   165
quaedam cum prima resecentur crimina barba;

indulge veniam pueris.   Lateranus ad illos
thermarum calices inscriptaque lintea vadit
maturus bello Armeniae Syriaeque tuendis
amnibus et Rheno atque Histro; praestare Neronem 170
securum valet haec aetas.   mitte Ostia, Caesar,
mitte, sed in magna legatum quaere popina;
invenies aliquo cum percussore jacentem,
permixtum nautis et furibus ac fugitivis,
inter carnifices et fabros sandapilarum   175
et resupinati cessantia tympana galli.
aequa ibi libertas, communia pocula, lectus
non alius cuiquam, nec mensa remotior ulli.
quid facias talem sortitus, Pontice, servum?
nempe in Lucanos aut Tusca ergastula mittas.   180
at vos, Trojugenae, vobis ignoscitis, et quae
turpia cerdoni, Volesos Brutumque decebunt.

   Quid, si numquam adeo foedis adeoque pudendis
utimur exemplis, ut non pejora supersint?
consumptis opibus vocem, Damasippe, locasti   185
sipario, clamosum ageres ut Phasma Catulli.
Laureolum velox etiam bene Lentulus egit,
judice me dignus vera cruce.   nec tamen ipsi
ignoscas populo: populi frons durior hujus,
qui sedet et spectat triscurria patriciorum,   190
planipedes audit Fabios, ridere potest qui
Mamercorum alapas.   quanti sua funera vendant,
quid refert? vendunt nullo cogente Nerone,
nec dubitant celsi praetoris vendere ludis.

finge tamen gladios inde atque hinc pulpita poni,   195
quid satius? mortem sic quisquam exhorruit, ut sit
zelotypus Thymeles, stupidi collega Corinthi?
res haut mira tamen citharoedo principe mimus
nobilis.   haec ultra quid erit nisi ludus? et illic
dedecus urbis habes, nec myrmillonis in armis,   200
nec clipeo Gracchum pugnantem aut falce supina.
damnat enim tales habitus, et damnat et odit,
nec galea faciem abscondit.   movet ecce tridentem,
postquam vibrata pendentia retia dextra
nequiquam effudit, nudum ad spectacula voltum   205
erigit, et tota fugit agnoscendus harena.
credamus tunicae, de faucibus aurea cum se
porrigat et longo jactetur spira galero?
ergo ignominiam graviorem pertulit omni
vulnere cum Graccho jussus pugnare secutor.   210
   Libera si dentur populo suffragia, quis tam
perditus, ut dubitet Senecam praeferre Neroni,
cujus supplicio non debuit una parari
simia nec serpens unus nec culleus unus?
par Agamemnonidae crimen, sed causa facit rem   215
dissimilem: quippe ille deis auctoribus ultor
patris erat caesi media inter pocula; sed nec
Electrae jugulo se polluit aut Spartani
sanguine conjugii, nullis aconita propinquis
miscuit, in scena numquam cantavit Orestes,   220
Troica non scripsit.   quid enim Verginius armis
debuit ulcisci magis, aut cum Vindice Galba,

quod Nero tam saeva crudaque tyrannide fecit?
haec opera atque hae sunt generosi principis artes,
gaudentis foedo peregrina ad pulpita cantu 225
prostitui Graiaeque apium meruisse coronae.
majorum effigies habeant insignia vocis,
ante pedes Domiti longum tu pone Thyestae
syrma vel Antigones aut personam Menalippes,
et de marmoreo citharam suspende colosso. 230

    Quid, Catilina, tuis natalibus atque Cethegi
inveniet quisquam sublimius? arma tamen vos
nocturna et flammas domibus templisque paratis,
ut Bracatorum pueri Senonumque minores,
ausi quod liceat tunica punire molesta. 235
sed vigilat consul vexillaque vestra coercet.
hic novus Arpinas, ignobilis et modo Romae
municipalis eques, galeatum ponit ubique
praesidium attonitis et in omni monte laborat.
tantum igitur muros intra toga contulit illi 240
nominis ac tituli, quantum vix Leucade, quantum
Thessaliae campis Octavius abstulit udo
caedibus assiduis gladio; set Roma parentem,
Roma patrem patriae Ciceronem libera dixit.
Arpinas alius Volscorum in monte solebat 245
poscere mercedes, alieno lassus aratro;
nodosam post haec frangebat vertice vitem,
si lentus pigra muniret castra dolabra:
hic tamen et Cimbros et summa pericula rerum
excipit, et solus trepidantem protegit urbem; 250

atque ideo, postquam ad Cimbros stragemque volabant
qui numquam attigerant majora cadavera corvi,
nobilis ornatur lauro collega secunda.
plebeiae Deciorum animae, plebeia fuerunt
nomina: pro totis legionibus hi tamen et pro   255
omnibus auxiliis atque omni pube Latina
sufficiunt dis infernis terraeque parenti;
pluris enim Decii, quam quae servantur ab illis.
ancilla natus trabeam et diadema Quirini
et fasces meruit, regum ultimus ille bonorum.   260
prodita laxabant portarum claustra tyrannis
exulibus juvenes ipsius consulis et quos
magnum aliquid dubia pro libertate deceret,
quod miraretur cum Coclite Mucius et quae
imperii fines Tiberinum virgo natavit.   265
occulta ad patres produxit crimina servus,
matronis lugendus; at illos verbera justis
adficiunt poenis et legum prima securis.

　　Malo pater tibi sit Thersites, dummodo tu sis
Aeacidae similis Vulcaniaque arma capessas,   270
quam te Thersitae similem producat Achilles.
et tamen, ut longe repetas longeque revolvas
nomen, ab infami gentem deducis asylo:
majorum primus, quisquis fuit ille, tuorum,
aut pastor fuit aut illud quod dicere nolo.   275

X.

Omnibus in terris, quae sunt a Gadibus usque
Auroram et Gangen, pauci dinoscere possunt
vera bona atque illis multum diversa, remota
erroris nebula.   quid enim ratione timemus
aut cupimus? quid tam dextro pede concipis, ut te   5
conatus non paeniteat votique peracti?
evertere domos totas optantibus ipsis
di faciles; nocitura toga, nocitura petuntur
militia; torrens dicendi copia multis
et sua mortifera est facundia; viribus ille   10
confisus periit admirandisque lacertis.
sed plures nimia congesta pecunia cura
strangulat et cuncta exuperans patrimonia census,
quanto delphinis balaena Britannica major.
temporibus diris igitur jussuque Neronis   15
Longinum et magnos Senecae praedivitis hortos
clausit et egregias Lateranorum obsidet aedes
tota cohors.   rarus venit in cenacula miles.
pauca licet portes argenti vascula puri,
nocte iter ingressus gladium contumque timebis,   20
et motae ad lunam trepidabis harundinis umbras:
cantabit vacuus coram latrone viator.
prima fere vota et cunctis notissima templis
divitiae, crescant ut opes, ut maxima toto
nostra sit arca foro.   sed nulla aconita bibuntur   25
fictilibus; tunc illa time, cum pocula sumes

F

gemmata et lato Setinum ardebit in auro.
jamne igitur laudas, quod de sapientibus alter
ridebat, quotiens de limine moverat unum
protuleratque pedem, flebat contrarius auctor?   30
sed facilis cuivis rigidi censura cachinni:
mirandum est, unde ille oculis suffecerit umor.
perpetuo risu pulmonem agitare solebat
Democritus, quamquam non essent urbibus illis
praetexta et trabeae, fasces, lectica, tribunal.   35
quid si vidisset praetorem curribus altis
exstantem, et medii sublimem pulvere circi
in tunica Jovis, et pictae Sarrana ferentem
ex umeris aulaea togae, magnaeque coronae
tantum orbem quanto cervix non sufficit ulla?   40
quippe tenet sudans hanc publicus et, sibi consul
ne placeat, curru servus portatur eodem.
da nunc et volucrem, sceptro quae surgit eburno,
illinc cornicines, hinc praecedentia longi
agminis officia et niveos ad frena Quirites,   45
defossa in loculis quos sportula fecit amicos.
tum quoque materiam risus invenit ad omnis
occursus hominum, cujus prudentia monstrat
summos posse viros et magna exempla daturos
vervecum in patria crassoque sub aëre nasci.   50
ridebat curas, nec non et gaudia vulgi,
interdum et lacrimas, cum Fortunae ipse minaci
mandaret laqueum mediumque ostenderet unguem.

  Ergo supervacua aut vel perniciosa petuntur:

propter quae fas est genua incerare deorum. 55

Quosdam praecipitat subjecta potentia magnae
invidiae; mergit longa atque insignis honorum
pagina. descendunt statuae restemque sequuntur,
ipsas deinde rotas bigarum inpacta securis
caedit, et inmeritis franguntur crura caballis: 60
jam strident ignes, jam follibus atque caminis
ardet adoratum populo caput, et crepat ingens
Sejanus; deinde ex facie toto orbe secunda
fiunt urceoli, pelves, sartago, matellae.
pone domi laurus, duc in Capitolia magnum 65
cretatumque bovem, Sejanus ducitur unco
spectandus! gaudent omnes. 'quae labra, quis illi
vultus erat! numquam, si quid mihi credis, amavi
hunc hominem. sed quo cecidit sub crimine? quisnam
delator? quibus indiciis, quo teste probavit?' 70
"nil horum, verbosa et grandis epistula venit
a Capreis." 'bene habet; nil plus interrogo. sed quid
turba Remi?' "sequitur fortunam, ut semper, et odit
damnatos; idem pópulus, si Nortia Tusco
favisset, si oppressa foret secura senectus 75
principis, hac ipsa Sejanum diceret hora
Augustum. jam pridem, ex quo suffragia nulli
vendimus, effudit curas; nam qui dabat olim
imperium, fasces, legiones, omnia, nunc se
continet atque duas tantum res anxius optat, 80
panem et circenses." 'perituros audio multos.'
"nil dubium, magna est fornacula." 'pallidulus mi

Brutidius meus ad Martis fuit obvius aram.
quam timeo, victus ne poenas exigat Ajax
ut male defensus! curramus praecipites et,   85
dum jacet in ripa, calcemus Caesaris hostem.
sed videant servi, ne quis neget et pavidum in jus
cervice obstricta dominum trahat.'   hi sermones
tunc de Sejano, secreta haec murmura vulgi.
visne salutari sicut Sejanus? habere   90
tantundem, atque illi summas donare curules,
illum exercitibus praeponere, tutor haberi
principis angusta Caprearum in rupe sedentis
cum grege Chaldaeo? vis certe pila, cohortes,
egregios equites, et castra domestica? quidni   95
haec cupias? et qui nolunt occidere quemquam,
posse volunt.   sed quae praeclara et prospera tanti,
ut rebus laetis par sit mensura malorum?
hujus, qui trahitur, praetextam sumere mavis,
an Fidenarum Gabiorumque esse potestas   100
et de mensura jus dicere, vasa minora
frangere, pannosus vacuis aedilis Ulubris?
ergo quid optandum foret, ignorasse fateris
Sejanum; nam qui nimios optabat honores
et nimias poscebat opes, numerosa parabat   105
excelsae turris tabulata, unda altior esset
casus et impulsae praeceps immane ruinae.
quid Crassos, quid Pompeios evertit, et illum
ad sua qui domitos deduxit flagra Quirites?
summus nempe locus nulla non arte petitus,   110

magnaque numinibus vota exaudita malignis.
ad generum Cereris sine caede ac vulnere pauci
descendunt reges et sicca morte tyranni.

Eloquium ac famam Demosthenis aut Ciceronis
incipit optare et totis quinquatribus optat, 115
quisquis adhuc uno parcam colit asse Minervam,
quem sequitur custos angustae vernula capsae.
eloquio sed uterque perit orator, utrumque
largus et exundans leto dedit ingenii fons.
ingenio manus est et cervix caesa, nec umquam 120
sanguine causidici maduerunt rostra pusilli.
'o fortunatam natam me consule Romam!'
Antoni gladios potuit contemnere, si sic
omnia dixisset. ridenda poemata malo,
quam te conspicuae, divina Philippica, famae, 125
volveris a prima quae proxima. saevus et illum
exitus eripuit, quem mirabantur Athenae
torrentem et pleni moderantem frena theatri:
dis ille adversis genitus fatoque sinistro,
quem pater ardentis massae fuligine lippus 130
a carbone et forcipibus gladiosque parante
incude et luteo Vulcano ad rhetora misit.

Bellorum exuviae, truncis adfixa tropaeis
lorica, et fracta de casside buccula pendens,
et curtum temone jugum, victaeque triremis 135
aplustre, et summo tristis captivos in arcu,
humanis majora bonis creduntur. ad hoc se
Romanus Graiusque et barbarus induperator

erexit : causas discriminis atque laboris
inde habuit.   tanto major famae sitis est quam   140
virtutis ; quis enim virtutem amplectitur ipsam,
praemia si tollas? patriam tamen obruit olim
gloria paucorum et laudis titulique cupido
haesuri saxis cinerum custodibus, ad quae
discutienda valent sterilis mala robora fici,   145
quandoquidem data sunt ipsis quoque fata sepulchris.
expende Hannibalem, quot libras in duce summo
invenies? hic est, quem non capit Africa Mauro
percussa Oceano Niloque admota tepenti,
rursus ad Aethiopum populos altosque elephantos.   150
additur imperiis Hispania, Pyrenaeum
transilit.   opposuit natura Alpemque nivemque,
diducit scopulos et montem rumpit aceto.
jam tenet Italiam, tamen ultra pergere tendit.
'actum,' inquit, 'nihil est, nisi Poeno milite portas   155
frangimus et media vexillum pono Subura.'
o qualis facies et quali digna tabella,
cum Gaetula ducem portaret belua luscum!
exitus ergo quis est? o gloria! vincitur idem
nempe et in exilium praeceps fugit atque ibi magnus 160
mirandusque cliens sedet ad praetoria regis,
donec Bithyno libeat vigilare tyranno.
finem animae, quae res humanas miscuit olim,
non gladii, non saxa dabunt, nec tela, sed ille
Cannarum vindex et tanti sanguinis ultor   165
anulus.   i, demens, et saevas curre per Alpes,

ut pueris placeas et declamatio fias!
unus Pellaeo juveni non sufficit orbis,
aestuat infelix angusto limite mundi,
ut Gyari clausus scopulis parvaque Seripho ;   170
cum tamen a figulis munitam intraverit urbem,
sarcophago contentus erit. mors sola fatetur,
quantula sint hominum corpuscula. creditur olim
velificatus Athos et quidquid Graecia mendax
audet in historia, constratum classibus isdem   175
suppositumque rotis solidum mare credimus, altos
defecisse amnes epotaque flumina Medo
prandente, et madidis cantat quae Sostratus alis.
ille tamen qualis rediit Salamine relicta,
in Corum atque Eurum solitus saevire flagellis   180
barbarus, Aeolio numquam hoc in carcere passos,
ipsum compedibus qui vinxerat Ennosigaeum —
mitius id sane, quod non et stigmate dignum
credidit. huic quisquam vellet servire deorum! —
sed qualis rediit? nempe una nave, cruentis   185
fluctibus, ac tarda per densa cadavera prora.
has totiens optata exegit gloria poenas!

   'Da spatium vitae, multos da, Juppiter, annos!'
hoc recto vultu, solum hoc et pallidus optas.
sed quam continuis et quantis longa senectus   190
plena malis! deformem et taetrum ante omnia vultum
dissimilemque sui, deformem pro cute pellem
pendentisque genas et talis aspice rugas,
quales, umbriferos ubi pandit Thabraca saltus,

in vetula scalpit jam mater simia bucca.   195
plurima sunt juvenum discrimina; pulchrior ille
hoc, atque ille alio, multum hic robustior illo;
una senum facies, cum voce trementia membra
et jam leve caput madidique infantia nasi,
frangendus misero gingiva panis inermi.   200
usque adeo gravis uxori natisque sibique,
ut captatori moveat fastidia Cosso.
non eadem vini atque cibi torpente palato   203
gaudia. . . . . aspice partis
nunc damnum alterius. nam quae cantante voluptas, 210
sit licet eximius citharoedus sitve Seleucus
et quibus aurata mos est fulgere lacerna?
quid refert, magni sedeat qua parte theatri,
qui vix cornicines exaudiet atque tubarum
concentus? clamore opus est, ut sentiat auris,   215
quem dicat venisse puer, quot nuntiet horas.
praeterea minimus gelido jam in corpore sanguis
febre calet sola; circumsilit agmine facto
morborum omne genus, quorum si nomina quaeras,
promptius expediam, quot amaverit Oppia moechos
quot Themison aegros autumno occiderit uno;   221
percurram citius, quot villas possideat nunc,   225
quo tondente gravis juveni mihi barba sonabat.
ille umero, hic lumbis, hic coxa debilis; ambos
perdidit ille oculos et luscis invidet; hujus
pallida labra cibum accipiunt digitis alienis,
ipse ad conspectum cenae diducere rictum   230

suetus hiat tantum, ceu pullus hirundinis, ad quem
ore volat pleno mater jejuna. sed omni
membrorum damno major dementia, quae nec
nomina servorum nec vultum agnoscit amici,
cum quo praeterita cenavit nocte, nec illos, 235
quos genuit, quos eduxit. nam codice saevo
heredes vetat esse suos, bona tota feruntur
ad Phialen; tantum artificis valet halitus oris,
quod steterat multis in carcere fornicis annis.
ut vigeant sensus animi, ducenda tamen sunt 240
funera natorum, rogus aspiciendus amatae
conjugis et fratris plenaeque sororibus urnae.
haec data poena diu viventibus, ut renovata
semper clade domus multis in luctibus inque
perpetuo maerore et nigra veste senescant. 245
rex Pylius, magno si quidquam credis Homero,
exemplum vitae fuit a cornice secundae.
felix nimirum, qui tot per saecula mortem
distulit atque suos jam dextra computat annos,
quique novum totiens mustum bibit. oro, parumper 250
attendas, quantum de legibus ipse queratur
fatorum et nimio de stamine, cum videt acris
Antilochi barbam ardentem, cum quaerit ab omni ·
quisquis adest socius, cur haec in tempora duret,
quod facinus dignum tam longo admiserit aevo? 255
haec eadem Peleus, raptum cum luget Achillem,
atque alius, cui fas Ithacum lugere natantem.
incolumi Troja Priamus venisset ad umbras

Assaraci magnis sollemnibus, Hectore funus
portante ac reliquis fratrum cervicibus inter   260
Iliadum lacrimas, ut primos edere planctus
Cassandra inciperet scissaque Polyxena palla,
si foret exstinctus diverso tempore, quo non
coeperat audaces Paris aedificare carinas.
longa dies igitur quid contulit? omnia vidit   265
eversa et flammis Asiam ferroque cadentem.
tunc miles tremulus posita tulit arma tiara
et ruit ante aram summi Jovis, ut vetulus bos,
qui domini cultris tenue et miserabile collum
praebet, ab ingrato jam fastiditus aratro.   270
exitus ille utcumque hominis, sed torva canino
latravit rictu, quae post hunc vixerat, uxor.
festino ad nostros, et regem transeo Ponti
et Croesum, quem vox justi facunda Solonis
respicere ad longae jussit spatia ultima vitae.   275
exilium et carcer Minturnarumque paludes
et mendicatus victa Carthagine panis
hinc causas habuere.   quid illo cive tulisset
natura in terris, quid Roma beatius umquam,
si circumducto captivorum agmine et omni   280
bellorum pompa animam exhalasset opimam,
cum de Teutonico vellet descendere curru?
provida Pompeio dederat Campania febres
optandas, sed multae urbes et publica vota
vicerunt; igitur fortuna ipsius et urbis   285
servatum victo caput abstulit. hoc cruciatu

Lentulus, hac poena caruit ceciditque Cethegus
integer, et jacuit Catilina cadavere toto.

    Formam optat modico pueris, majore puellis
murmure, cum Veneris fanum videt, anxia mater   290
usque ad delicias votorum. ' cur tamen,' inquit,
' corripias? pulchra gaudet Latona Diana.'
sed vetat optari faciem Lucretia, qualem
ipsa habuit; cuperet Rutilae Verginia gibbum
accipere atque suam Rutilae dare. filius autem   295
corporis egregii miseros trepidosque parentes
semper habet; rara est adeo concordia formae
atque pudicitiae. sanctos licet horrida mores
tradiderit domus ac veteres imitata Sabinos,
praeterea castum ingenium vultumque modesto   300
sanguine ferventem tribuat natura benigna
larga manu — quid enim puero conferre potest plus
custode et cura natura potentior omni? —
non licet esse viro; nam prodiga corruptoris
improbitas ipsos audet temptare parentes.   305
' sed casto quid forma nocet?' quid profuit immo   324
Hippolyto grave propositum, quid Bellerophonti?
erubuit nempe haec, ceu fastidita, repulsa
nec Stheneboea minus quam Cressa excanduit, et se
concussere ambae. mulier saevissima tunc est,
cum stimulos odio pudor admovet. elige, quidnam
suadendum esse putes, cui nubere Caesaris uxor   330
destinat. optimus hic et formosissimus idem
gentis patriciae rapitur miser exstinguendus

Messalinae oculis; dudum sedet illa parato
flammeolo, Tyriusque palam genialis in hortis
sternitur, et ritu decies centena dabuntur   335
antiquo, veniet cum signatoribus auspex.
haec tu secreta et paucis commissa putabas?
uon nisi legitime vult nubere. quid placeat, dic:
ni parere velis, pereundum erit ante lucernas;
si scelus admittas, dabitur mora parvula, dum res   340
nota urbi et populo contingat principis aurem.
dedecus ille domus sciet ultimus; interea tu
obsequere imperio, si tanti vita dierum
paucorum. quidquid levius meliusque putaris,
praebenda est gladio pulchra haec et candida cervix. 345
   'Nil ergo optabunt homines?' si consilium vis,
permittes ipsis expendere numinibus, quid
conveniat nobis rebusque sit utile nostris.
nam pro jucundis aptissima quaeque dabunt di.
carior est illis homo, quam sibi. nos animorum   350
inpulsu et caeca magnaque cupidine ducti
conjugium petimus partumque uxoris; at illis
notum, qui pueri qualisque futura sit uxor.
ut tamen et poscas aliquid voveasque sacellis
exta et candiduli divina tomacula porci,   355
orandum est, ut sit mens sana in corpore sano.
fortem posce animum, mortis terrore carentem,
qui spatium vitae extremum inter munera ponat
naturae, qui ferre queat quoscumque labores,
nesciat irasci, cupiat nihil, et potiores   360

Herculis aerumnas credat saevosque labores
et Venere et cenis et pluma Sardanapalli.
monstro quod ipse tibi possis dare : semita certe
tranquillae per virtutem patet unica vitae.
nullum numen habes, si sit prudentia ; nos te,   365
nos facimus, Fortuna, deam caeloque locamus.

XI.

Atticus eximie si cenat, lautus habetur ;
si Rutilus, demens.   quid enim majore cachinno
excipitur vulgi, quam pauper Apicius? omnis
convictus, thermae, stationes, omne theatrum
de Rutilo.   nam dum valida ac juvenalia membra   5
sufficiunt galeae dumque ardent sanguine, fertur
(non cogente quidem, sed nec prohibente tribuno)
scripturus leges et regia verba lanistae.
multos porro vides, quos saepe elusus ad ipsum
creditor introitum solet exspectare macelli,   10
et quibus in solo vivendi causa palato est.
egregius cenat meliusque miserrimus horum
et cito casurus jam perlucente ruina.
interea gustus elementa per omnia quaerunt,
numquam animo pretiis obstantibus ; interius si   15
adtendas, magis illa juvant quae pluris emuntur.
ergo haut difficile est perituram arcessere summam
lancibus oppositis vel matris imagine fracta,
et quadringentis nummis condire gulosum
fictile : sic veniunt ad miscellanea ludi,   20

G

Refert ergo, quis haec eadem paret: in Rutilo nam
luxuria est, in Ventidio laudabile nomen
sumit et a censu famam trahit. illum ego jure
despiciam, qui scit, quanto sublimior Atlas
omnibus in Libya sit montibus, hic tamen idem   25
ignoret, quantum ferrata distet ab arca
sacculus. e caelo descendit γνῶθι σεαυτόν,
figendum et memori tractandum pectore, sive
conjugium quaeras vel sacri in parte senatus
esse velis; neque enim loricam poscit Achillis   30
Thersites, in qua se transducebat Ulixes;
ancipitem seu tu magno discrimine causam
protegere adfectas, te consule, dic tibi qui sis,
orator vehemens, an Curtius et Matho buccae.
noscenda est mensura sui spectandaque rebus   35
in summis minimisque, etiam cum piscis emetur;
ne mullum cupias, cum sit tibi gobio tantum
in loculis. quis enim te deficiente crumina
et crescente gula manet exitus, aere paterno
ac rebus mersis in ventrem fenoris atque   40
argenti gravis et pecorum agrorumque capacem?
talibus a dominis post cuncta novissimus exit
anulus, et digito mendicat Pollio nudo.
non praematuri cineres nec funus acerbum
luxuriae, sed morte magis metuenda senectus.   45
hi plerumque gradus: conducta pecunia Romae
et coram dominis consumitur; inde ubi paulum
nescio quid superest et pallet fenoris auctor,

qui vertere solum, **Baias** et ad ostrea currunt.
cedere namque foro jam non est deterius quam   50
Esquilias a ferventi migrare Subura.
ille dolor solus patriam fugientibus, illa
maestitia est, caruisse anno circensibus uno.
sanguinis in facie non haeret gutta; morantur
pauci ridiculum et fugientem ex urbe pudorem.   55
   Experiere hodie, numquid pulcherrima dictu,
Persice, non praestem vita vel moribus et re,
si laudem siliquas occultus ganeo, pultes
coram aliis dictem puero, sed in aure placentas.
nam cum sis conviva mihi promissus, habebis   60
Euandrum, venies Tirynthius aut minor illo
hospes, et ipse tamen contingens sanguine caelum,
alter aquis, alter flammis ad sidera missus.
fercula nunc audi nullis ornata macellis.
de Tiburtino veniet pinguissimus agro   65
haedulus et toto grege mollior, inscius herbae,
necdum ausus virgas humilis mordere salicti,
qui plus lactis habet quam sanguinis, et montani
asparagi, posito quos legit vilica fuso;
grandia praeterea tortoque calentia faeno   70
ova adsunt ipsis cum matribus, et servatae
parte anni quales fuerant in vitibus uvae,
Signinum Syriumque pirum, de corbibus îsdem
aemula Picenis et odoris mala recentis,
nec metuenda tibi, siccatum frigore postquam   75
autumnum et crudi posuere pericula suci.

haec olim nostri jam luxuriosa senatus
cena fuit.   Curius parvo quae legerat horto
ipse focis brevibus ponebat holuscula, quae nunc
squalidus in magna fastidit compede fossor,   80
qui meminit, calidae sapiat quid vulva popinae.
sicci terga suis, rara pendentia crate,
moris erat quondam festis servare diebus
et natalicium cognatis ponere lardum,
accedente nova, si quam dabat hostia, carne.   85
cognatorum aliquis titulo ter consulis atque
castrorum imperiis et dictatoris honore
functus ad has epulas solito maturius ibat,
erectum domito referens a monte ligonem.
cum tremerent autem Fabios durumque Catonem   90
et Scauros et Fabricios, postremo severos
censoris mores etiam collega timeret,
nemo inter curas et seria duxit habendum,
qualis in Oceani fluctu testudo nataret,
clarum Trojugenis factura et nobile fulcrum,   95
sed nudo latere et parvis frons aerea lectis
vile coronati caput ostendebat aselli,
ad quod lascivi ludebant ruris alumni.
tales ergo cibi, qualis domus atque supellex.
tunc rudis et Graias mirari nescius artes   100
urbibus eversis praedarum in parte reperta
magnorum artificum frangebat pocula miles,
ut phaleris gauderet ecus, caelataque cassis
Romuleae simulacra ferae mansuescere jussae

imperii fato, geminos sub rupe Quirinos, 105
ac nudam effigiem clipeo venientis et hasta
pendentisque dei perituro ostenderet hosti.
ponebant igitur Tusco farrata catino;
argenti quod erat, solis fulgebat in armis.
omnia tunc, quibus invideas, si lividulus sis. 110
templorum quoque majestas praesentior et vox
nocte fere media mediamque audita per urbem,
litore ab Oceani Gallis venientibus et dîs
officium vatis peragentibus. his monuit nos,
hanc rebus Latiis curam praestare solebat 115
fictilis et nullo violatus Juppiter auro.
illa domi natas nostraque ex arbore mensas
tempora viderunt; hos lignum stabat ad usus,
annosam si forte nucem dejecerat eurus.
at nunc divitibus cenandi nulla voluptas, 120
nil rhombus, nil dama sapit, putere videntur
unguenta atque rosae, latos nisi sustinet orbes
grande ebur et magno sublimis pardus hiatu,
dentibus ex illis, quos mittit porta Syenes
et Mauri celeres et Mauro obscurior Indus, 125
et quos deposuit Nabataeo belua saltu,
jam nimios capitique graves. hinc surgit orexis,
hinc stomacho vires; nam pes argenteus illis,
anulus in digito quod ferreus. ergo superbum
convivam caveo, qui me sibi comparat et res 130
despicit exiguas. adeo nulla uncia nobis
est eboris, nec tessellae, nec calculus ex hac

materia, quin ipsa manubria cultellorum
ossea; non tamen his ulla umquam obsonia fiunt
rancidula, aut ideo pejor gallina secatur.   135
sed nec structor erit, cui cedere debeat omnis
pergula, discipulus Trypheri doctoris, aput quem
sumine cum magno lepus atque aper et pygargus
et Scythicae volucres et phoenicopterus ingens
et Gaetulus oryx hebeti lautissima ferro   140
caeditur et tota sonat ulmea cena Subura.
nec frustum capreae subducere nec latus Afrae
novit avis noster, tirunculus ac rudis omni
tempore et exiguae furtis inbutus ofellae.
plebeios calices et paucis assibus emptos   145
porriget incultus puer atque a frigore tutus;
non Phryx aut Lycius, non a mangone petitus
quisquam erit et magno.   cum posces, posce Latine.
idem habitus cunctis, tonsi rectique capilli
atque hodie tantum propter convivia pexi.   150
pastoris duri hic est filius, ille bubulci.
suspirat longo non visam tempore matrem,
et casulam et notos tristis desiderat haedos,
ingenui vultus puer ingenuique pudoris,
quales esse decet quos ardens purpura vestit.   155
hic tibi vina dabit diffusa in montibus illis,   159
a quibus ipse venit, quorum sub vertice lusit;
namque una atque eadem est vini patria atque ministri.

    Nostra dabunt alios hodie convivia ludos: 179
conditor Iliados cantabitur atque Maronis

altisoni dubiam facientia carmina palmam.
quid refert, tales versus qua voce legantur?

   Sed nunc dilatis averte negotia curis   183
et gratam requiem dona tibi, quando licebit
per totum cessare diem.   non fenoris ulla
mentio, nec, prima si luce egressa reverti
nocte solet, tacito bilem tibi contrahat uxor.   187
protinus ante meum quidquid dolet exue limen;   190
pone domum et servos et quidquid frangitur illis
aut perit; ingratos ante omnia pone sodales.
interea Megalesiacae spectacula mappae,
Idaeum sollemne, colunt, similisque triumpho
praeda caballorum praetor sedet ac, mihi pace   195
immensae nimiaeque licet si dicere plebis,
totam hodie Romam circus capit et fragor aurem
percutit, eventum viridis quo colligo panni:
nam si deficeret, maestam attonitamque videres
hanc urbem, veluti Cannarum in pulvere victis   200
consulibus.   spectent juvenes, quos clamor et audax
sponsio, quos cultae decet adsedisse puellae;
nostra bibat vernum contracta cuticula solem
effugiatque togam.   jam nunc in balnea salva
fronte licet vadas, quamquam solida hora supersit   205
ad sextam.   facere hoc non possis quinque diebus
continuis, quia sunt talis quoque taedia vitae
magna; voluptates commendat rarior usus.

XIII.

Exemplo quodcumque malo committitur, ipsi
displicet auctori.   prima est haec ultio, quod se
judice nemo nocens absolvitur, improba quamvis
gratia fallaci praetoris vicerit urna.
quid sentire putas omnes, Calvine, recenti   5
de scelere et fidei violatae crimine ? sed nec
tam tenuis census tibi contigit, ut mediocris
jacturae te mergat onus, nec rara videmus
quae pateris; casus multis hic cognitus ac jam
tritus et e medio fortunae ductus acervo.   10
ponamus nimios gemitus: flagrantior aequo
non debet dolor esse viri, nec vulnere major.
tu quamvis levium minimam exiguamque malorum
particulam vix ferre potes, spumantibus ardens
visceribus, sacrum tibi quod non reddat amicus   15
depositum.   stupet haec, qui jam post terga reliquit
sexaginta annos, Fonteio consule natus?
an nihil in melius tot rerum proficit usus?
magna quidem, sacris quae dat praecepta libellis,
victrix fortunae sapientia; ducimus autem   20
hos quoque felices, qui ferre incommoda vitae
nec jactare jugum vita didicere magistra.
quae tam festa dies, ut cesset prodere furem,
perfidiam, fraudes, atque omni ex crimine lucrum
quaesitum, et partos gladio vel puxide nummos?   25
rari quippe boni; numero vix sunt totidem quot

Thebarum portae vel divitis ostia Nili.
nona aetas agitur pejoraque saecula ferri
temporibus, quorum sceleri non invenit ipsa
nomen et a nullo posuit natura metallo.   30
nos hominum divumque fidem clamore ciemus,
quanto Faesidium laudat vocalis agentem
sportula.   dic, senior bulla dignissime, nescis,
quas habeat veneres aliena pecunia? nescis,
quem tua simplicitas risum vulgo moveat, cum   35
exigis a quoquam ne pejeret et putet ullis
esse aliquod numen templis araeque rubenti?
quondam hoc indigenae vivebant more, priusquam
sumeret agrestem posito diademate falcem
Saturnus fugiens, tunc, cum virguncula Juno   40
et privatus adhuc Idaeis Juppiter antris,
nulla super nubes convivia caelicolarum,
nec puer Iliacus, formonsa nec Herculis uxor
ad cyathos, et jam siccato nectare tergens
bracchia Vulcanus Liparaea nigra taberna.   45
prandebat sibi quisque deus, nec turba deorum
talis ut est hodie, contentaque sidera paucis
numinibus miserum urguebant Atlanta minori
pondere.   nondum aliquis sortitus triste profundi
imperium, aut Sicula torvus cum conjuge Pluton,   50
nec rota nec Furiae nec saxum aut vulturis atri
poena, sed infernis hilares sine regibus umbrae.
inprobitas illo fuit admirabilis aevo,
credebant quo grande nefas et morte piandum,
6— Juv.

si juvenis vetulo non assurrexerat et si　　　　　　55
barbato cuicumque puer, licet ipse videret
plura domi fraga et majores glandis acervos.
tam venerabile erat praecedere quattuor annis,
primaque par adeo sacrae lanugo senectae.
nunc, si depositum non infitietur amicus,　　　　　60
si reddat veterem cum tota aerugine follem,
prodigiosa fides et Tuscis digna libellis,
quaeque coronata lustrari debeat agna.
egregium sanctumque virum si cerno, bimembri
hoc monstrum puero vel miranti sub aratro　　　65
piscibus inventis et fetae conparo mulae,
sollicitus, tamquam lapides effuderit imber
examenque apium longa consederit uva
culmine delubri, tamquam in mare fluxerit amnis
gurgitibus miris et lactis vertice torrens.　　　　70
　　Intercepta decem quereris sestertia fraude
sacrilega? quid si bis centum perdidit alter
hoc arcana modo? majorem tertius illa
summam, quam patulae vix ceperat angulus arcae?
tam facile et pronum est superos contemnere testes,　75
si mortalis idem nemo sciat! aspice, quanta
voce neget, quae sit ficti constantia vultus.
per Solis radios Tarpeiaque fulmina jurat
et Martis frameam et Cirraei spicula vatis,
per calamos venatricis pharetramque puellae,　　　80
perque tuum, pater Aegaei Neptune, tridentem;
addit et Herculeos arcus hastamque Minervae,

quidquid habent telorum armamentaria caeli.
si vero et pater est, ' comedam,' inquit, ' flebile nati
sinciput elixi Pharioque madentis aceto.'   85
   Sunt in fortunae qui casibus omnia ponant
et nullo credant mundum rectore moveri,
natura volvente vices et lucis et anni,
atque ideo intrepidi quaecumque altaria tangunt.
[est alius metuens, ne crimen poena sequatur ;]   90
hic putat esse deos et pejerat, atque ita secum :
' decernat quodcumque volet de corpore nostro
Isis et irato feriat mea lumina sistro,
dummodo vel caecus teneam quos abnego nummos.
et phthisis et vomicae putres et dimidium crus   95
sunt tanti.   pauper locupletem optare podagram
nec dubitet Ladas, si non eget Anticyra nec
Archigene; quid enim velocis gloria plantae
praestat et esuriens Pisaeae ramus olivae?
ut sit magna, tamen certe lenta ira deorum est: 100
si curant igitur cunctos punire nocentes,
quando ad me venient? sed et exorabile numen
fortasse experiar; solet his ignoscere.   multi
committunt eadem diverso crimina fato ;
ille crucem sceleris pretium tulit, hic diadema.'   105
sic animum dirae trepidum formidine culpae
confirmat, tunc te sacra ad delubra vocantem
praecedit, trahere immo ultro ac vexare paratus.
nam cum magna malae superest audacia causae,
creditur a multis fiducia.   mimum agit ille,   110

urbani qualem fugitivus scurra Catulli;
tu miser exclamas, ut Stentora vincere possis,
vel potius quantum Gradivus Homericus : 'audis,
Juppiter, haec, nec labra moves, cum mittere vocem
debueris vel marmoreus vel aeneus? aut cur   115
in carbone tuo charta pia tura soluta
ponimus et sectum vituli jecur albaque porci
omenta? ut video, nullum discrimen habendum est
effigies inter vestras statuamque Vagelli.'

   Accipe, quae contra valeat solacia ferre   120
et qui nec cynicos nec stoica dogmata legit
a cynicis tunica distantia, non Epicurum
suspicit exigui laetum plantaribus horti.
curentur dubii medicis majoribus aegri;
tu venam vel discipulo committe Philippi.   125
si nullum in terris tam detestabile factum
ostendis, taceo, nec pugnis caedere pectus
te veto, nec plana faciem contundere palma,
quandoquidem accepto claudenda est janua damno,
et majore domus gemitu, majore tumultu   130
planguntur nummi quam funera.   nemo dolorem
fingit in hoc casu, vestem diducere summam
contentus, vexare oculos umore coacto:
ploratur lacrimis amissa pecunia veris.
sed si cuncta vides simili fora plena querella,   135
si deciens lectis diversa parte tabellis
vana supervacui dicunt chirographa ligni,
arguit ipsorum quos littera gemmaque princeps

sardonychum, loculis quae custoditur eburnis:
ten' (o delicias!) extra communia censes 140
ponendum, quia tu gallinae filius albae,
nos viles pulli nati infelicibus ovis?
rem pateris modicam et mediocri bile ferendam,
si flectas oculos majora ad crimina. confer
conductum latronem, incendia sulpure coepta 145
atque dolo, primos cum janua colligit ignes;
confer et hos, veteris qui tollunt grandia templi
pocula adorandae robiginis et populorum
dona vel antiquo positas a rege coronas.
haec ibi si non sunt, minor exstat sacrilegus, qui 150
radat inaurati femur Herculis et faciem ipsam
Neptuni, qui bratteolam de Castore ducat;
an dubitet? solitum*st* totum conflare tonantem.
confer et artifices mercatoremque veneni
et deducendum corio bovis in mare, cum quo 155
clauditur adversis innoxia simia fatis.
haec quota pars scelerum, quae custos Gallicus urbis
usque a lucifero donec lux occidat audit?
humani generis mores tibi nosse volenti
sufficit una domus; paucos consume dies, et 160
dicere te miserum, postquam illinc veneris, aude.
quis tumidum guttur miratur in Alpibus? aut quis
in Meroë crasso majorem infante mamillam?
caerula quis stupuit Germani lumina, flavam
caesariem et madido torquentem cornua cirro? 165
nempe quod haec illis natura est omnibus una.

H

ad subitas Thracum volucres nubemque sonoram
Pygmaeus parvis currit bellator in armis,
mox impar hosti raptusque per aera curvis
unguibus a saeva fertur grue. si videas hoc   170
gentibus in nostris, risu quatiare; sed illic,
quamquam eadem assidue spectentur proelia, ridet
nemo, ubi tota cohors pede non est altior uno.

   Nullane perjuri capitis fraudisque nefandae
poena erit?— abreptum crede hunc graviore catena 175
protinus et nostro — quid plus velit ira?— necari
arbitrio; manet illa tamen jactura, nec umquam
depositum tibi sospes erit, sed corpore trunco
invidiosa dabit minimus solacia sanguis.
'at vindicta bonum vita jucundius ipsa.'   180
nempe hoc indocti, quorum praecordia nullis
interdum aut levibus videas flagrantia causis:
[quantulacumque adeo est occasio, sufficit irae.]
Chrysippus non dicet idem nec mite Thaletis
ingenium dulcique senex vicinus Hymetto,   185
qui partem acceptae saeva inter vincla cicutae
accusatori nollet dare. [plurima felix
paulatim vitia atque errores exuit omnes,
prima docet rectum sapientia.] quippe minuti
semper et infirmi est animi exiguique voluptas   190
ultio: continuo sic collige, quod vindicta
nemo magis gaudet quam femina. cur tamen hos tu
evasisse putes, quos diri conscia facti
mens habet attonitos et surdo verbere caedit.

occultum quatiente animo tortore flagellum?   195
poena autem vehemens ac multo saevior illis,
quas et Caedicius gravis invenit et Rhadamanthus,
nocte dieque suum gestare in pectore testem.
Spartano cuidam respondit Pythia vates,
haut impunitum quondam fore, quod dubitaret   200
depositum retinere et fraudem jure tueri
jurando.   quaerebat enim, quae numinis esset
mens, et an hoc illi facinus suaderet Apollo?
reddidit ergo metu, non moribus; et tamen omnem
vocem adyti dignam templo veramque probavit,   205
extinctus tota pariter cum prole domoque
et quamvis longa deductis gente propinquis.
has patitur poenas peccandi sola voluntas.
nam scelus intra se tacitum qui cogitat ullum,
facti crimen habet: cedo, si conata peregit?   210
perpetua anxietas nec mensae tempore cessat,
faucibus ut morbo siccis interque molares
difficili crescente cibo; Setina misellus
expuit, Albani veteris pretiosa senectus
displicet; ostendas melius, densissima ruga   215
cogitur in frontem, velut acri ducta Falerno.
nocte brevem si forte indulsit cura soporem
et toto versata toro jam membra quiescunt,
continuo templum et violati numinis aras
et, quod praecipuis mentem sudoribus urguet,   220
te videt in somnis; tua sacra et major imago
humana turbat pavidum cogitque fateri.

hi sunt, qui trepidant et ad omnia fulgura pallent,
cum tonat, exanimes primo quoque murmure caeli;
non quasi fortuitus nec ventorum rabie, set   225
iratus cadat in terras et vindicet ignis.
illa nihil nocuit, cura graviore timetur
proxima tempestas, velut hoc dilata sereno.
praeterea lateris vigili cum febre dolorem
si coepere pati, missum ad sua corpora morbum   230
infesto credunt a numine; saxa deorum
haec et tela putant.   pecudem spondere sacello
balantem et Laribus cristam promittere galli
non audent; quid enim sperare nocentibus aegris
concessum? vel quae non dignior hostia vita?   235
mobilis et varia est ferme natura malorum.
cum scelus admittunt, superest constantia; quid fas
atque nefas, tandem incipiunt sentire peractis
criminibus.   tamen ad mores natura recurrit
damnatos, fixa et mutari nescia   nam quis   240
peccandi finem posuit sibi? quando recepit
ejectum semel attrita de fronte ruborem?
quisnam hominum est, quem tu contentum videris uno
flagitio? dabit in laqueum vestigia noster
perfidus, et nigri patietur carceris uncum,   245
aut maris Aegaei rupem scopulosque frequentes
exulibus magnis.   poena gaudebis amara
nominis invisi, tandemque fatebere laetus
nec surdum nec Tiresian quemquam esse deorum.

XIV.

Plurima sunt, Fuscine, et fama digna sinistra
et nitidis maculam haesuram figentia rebus,
quae monstrant ipsi pueris traduntque parentes.
si damnosa senem juvat alea, ludit et heres
bullatus parvoque eadem movet arma fritillo. 5
nec melius de se cuiquam sperare propinquo
concedet juvenis, qui radere tubera terrae,
boletum condire et eodem jure natantis
mergere ficellas didicit, nebulone parente
et cana monstrante gula. cum septimus annus 10
transierit puerum, nondum omni dente renato,
barbatos licet admoveas mille inde magistros,
hinc totidem, cupiet lauto cenare paratu
semper et a magna non degenerare culina.
mitem animum et mores modicis erroribus aequos 15
praecipit, atque animas servorum et corpora nostra
materia constare putat paribusque elementis,
an saevire docet Rutilus, qui gaudet acerbo
plagarum strepitu et nullam Sirena flagellis
conparat, Antiphates trepidi laris ac Polyphemus, 20
tunc felix, quotiens aliquis tortore vocato
uritur ardenti duo propter lintea ferro?
quid suadet juveni laetus stridore catenae,
quem mire afficiunt inscripta ergastula, carcer? 24
sic natura jubet: velocius et citius nos 31
corrumpunt vitiorum exempla domestica, magnis

cum subeant animos auctoribus.   unus et alter
forsitan haec spernant juvenes, quibus arte benigna
et meliore luto finxit praecordia Titan ;   35
sed reliquos fugienda patrum vestigia ducunt
et monstrata diu veteris trahit orbita culpae.
abstineas igitur damnandis.   hujus enim vel
una potens ratio est, ne crimina nostra sequantur
ex nobis geniti, quoniam dociles imitandis   40
turpibus ac pravis omnes sumus, et Catilinam
quocumque in populo videas, quocumque sub axe,
sed nec Brutus erit, Bruti nec avunculus usquam.
nil dictu foedum visuque haec limina tangat,
intra quae pater est.   procul, a procul inde puellae   45
lenonum et cantus pernoctantis parasiti !
maxima debetur puero reverentia.   si quid   ·
turpe paras, ne tu pueri contempseris annos,
sed peccaturo obstet tibi filius infans.
nam si quid dignum censoris fecerit ira   50
quandoque et similem tibi se non corpore tantum
nec vultu dederit, morum quoque filius et qui
omnia deterius tua per vestigia peccet,
corripies nimirum et castigabis acerbo
clamore ac post haec tabulas mutare parabis.   55
unde tibi frontem libertatemque parentis,
cum facias pejora senex, vacuumque cerebro
jam pridem caput hoc ventosa cucurbita quaerat?
    Hospite venturo cessabit nemo tuorum.
' verre pavimentum, nitidas ostende columnas,   60

arida cum **tota descendat** aranea tela,
hic leve argentum, vasa aspera tergeat alter!'
vox domini furit instantis virgamque tenentis.
ergo miser trepidas, ne stercore foeda canino
atria displiceant oculis venientis amici,   65
ne perfusa luto sit porticus; et tamen uno
semodio scobis haec emendat servulus unus:
illud non **agitas,** ut sanctam filius **omni**
aspiciat sine labe domum vitioque carentem?
gratum est quod patriae civem populoque dedisti,   70
si facis ut patriae sit idoneus, utilis agris,
utilis et bellorum et pacis rebus agendis.
plurimum enim **intererit, quibus** artibus et **quibus**
     hunc **tu**
moribus instituas. serpente ciconia pullos
nutrit et inventa per devia rura lacerta: 75
illi eadem sumptis quaerunt animalia pinnis.
vultur jumento et canibus crucibusque relictis
ad fetus properat partemque cadaveris adfert:
hic est ergo cibus magni quoque vulturis et se
pascentis, propria cum jam facit arbore nidos.   80
sed **leporem** aut capream famulae Jovis et generosae
in saltu venantur aves, hinc praeda cubili
ponitur: inde autem cum se matura levavit
progenies, stimulante fame festinat ad illam,
quam primum praedam rupto gustaverat ovo.   85
    Aedificator erat Cretonius, et modo curvo
litore Caietae, summa nunc Tiburis arce,

nunc Praenestinis in montibus alta parabat
culmina villarum Graecis longeque petitis
marmoribus, vincens Fortunae atque Herculis aedem,   90
ut spado vincebat Capitolia nostra Posides.
dum sic ergo habitat Cretonius, inminuit rem,
fregit opes ; nec parva tamen mensura relictae
partis erat : totam hanc turbavit filius amens,
dum meliore novas attollit marmore villas.   95

    Quidam sortiti metuentem sabbata patrem
nil praeter nubes et caeli numen adorant,
nec distare putant humana carne suillam,
qua pater abstinuit ; mox et praeputia ponunt
Romanas autem soliti contemnere leges   100
Judaicum ediscunt et servant ac metuunt jus,
tradidit arcano quodcumque volumine Moyses,
non monstrare vias eadem nisi sacra colenti,
quaesitum ad fontem solos deducere verpos.
sed pater in causa, cui septima quaeque fuit lux   105
ignava et partem vitae non attigit ullam.

    Sponte tamen juvenes imitantur cetera, solam
inviti quoque avaritiam exercere jubentur.
fallit enim vitium specie virtutis et umbra,
cum sit triste habitu vultuque et veste severum,   110
nec dubie tamquam frugi laudetur avarus,
tamquam parcus homo et rerum tutela suarum
certa magis quam si fortunas servet easdem
Hesperidum serpens aut Ponticus. adde quod hunc, de
quo loquor, egregium populus putat adquirendi   115

artificem; quippe his crescunt patrimonia fabris,
sed crescunt quocumque modo, majoraque fiunt
incude assidua semperque ardente camino.
et pater ergo animi felices credit avaros,
qui miratur opes, qui nulla exempla beati   120
pauperis esse putat; juvenes hortatur ut illam
ire viam pergant et eidem incumbere sectae.
sunt quaedam vitiorum elementa: his protinus illos
inbuit et cogit minimas ediscere sordes,
[mox adquirendi docet insatiabile votum.]   125
servorum ventres modio castigat iniquo,
ipse quoque esuriens; neque enim omnia sustinet
    umquam
mucida caerulei panis consumere frusta,
hesternum solitus medio servare minutal
Septembri, nec non differre in tempora cenae   130
alterius conchem aestivi cum parte lacerti
signatam vel dimidio putrique siluro,
filaque sectivi numerata includere porri:
invitatus ad haec aliquis de ponte negabit.
sed quo divitias haec per tormenta coactas,   135
cum furor haut dubius, cum sit manifesta phrenesis,
ut locuples moriaris, egentis vivere fato?
interea pleno cum turget sacculus ore,
crescit amor nummi, quantum ipsa pecunia crevit,
et minus hanc optat qui non habet. ergo paratur   140
altera villa tibi, cum rus non sufficit unum,
et proferre libet fines, majorque videtur

et melior vicina seges : mercaris et hanc et
arbusta et densa montem qui canet oliva.
quorum si pretio dominus non vincitur ullo,   145
nocte boves macri lassoque famelica collo
jumenta ad virides hujus mittentur aristas,
nec prius inde domum quam tota novalia saevos
in ventres abeant, ut credas falcibus actum.
dicere vix possis quam multi talia plorent,   150
et quot venales injuria fecerit agros.
sed qui sermones, quam foedae bucina famae!
'quid nocet haec?' inquit, 'tunicam mihi malo lupini,
quam si me toto laudet vicinia pago
exigui ruris paucissima farra secantem.'   155
scilicet et morbis et debilitate carebis,
et luctum et curam effugies, et tempora vitae
longa tibi posthac fato meliore dabuntur,
si tantum culti solus possederis agri,
quantum sub Tatio populus Romanus arabat.   160
mox etiam fractis aetate ac Punica passis
proelia vel Pyrrum inmanem gladiosque Molossos
tandem pro multis vix jugera bina dabantur
vulneribus.   merces haec sanguinis atque laboris
nullis visa umquam meritis minor aut ingratae   165
curta fides patriae.   saturabat glebula talis
patrem ipsum turbamque casae, qua feta jacebat
uxor et infantes ludebant quattuor, unus
vernula, tres domini ; sed magnis fratribus horum
a scrobe vel sulco redeuntibus altera cena   170

amplior et grandes fumabant pultibus ollae:
nunc modus hic agri nostro non sufficit horto.
inde fere scelerum causae; nec plura venena
miscuit aut ferro grassatur saepius ullum
humanae mentis vitium quam saeva cupido   175
inmodici census. nam dives qui fieri vult,
et cito vult fieri : sed quae reverentia legum,
quis metus aut pudor est umquam properantis avari?
'vivite contenti casulis et collibus istis,
o pueri!' Marsus dicebat et Hernicus olim   180
Vestinusque senex; 'panem quaeramus aratro,
qui satis est mensis: laudant hoc numina ruris,
quorum ope et auxilio gratae post munus aristae
contingunt homini veteris fastidia quercus.
nil vetitum fecisse volet, quem non pudet alto   185
per glaciem perone tegi, qui summovet euros
pellibus inversis; peregrina ignotaque nobis
ad scelus atque nefas, quaecumque est, purpura ducit.'
haec illi veteres praecepta minoribus : at nunc
post finem autumni media de nocte supinum   190
clamosus juvenem pater excitat: 'accipe ceras,
scribe, puer, vigila, causas age, perlege rubras
majorum leges aut vitem posce libello.
sed caput intactum buxo naresque pilosas
adnotet et grandes miretur Laelius alas.   195
dirue Maurorum attegias, castella Brigantum,
ut locupletem aquilam tibi sexagensimus annus
adferat; aut, longos castrorum ferre labores

si piget et trepidum solvunt tibi cornua ventrem
cum lituis audita, pares quod vendere possis   200
pluris dimidio, nec te fastidia mercis
ullius subeant ablegandae Tiberim ultra,
neu credas ponendum aliquid discriminis inter
unguenta et corium: lucri bonus est odor ex re
qualibet. illa tuo sententia semper in ore   205
versetur, dis atque ipso Jove digna poeta,
"unde habeas, quaerit nemo, sed oportet habere." '
hoc monstrant vetulae pueris repentibus assae,
hoc discunt omnes ante alpha et beta puellae!
talibus instantem monitis quemcumque parentem   210
sic possem adfari: 'dic, o vanissime, quis te
festinare jubet? meliorem praesto magistro
discipulum.   securus abi, vinceris, ut Ajax
praeteriit Telamonem, ut Pelea vicit Achilles.
parcendum est teneris: nondum implevere medullas 215
maturae mala nequitiae: ast cum pectere barbam
coeperit et longi mucronem admittere cultri,
falsus erit testis, vendet perjuria summa
exigua et Cereris tangens aramque pedemque.
elatam jam crede nurum, si limina vestra   220
mortifera cum dote subit.   quibus illa premetur
per somnum digitis! nam quae terraque marique
adquirenda putas, brevior via conferet illi;
nullus enim magni sceleris labor. "haec ego numquam
mandavi," dices olim, "nec talia suasi."   225
mentis causa malae tamen est et origo penes te.

nam quisquis magni census praecepit amorem,
et laevo monitu pueros producit avaros,
[et qui per fraudes patrimonia couduplicare,]
dat libertatem et totas effundit habenas   230
curriculo; quem si revoces, subsistere nescit
et te contempto rapitur metisque relictis.
nemo satis credit tantum delinquere, quantum
permittas; adeo indulgent sibi latius ipsi.
cum dicis juveni stultum, qui donet amico,   235
qui paupertatem levet attollatque propinqui,
et spoliare doces et circumscribere et omni
crimine divitias adquirere, quarum amor in te
quantus erat patriae Deciorum in pectore, quantum
dilexit Thebas, si Graecia vera, Menoeceus;   240
in quorum sulcis legiones dentibus anguis
cum clipeis nascuntur et horrida bella capessunt
continuo, tamquam et tubicen surrexerit una.
ergo ignem, cujus scintillas ipse dedisti,   .
flagrantem late et rapientem cuncta videbis;   245
nec tibi parcetur misero, trepidumque magistrum
in cavea magno fremitu leo tollet alumnus.
nota mathematicis genesis tua; sed grave tardas
exspectare colus: morieris stamine nondum
abrupto.   jam nunc obstas et vota moraris,   250
jam torquet juvenem longa et cervina senectus.
ocius Archigenen quaere atque eme quod Mithridates
composuit, si vis aliam decerpere ficum
atque alias tractare rosas.   medicamen habendum est,

    7 — Juv.   I

sorbere ante cibum quod debeat et pater et rex.'   255
   Monstro voluptatem egregiam, cui nulla theatra,
nulla aequare queas praetoris pulpita lauti,
si spectes quanto capitis discrimine constent
incrementa domus, aerata multus in arca
fiscus et ad vigilem ponendi Castora nummi,   260
ex quo Mars ultor galeam quoque perdidit et res
non potuit servare suas.   ergo omnia Florae
et Cereris licet et Cybeles aulaea relinquas;
tanto majores humana negotia ludi.
an magis oblectant animum jactata petauro   265
corpora quique solet rectum descendere funem,
quam tu, Corycia semper qui puppe moraris
atque habitas, coro semper tollendus et austro,
perditus ac vilis sacci mercator olentis,
qui gaudes pingue antiquae de litore Cretae   270
passum et municipes Jovis advexisse lagonas?
hic tamen ancipiti figens vestigia planta
victum illa mercede parat brumamque famemque
illa reste cavet; tu propter mille talenta
et centum villas temerarius.   aspice portus   275
et plenum magnis trabibus mare; plus hominum
       est jam
in pelago; veniet classis, quocumque vocarit
spes lucri, nec Carpathium Gaetulaque tantum
aequora transiliet, sed longe Calpe relicta
audiet Herculeo stridentem gurgite solem.   280
grande operae pretium est, ut tenso folle reverti

inde domum possis tumidaque superbus aluta,
Oceani monstra et juvenes vidisse marinos.
non unus mentes agitat furor. ille sororis
in manibus vultu Eumenidum terretur et igni,   285
hic bove percusso mugire Agamemnona credit.
aut Ithacum. parcat tunicis licet atque lacernis,
curatoris eget qui navem mercibus implet
ad summum latus et tabula distinguitur unda,
cum sit causa mali tanti et discriminis hujus   290
concisum argentum in titulos faciesque minutas.
occurrunt nubes et fulgura, 'solvite funem,'
frumenti dominus clamat piperisve coempti,
'nil color hic caeli, nil fascia nigra minatur ;
aestivum tonat.' infelix hac forsitan ipsa   295
nocte cadit fractis trabibus, fluctuque premetur
obrutus et zonam laeva morsuque tenebit.
sed cujus votis modo non suffecerat aurum,
quod Tagus et rutila volvit Pactolus harena,
frigida sufficient velantes inguina panni   300
exiguusque cibus, mersa rate naufragus assem
dum rogat et picta se tempestate tuetur

Tantis parta malis cura majore metuque
servantur. misera est magni custodia census.
dispositis praedives amis vigilare cohortem   305
servorum noctu Licinus jubet, attonitus pro
electro signisque suis Phrygiaque columna
atque ebore et lata testudine. dolia nudi
non ardent cynici ; si fregeris, altera fiet

cras domus, atque eadem plumbo commissa manebit. 310
sensit Alexander, testa cum vidit in illa
magnum habitatorem, quanto felicior hic, qui
nil cuperet, quam qui totum sibi posceret orbem,
passurus gestis aequanda pericula rebus.
nullum numen habes, si sit prudentia; nos te,   315
nos facimus, Fortuna, deam. mensura tamen quae
sufficiat census, si quis me consulat, edam:
in quantum sitis atque fames et frigora poscunt,
quantum, Epicure, tibi parvis suffecit in hortis,
quantum Socratici ceperunt ante penates.   320
numquam aliut natura, aliut sapientia dicit.
acribus exemplis videor te cludere? misce
ergo aliquid nostris de moribus, effice summam,
bis septem ordinibus quam lex dignatur Othonis.
haec quoque si rugam trahit extenditque labellum,   325
sume duos equites, fac tertia quadringenta.
si nondum inplevi gremium, si panditur ultra,
nec Croesi fortuna umquam nec Persica regna
sufficient animo nec divitiae Narcissi,
indulsit Caesar cui Claudius omnia, cujus   330
paruit imperiis uxorem occidere jussus.

XV.

Quis nescit, Volusi Bithynice, qualia demens
Aegyptus portenta colat? crocodilon adorat
pars haec, illa pavet saturam serpentibus ibin.
effigies sacri nitet aurea cercopitheci,

dimidio magicae resonant ubi Memnone chordae   5
atque vetus Thebe centum jacet obruta portis.
illic aeluros, hic piscem fluminis, illic
oppida tota canem venerantur, nemo Dianam.
porrum et cepe nefas violare et frangere morsu :
o sanctas gentes, quibus haec nascuntur in hortis   10
numina! lanatis animalibus abstinet omnis
mensa, nefas illic fetum jugulare capellae :
carnibus humanis vesci licet. attonito cum
tale super cenam facinus narraret Ulixes
Alcinoo, bilem aut risum fortasse quibusdam   15
moverat, ut mendax aretalogus. 'in mare nemo
hunc abicit saeva dignum veraque Charybdi,
fingentem inmanis Laestrygonas atque Cyclopas?
nam citius Scyllam vel concurrentia saxa
Cyaneis, plenos et tempestatibus utres   20
crediderim, aut tenui percussum verbere Circes
et cum remigibus grunnisse Elpenora porcis.
tam vacui capitis populum Phaeaca putavit?'
sic aliquis merito nondum ebrius et minimum qui
de Corcyraea temetum duxerat urna ;   25
solus enim haec Ithacus nullo sub teste canebat.
nos miranda quidem, set nuper consule Junco
gesta super calidae referemus moenia Copti,
nos volgi scelus et cunctis graviora cothurnis ;
nam scelus, a Pyrra quamquam omnia syrmata volvas, 30
nullus aput tragicos populus facit. accipe nostro
dira quod exemplum feritas produxerit aevo.

Inter finitimos vetus atque antiqua simultas,
inmortale odium et numquam sanabile vulnus
ardet adhuc, Ombos et Tentyra. summus utrimque   35
inde furor vulgo, quod numina vicinorum
odit uterque locus, cum solos credat habendos
esse deos, quos ipse colit. set tempore festo
alterius populi rapienda occasio cunctis
visa inimicorum primoribus ac ducibus, ne   40
laetum hilaremque diem, ne magnae gaudia cenae
sentirent, positis ad templa et compita mensis
pervigilique toro, quem nocte ac luce jacentem
septimus interdum sol invenit. (horrida sane.
Aegyptos, sed luxuria, quantum ipse notavi,   45
barbara famoso non cedit turba Canopo.)
adde quod et facilis victoria de madidis et
blaesis atque mero titubantibus. inde virorum
saltatus nigro tibicine, qualiacumque
unguenta et flores multaeque in fronte coronae;   50
hinc jejunum odium. sed jurgia prima sonare
incipiunt animis ardentibus, haec tuba rixae.
dein clamore pari concurritur, et vice teli
saevit nuda manus. paucae sine vulnere malae,
vix cuiquam aut nulli toto certamine nasus   55
integer; aspiceres jam cuncta per agmina vultus
dimidios, alias facies et hiantia ruptis
ossa genis, plenos oculorum sanguine pugnos.
ludere se credunt ipsi tamen et pueriles
exercere acies, quod nulla cadavera calcent: 60

et sane quo tot rixantis milia turbae,
si vivunt omnes? ergo acrior impetus, et jam
saxa inclinatis per humum quaesita lacertis
incipiunt torquere, domestica seditioni
tela, nec hunc lapidem qualis et Turnus et Ajax,   65
vel quo Tydides percussit pondere coxam
Aeneae, sed quem valeant emittere dextrae
illis dissimiles et nostro tempore natae.
nam genus hoc vivo jam decrescebat Homero;
terra malos homines nunc educat atque pusillos,   70
ergo deus, quicumque aspexit, ridet et odit.

    A deverticulo repetatur fabula.   postquam,
subsidiis aucti, pars altera promere ferrum
audet et infestis pugnam instaurare sagittis:
terga fuga celeri praestant instantibus Ombis   75
qui vicina colunt umbrosae Tentyra palmae.
labitur hinc quidam nimia formidine cursum
praecipitans, capiturque.   ast illum in plurima sectum
frusta et particulas, ut multis mortuus unus
sufficeret, totum corrosis ossibus edit   80
victrix turba; nec ardenti decoxit aeno
aut veribus; longum usque adeo tardumque putavit
expectare focos, contenta cadavere crudo.
hic gaudere libet, quod non violaverit ignem,
quem summa caeli raptum de parte Prometheus   85
donavit terris: elemento gratulor, et te
exultare reor.   sed qui mordere cadaver
sustinuit, nil umquam hac carne libentius edit.

nam scelere in tanto ne quaeras et dubites an
prima voluptatem gula senserit; ultimus autem 90
qui stetit absumpto jam toto corpore, ductis
per terram digitis aliquid de sanguine gustat.
Vascones, haec fama est, alimentis talibus olim
produxere animas: sed res diversa, sed illic
fortunae invidia est bellorumque ultima, casus 95
extremi, longae dira obsidionis egestas.
[hujus enim, quod nunc agitur, miserabile debet
exemplum esse cibi, sicut modo dicta mihi gens]
post omnes herbas, post cuncta animalia, quidquid
cogebat vacui ventris furor, hostibus ipsis 100
pallorem ac maciem et tenues miserantibus artus,
membra aliena fame lacerabant, esse parati
et sua.   quisnam hominum veniam dare quisve deorum
ventribus abnueret dira atque inmania passis,
et quibus illorum poterant ignoscere manes, 105
quorum corporibus vescebantur? melius nos
Zenonis praecepta monent; nec enim omnia, quaedam
pro vita facienda putant: sed Cantaber unde
stoicus, antiqui praesertim aetate Metelli?
nunc totus Graias nostrasque habet orbis Athenas, 110
Gallia causidicos docuit facunda Britannos,
de conducendo loquitur jam rhetore Thyle.
nobilis ille tamen populus, quem diximus, et par
virtute atque fide, sed major clade, Zagynthos,
tale quid excusat: Maeotide saevior ara 115
Aegyptos.   quippe illa nefandi Taurica sacri

inventrix homines (ut jam quae carmina tradunt
digna fide credas) tantum immolat, ulterius nil
aut gravius cultro timet hostia.   quis modo casus
impulit hos? quae tanta fames infestaque vallo   120
arma coegerunt tam detestabile monstrum
audere? anne aliam terra Memphitide sicca
invidiam facerent nolenti surgere Nilo?
qua nec terribiles Cimbri nec Britones umquam
Sauromataeque truces aut immanes Agathyrsi,   125
hac saevit rabie inbelle et inutile vulgus,
parvula fictilibus solitum dare vela phaselis
et brevibus pictae remis incumbere testae.
nec poenam sceleri invenies, nec digna parabis
supplicia his populis, in quorum mente pares sunt   130
et similes ira atque fames.   mollissima corda
humano generi dare se natura fatetur,
quae lacrimas dedit; haec nostri pars optima sensus.
plorare ergo jubet causam dicentis amici
squaloremque rei, pupillum ad jura vocantem   135
circumscriptorem, cujus manantia fletu
ora puellares faciunt incerta capilli.
naturae imperio gemimus, quum funus adultae
virginis occurrit vel terra clauditur infans
et minor igne rogi.   quis enim bonus et face dignus 140
arcana, qualem Cereris vult esse sacerdos,
ulla aliena sibi credit mala? separat hoc nos
a grege mutorum, atque ideo venerabile soli
sortiti ingenium divinorumque capaces

atque exercendis capiendisque artibus apti   145
sensum a caelesti demissum traximus arce,
cujus egent prona et terram spectantia.   mundi
principio indulsit communis conditor illis
tantum animas, nobis animum quoque, mutuus ut nos
adfectus petere auxilium et praestare juberet,   150
dispersos trahere in populum, migrare vetusto
de nemore et proavis habitatas linquere silvas,
aedificare domos, laribus conjungere nostris
tectum aliud, tutos vicino limine somnos
ut conlata daret fiducia, protegere armis   155
lapsum aut ingenti nutantem vulnere civem,
communi dare signa tuba, defendier îsdem
turribus atque una portarum clave teneri.
sed jam serpentum major concordia.   parcit
cognatis maculis similis fera.   quando leoni   160
fortior eripuit vitam leo? quo nemore umquam
exspiravit aper majoris dentibus apri?
Indica tigris agit rabida cum tigride pacem
perpetuam, saevis inter se convenit ursis.
ast homini ferrum letale incude nefanda   165
produxisse parum est, cum rastra et sarcula tantum
adsueti coquere et marris ac vomere lassi
nescierint primi gladios extendere fabri.
aspicimus populos, quorum non sufficit irae
occidisse aliquem, sed pectora, brachia, vultum   170
crediderint genus esse cibi.   quid diceret ergo,
vel quo non fugeret, si nunc haec monstra videret

Pythagoras, cunctis animalibus abstinuit qui
tamquam homine et ventri indulsit non omne legumen?

XVI.

Quis numerare queat felicis praemia, Galli,
militiae? nam si subeuntur prospera castra,
me pavidum excipiat tironem porta secundo
sidere. plus etenim fati valet hora benigni,
quam si nos Veneris commendet epistula Marti   5
et Samia genetrix quae delectatur harena.
  Commoda tractemus primum communia, quorum
haut minimum illud erit, ne te pulsare togatus
audeat, immo etsi pulsetur, dissimulet, nec
audeat excussos praetori ostendere dentes,   10
et nigram in facie tumidis livoribus offam,
atque oculum medico nil promittente relictum.
Bardaicus judex datur haec punire volenti
calceus et grandes magna ad subsellia surae,
legibus antiquis castrorum et more Camilli   15
servato, miles ne vallum litiget extra
et procul a signis. justissima centurionum
cognitio est igitur de milite, nec mihi derit
ultio, si justae defertur causa querellae:
tota cohors tamen est inimica, omnesque manipli   20
consensu magno efficiunt, curabilis ut sit
vindicta et gravior quam injuria. dignum erit ergo
declamatoris mulino corde Vagelli,
cum duo crura habeas, offendere tot caligas, tot

milia clavorum.   quis tam procul absit ab urbe   25
praeterea, quis tam Pylades, molem aggeris ultra
ut veniat? lacrimae siccentur protinus, et se
excusaturos non sollicitemus amicos.
'da testem' judex cum dixerit, audeat ille
nescio quis, pugnos qui vidit, dicere 'vidi,'   30
et credam dignum barba dignumque capillis
majorum.   citius falsum producere testem
contra paganum possis, quam vera loquentem
contra fortunam armati contraque pudorem.

   Praemia nunc alia atque alia emolumenta notemus 35
sacramentorum.   convallem ruris aviti
improbus aut campum mihi si vicinus ademit,
et sacrum effodit medio de limite saxum,
quod mea cum patulo coluit puls annua libo,
debitor aut sumptos pergit non reddere nummos,   40
vana supervacui dicens chirographa ligni,
expectandus erit qui lites inchoet annus
totius populi.   sed tunc quoque mille ferenda
taedia, mille morae: totiens subsellia tantum
sternuntur; jam facundo ponente lacernas   45
Caedicio et Fusco jam micturiente, parati
digredimur, lentaque fori pugnamus harena.
ast illis, quos arma tegunt et balteus ambit,
quod placitum est ipsis praestatur tempus agendi,
nec res atteritur longo sufflamine litis.   50

   Solis praeterea testandi militibus jus
vivo patre datur; nam quae sunt parta labore

militiae, placuit non esse in corpore census,
omne tenet cujus regimen pater.   ergo Coranum
signorum comitem castrorumque aera merentem   55
quamvis jam tremulus captat pater. hunc favor aequus
provehit et pulchro reddit sua dona labori.
ipsius certe ducis hoc referre videtur,
ut, qui fortis erit, sit felicissimus idem,
ut laeti phaleris omnes et torquibus omnes.   60

K

A. PERSII FLACCI
SATVRA V.

———◦◦ː◦ːː◦◦———

VATIBUS hic mos est, centum sibi poscere voces,
centum ora et linguas optare in carmina centum,
fabula seu maesto ponatur hianda tragoedo,
vulnera seu Parthi ducentis ab inguine ferrum.
  ' Quorsum haec? aut quantas robusti carminis offas 5
ingeris, ut par sit centeno gutture niti?
grande locuturi nebulas Helicone legunto,
si quibus aut Prognes, aut si quibus olla Thyestae
fervebit, saepe insulso cenanda Glyconi;
tu neque anhelanti, coquitur dum massa camino,   10
folle premis ventos, nec clauso murmure raucus
nescio quid tecum grave cornicaris inepte,
nec stloppo tumidas intendis rumpere buccas.
verba togae sequeris, junctura callidus acri,
ore teres modico, pallentis radere mores   15
doctus, et ingenuo culpam defigere ludo.
hinc trahe quae dicis, mensasque relinque Mycenis
cum capite et pedibus, plebeiaque prandia nôris.'
  Non equidem hoc studeo, bullatis ut mihi nugis

pagina turgescat, dare pondus idonea fumo.   20
secreti loquimur; tibi nunc, hortante Camena,
excutienda damus praecordia, quantaque nostrae
pars tua sit, Cornute, animae, tibi, dulcis amice,
ostendisse juvat: pulsa, dinoscere cautus,
quid solidum crepet et pictae tectoria linguae.   25
hic ego centenas ausim deposcere voces,
ut, quantum mihi te sinuoso in pectore fixi,
voce traham pura, totumque hoc verba resignent,
quod latet arcana non enarrabile fibra.
  Cum primum pavido custos mihi purpura cessit,   30
bullaque succinctis Laribus donata pependit,
cum blandi comites, totaque impune Subura
permisit sparsisse oculos jam candidus umbo,
cumque iter ambiguum est, et vitae nescius error
deducit trepidas ramosa in compita mentes,   35
me tibi supposui: teneros tu suscipis annos
Socratico, Cornute, sinu; tum fallere sollers
adposita intortos extendit regula mores,
et premitur ratione animus, vincique laborat,
artificemque tuo ducit sub pollice vultum.   40
tecum etenim longos memini consumere soles,
et tecum primas epulis decerhere noctes:
unum opus et requiem pariter disponimus ambo,
atque verecunda laxamus seria mensa.
non equidem hoc dubites, amborum foedere certo   45
consentire dies et ab uno sidere duci:
nostra vel aequali suspendit tempora Libra

Parca tenax veri, seu nata fidelibus hora
dividit in Geminos concordia fata duorum,
Saturnumque gravem nostro Jove frangimus una :   50
nescio quod, certe est, quod me tibi temperat astrum.

    Mille hominum species, et rerum discolor usus ;
velle suum cuique est, nec voto vivitur uno.
mercibus hic Italis mutat sub sole recenti
rugosum piper et pallentis grana cumini,   55
hic satur inriguo mavult turgescere somno,
hic campo indulget, hunc alea decoquit, ille
in Venerem putris ; sed cum lapidosa cheragra
fregerit articulos, veteris ramalia fagi,
tunc crassos transisse dies, lucemque palustrem,   60
et sibi jam seri vitam ingemuere relictam.

    At te nocturnis juvat inpallescere chartis ;
cultor enim juvenum purgatas inseris aures
fruge Cleanthea.   petite hinc, puerique senesque,
finem animo certum, miserisque viatica canis !   65
'Cras hoc fiet.'   Idem cras fiet.   'Quid ? quasi magnum
nempe diem donas ? '   Sed cum lux altera venit,
jam cras hesternum consumpsimus : ecce aliud cras
egerit hos annos, et semper paulum erit ultra.
nam quamvis prope te, quamvis temone sub uno   70
vertentem sese, frustra sectabere cantum,
cum rota posterior curras et in axe secundo.

    Libertate opus est : non hac, ut, quisque Velina
Publius emeruit, scabiosum tesserula far
possidet.   heu steriles veri, quibus una Quiritem   75

vertigo facit! hic Dama est non tressis agaso,
vappa lippus, et in tenui farragine mendax :
verterit hunc dominus, momento turbinis exit
Marcus Dama.   papae! Marco spondente, recusas
credere tu nummos? Marco sub judice palles?   80
Marcus dixit: ita est; adsigna, Marce, tabellas.
haec mera libertas! hoc nobis pillea donant!
'An quisquam est alius liber, nisi ducere vitam
cui licet, ut voluit? licet ut volo vivere: non sum
liberior Bruto?' "Mendose colligis," inquit   85
stoicus hic, aurem mordaci lotus aceto ;
"haec reliqua accipio; *licet* illud et *ut volo* tolle."
'Vindicta postquam meus a praetore recessi,
cur mihi non liceat, jussit quodcumque voluntas,
excepto si quid Masuri rubrica vetavit?'   90

   Disce, sed ira cadat naso rugosaque sanna,
dum veteres avias tibi de pulmone revello.
non praetoris erat stultis dare tenuia rerum
officia, atque usum rapidae permittere vitae:
sambucam citius caloni aptaveris alto.   95
stat contra ratio, et secretam garrit in aurem
ne liceat facere id quod quis vitiabit agendo.
publica lex hominum naturaque continet hoc fas,
ut teneat vetitos inscitia debilis actus.
diluis helleborum, certo conpescere puncto   100
nescius examen? vetat hoc natura medendi.
navem si poscat sibi peronatus arator,
luciferi rudis, exclamet Melicerta perisse
   8 — Juv.   K 2

frontem de rebus.   tibi recto vivere talo
ars dedit? et veri speciem dinoscere calles,   105
ne qua subaerato mendosum tinniat auro?
quaeque sequenda forent, quaeque evitanda vicissim,
illa prius creta, mox haec carbone, notasti?
es modicus voti? presso lare? dulcis amicis?
jam nunc astringas, jam nunc granaria laxes?   110
inque luto fixum possis transcendere nummum,
nec glutto sorbere salivam Mercurialem?
'haec mea sunt, teneo' cum vere dixeris, esto
liberque ac sapiens, praetoribus ac Jove dextro;
sin tu, cum fueris nostrae paulo ante farinae,   115
pelliculam veterem retines, et fronte politus
astutam vapido servas in pectore vulpem,
quae dederam supra relego, funemque reduco:
nil tibi concessit ratio; digitum exere, peccas,
et quid tam parvum est? sed nullo ture litabis,   120
haereat in stultis brevis ut semuncia recti.
haec miscere nefas; nec, cum sis cetera fossor,
tris tantum ad numeros satyrum moveare Bathylli.
'Liber ego.' Unde datum hoc sentis, tot subdite rebus?
an dominum ignoras, nisi quem vindicta relaxat   125
'I, puer, et strigiles Crispini ad balnea defer!'
si increpuit, 'cessas nugator?' servitium acre
te nihil inpellit, nec quicquam extrinsecus intrat,
quod nervos agitet; sed si intus et in jecore aegro
nascuntur domini, quî tu impunitior exis   130
atque hic, quem ad strigiles scutica et metus egit erilis?

Mane piger stertis. 'Surge!' inquit Avaritia,'heia
surge!' Negas; instat, 'Surge!' inquit. "Non queo."
    'Surge!'
"Et quid agam?" 'Rogitas? en saperdam advehe
    Ponto,
castoreum, stuppas, hebenum, tus, lubrica Coa;   135
tolle recens primus piper ex sitiente camello;
verte aliquid; jura.' "Sed Juppiter audiet." 'Eheu!
baro, regustatum digito terebrare salinum
contentus perages, si vivere cum Jove tendis!'
jam pueris pellem succinctus et oenophorum aptas: 140
'Ocius ad navem!' nihil obstat, quin trabe vasta
Aegaeum rapias, ni sollers Luxuria ante
seductum moneat 'Quo deinde, insane, ruis? quo?
quid tibi vis? calido sub pectore mascula bilis
intumuit, quod non extinxerit urna cicutae?   145
tun' mare transilias? tibi torta cannabe fulto
cena sit in transtro, Veientanumque rubellum
exalet vapida laesum pice sessilis obba?
quid petis? ut nummi, quos hic quincunce modesto
nutrieras, pergant avidos sudare deunces?   150
indulge Genio, carpamus dulcia! nostrum est
quod vivis; cinis et manes et fabula fies.
vive memor leti! fugit hora; hoc quod loquor inde est.'
en quid agis? duplici in diversum scinderis hamo.
huncine, an hunc sequeris? subeas alternus oportet 155
ancipiti obsequio dominos, alternus oberres.
nec tu, cum obstiteris semel instantique negaris

parere imperio, 'rupi jam vincula' dicas;
nam et luctata canis nodum abripit; et tamen illi,
cum fugit, a collo trahitur pars longa catenae.　　　160
　'Dave, cito, hoc credas jubeo, finire dolores
praeteritos meditor:' crudum Chaerestratus unguem
abrodens ait haec.　'An siccis dedecus obstem
cognatis? an rem patriam rumore sinistro
limen ad obscenum frangam, dum Chrysidis udas　165
ebrius ante fores exstincta cum face canto?'
"Euge, puer, sapias; dis depellentibus agnam
percute."　'Sed censen' plorabit, Dave, relicta?'
"Nugaris; solea, puer, objurgabere rubra.
ne trepidare velis atque artos rodere casses!　　170
nunc ferus et violens; at si vocet, haud mora, dicas,
Quidnam igitur faciam? nec nunc, cum arcessat et ultro
supplicet, accedam?　Si totus et integer illinc
exieras, nec nunc."　hic, hic, quem quaerimus, hic est,
non in festuca, lictor quam jactat ineptus.　　175
　Jus habet ille sui palpo, quem ducit hiantem
cretata ambitio? vigila, et cicer ingere large
rixanti populo, nostra ut Floralia possint
aprici meminisse senes.　quid pulchrius? at cum
Herodis venere dies, unctaque fenestra　　180
dispositae pinguem nebulam vomuere lucernae
portantes violas, rubrumque amplexa catinum
cauda natat thynni, tumet alba fidelia vino:
labra moves tacitus, recutitaque sabbata palles.
tum nigri lemures, ovoque pericula rupto,　　185

tum grandes Galli et cum sistro lusca sacerdos
incussere deos inflantis corpora, si non
praedictum ter mane caput gustaveris alli.

Dixeris haec inter varicosos centuriones,
continuo crassum ridet Fulfennius ingens,   190
et centum Graecos curto centusse licetur.

NOTES.

P codicis Pithoeani nunc Montepessulani lectio genuina . ubi quid erasum est neque legi potuit * * indicatum est.

S scholiorum lectiones ipsis litteris, lemmatibus maxime, scriptae.

Σ scholiorum lectiones, de quibus interpretatione coniecturam capere licet.

ω codices interpolati uel omnes uel plurimi.

ς codices interpolati aliquot, maxime recentiores. Ad hos pertinent

    p codicis Pithoeani manus secunda.

    r codicis Vaticani palimpsesti fragmentum.

    a codex bibliothecae Laurentianae, saec. xi.

    b codex bibliothecae Sangallensis, saec. ix.

    c codex bibliothecae Einsiedlensis, saec. x.

    d codex bibliothecae Parisiensis 8070, saec. xii.

    c codex bibliothecae Parisiensis 4883 A.

    f codex bibliothecae Parisiensis 8071, saec. x.

    g codex bibliothecae Parisiensis 7900, saec. ix.

    h codex bibliothecae Vaticanae Vrbinas 661.

    v excerpta e codice Vossiano apud Cortium et Fabricium.—
    JAHN.

NOTES.

SATIRE I.

————◦○⦂❋⦂○◦————

ARGUMENT.

1-14. "Must I be forever a passive listener to epics, comedies, elegies, and tragedies? Am I never to retaliate upon those wretched poetasters by whom, at every turn, the legends of the Argonauts and Centaurs are dinned in our ears?

15-18. "I, too, have flinched from the master's cane; I, too, in the school of rhetoric, have urged Sulla to abdicate. Why should not I, then, waste ink and paper with the rest of the world?

19-50. "I will follow in the track of Lucilius. As a eunuch weds, as a virago spears boars in the amphitheatre, as my old barber vies with Rome's whole nobility in his single wealth, as Crispinus, the spawn of the Nile, flaunts it in a purple cloak, and daintily airs light summer-rings, 'tis hard not to write satire. Who could hold his peace when Matho fills his new sedan with his swollen self, and the spy of spies goes by, who will soon despatch the remnant of Rome's nobles, as he has already betrayed his lord and friend? when a scoundrel robs his ward, and compels him to eat the bread of shame? when Marius, mulcted in fame not in purse, sits down in exile to carouse a full hour before Rome dines, while plundered Africa cries out upon the barren verdict?

51-72. "These themes, surely, are worthier the midnight lamp of Horace than all the threadbare romances, labors of Hercules, ' return' of Diomed, the Minotaur's bellowing, the airy voyage of Daedalus, and the headlong plunge of Icarus. Is it a time for toys like these, when the gallant's estate, denied by law to the wife, is taken by the pander husband, who winks at his own shame? when a youth of ancient lineage holds it no sin by the profits of a military command to retrieve his inheritance wasted upon grooms, or furious drives along the Flaminian way, himself stooping to guide the reins, showing off his skill to his mistress? Fain must I fill every leaf of my tablets, even in the middle of the street, as there sweeps lordly by, lolling in an open sedan, courting the public gaze, the forger, enriched at the cost of a few lines of writing and a moistened signet. The matron fronts us to our face, who, when her lord calls for wine, drugs the cup with toad's juice, and trains country cousins to carry out their husbands' spotted corpses amid the whispers of the crowd.

73-80. "Stoutly sin, if you would be something in this world. Virtue is praised, and starves. 'T is crime that wins parks, mansions, costly tablets, embossed beakers. Who can sleep, for incest and precocious crime? If nature is grudging, scorn indites the verse, the best it can, such as I write — or Cluvienus.

81-150. "The whole range of human life since the flood, all its passions and interests, is my theme. The gambler stakes his fortune, leaving his page the while in tatters; the great add palace to palace, luxury to luxury, but for themselves alone; poor retainers may not pass the threshold, where, after a jealous scrutiny, the fixed pittance is doled out; praetors and tribunes themselves attend the levée, and are served in the order of their rank; but a wealthy freedman claims precedence, for Mammon is the god we worship. The dole is an item in a consul's revenue; can the poor man scorn it, who has nothing else? Great ladies in their palanquins follow their husbands for a second dole; sometimes the empty palanquin deceives the steward. After a long day's attendance, clients disperse to their dinner of herbs; while the 'king' and patron devours an estate at a solitary board. Excess will cut short his days, and he will die unwept. Nothing will remain for after times to add to our corruption; posterity will but ape our acts and our desires; all vice has settled at its zenith : poet, hoist sail, shake out every stitch of canvas!

150-171. "Here, perhaps, you may ask, 'Whence a genius equal to the theme? whence that bluntness wherewith the ancients wrote off as their blood boiled within them whatever they list? Set forth Tigellinus, and you will light up the amphitheatre by night amidst those pine fagots, by which they burn as they stand, who smoke with pierced breast, and your body will be dragged with a hook through the midst of the arena.' What, should he who administered poison to three uncles ride past slung upon his downy pillow, and thence look down with disdain upon *me?* 'When he shall meet you, lay your finger on your lip. 'T is defamation but to say, That's he! You may pit Aeneas against Turnus, and safely; you may wound Achilles in epic verse; Hylas may drop his pitcher, and none will cry, not if he drown himself for company; but let Lucilius once in a glow of anger draw his sword and thunder in verse, the hearer, whose soul is chill with guilt, blushes, his heart sweats under his secret sins. Count well the cost, then, before the trumpet sounds to battle; the plumed combatant repents too late.'

"If it be so hazardous to touch the living, I will try what may be said against those whose ashes lie entombed by the highway side." — MAYOR (*with modifications*).

This satire must have been published after A. D. 100, in which year Marius Priscus was condemned for oppression in proconsular Africa. The greater part of it may have been *written* before that date.

1. Auditor. Recitations by authors were in vogue from the days of Augustus to those of Hadrian. The reciters summoned their friends to hired rooms, or to a private house lent for the purpose by a wealthy patron, or to some public place, as the forum, a bath, a temple, or a theatre ; sometimes they button-holed those they chanced to meet in such places, and assailed their ears with their verses; sometimes a host would inflict his poems on his guests at a dinner-party. The author of the Aeneid used to recite his lines; but in Juvenal's time there were more Corduses than Virgils.

Tantum, *only.* When used as a restrictive particle, *tantum*, like *quoque,* generally stands after the word which it limits; yet not without exception.

Numquamne reponam, shall I never retaliate ? Cf. Horat. *Ep.* i. 19, 39 : scriptorum auditor *et ultor.* Literally, shall I never pay back ? A metaphor derived from mercantile language. The verb may be either in the future indicative or the deliberative subjunctive ; preferably the latter.

2. Totiens (= *toties*). The poem was so long that it lasted through a number of recitations.

Rauci. The wretched poet is *hoarse* from his long reading and pompous mouthing.

Cordi. Probably a fictitious name. The **Theseis** would be an epic poem on the exploits of Theseus; the name being formed as are *Aeneis, Achilleis, Heracleis.* Another reading here is *Codri.*

3. Notice the emphatic position of impune.—Ergo, as it does often, denotes indignant feeling.—Recitaverit is fut. perf. indicative : "shall it go for nothing that one has recited," etc. So also **consumpserit.**

Togatas, sc. *fabulas, his comedies.* In these plays the actors appear in the *toga,* and the manners of the middle or lower classes of Rome are represented. The *praetexta* was the symbol of tragedy ; the *pallium* of Greek subjects.

4. Diem. Auditur toto saepe poeta die. Mart. xi. 70.

4, 5. Telephus, king of Mysia and son of Hercules, was wounded by the spear of Achilles, and was the hero of many tragedies, both Greek and Roman. **Ingens** refers probably to the length of the poem ("the everlasting Telephus," E.) ; some have taken it, however, of the size of the hero (*giant*), others of his prowess (*mighty*).

5, 6. Summi — tergo (the tragedy of Orestes), *written even on the back* (of the paper), *as the border to the very end of the roll is already full.* The ancients wrote usually on one side only of the papyrus or parchment, leaving a good margin. Books written on both sides were called *opisthographi*, and were also said to be written *in aversa charta* (Mart. viii. 62). **Summus** is used here in the sense of *extremus*. Cf. Verg. *Aen.* ii. 324: *venit summa dies*. Plena margine is abl. absolute. Priscian cites this passage as an example of the use of margo as feminine. For **scriptus**, J. and My. read with P, *scribtus*. The participle might have been in the feminine gender, as *Orestes* is the name of a play (*fabula*). Cf. Suet. *vit. Ter.* 2: Eunuchus bis die acta est.

7-9. There were several *groves of Mars*, any of which may be meant: as that at Colchis, in which hung the golden fleece guarded by a dragon; and that "in quo Ilia peperit." The *rocks of Aeolus* are Strongyle, the modern Stromboli, one of the *Aeoliae insulae* (now Lipari islands), the abode of the king of the winds; *Vulcan's cave* was in the southernmost of these islands, Hiera, which was regarded as the forge of Vulcan. Cf. Verg. *Aen.* viii. 416 sqq. Mayor connects the allusions in these verses with the Argonauts, who visited Vulcan's forge and the isle of Aeolus.

9. Agant, *are about*, purpose, are contriving. See Val. Fl. i. 574 sqq. **Venti.** The name of their king, in the adjective *Aeoliis*, suggests the winds. Cf. Verg. *Aen.* i. 81-123, 131-141. Early examples of descriptions of storms were found in the *Nostoi*, as the poems in the Epic Cycle were called, which described the homeward journeys of the Greek heroes after the taking of Troy.

Torqueat, *examines by torture*, as a *judex quaestionis*.

10. Alius, i. e. Jason. Juvenal, in his ill-humor, speaking slightingly of the whole story, does not mention the name of the hero, but simply calls him *another*. So he refers to the golden fleece satirically in *furtivae*, and contemptuously in the diminutive *pelliculae* (that sorry fleece).

11. Monychus. A leader of the Centaurs who hurled trees upon the Lapithae in the quarrel at the marriage of Peirithous. The name retains, of course, the quantity of the Greek word, which is formed by syncope.

12. Fronto was some rich patron, who lent his grounds for recitation; perhaps Fronto Catius, whose oratory is praised by Pliny.

Platani. The plane was much admired for its beauty and shade.

Marmora. The marbles, which shake at the shouts of the audience and re-echo the recited verses, are marble panels inlaid in the walls of the porticus, or slabs in the pavement. The manifest exaggeration in the terms *convulsa* and *ruptae* corresponds with the poet's excited feeling. Virgil, however, says *cantu querulae rumpent arbusta cicadae* (Georg. iii. 328), "shall make the woodlands ring."

13. Adsiduo (= assiduo) **ruptae lectore.** This construction is to be distinguished from the ablative of the voluntary agent with *ab*. When the agent is regarded simply as a means or instrument, the preposition is omitted; this seldom happens, however, unless the noun is accompanied with an adjective or pronoun, so that it might (in many cases) be considered as an ablative absolute of cause. The adjective here is a prominent part of the meaning: the columns are "split" by the *persistency* of the recitations.

14. Exspectes. The subjunctive, of a general condition, in the *second person singular*, to denote the act of an indefinite subject : (*you = any one.*)

Eadem, "sc. ut carmina et scribant et recitent."

15. Et nos ergo, *Well, then ; I too* have been to a grammar-school. —**Et nos,** consilium, etc.; *I too* have written themes in the schools of rhetoric.

16. The theses for original declamations in the schools of rhetoric were (1) *suasoriae* (as in this instance), generally on historical or legendary subjects (cf. Quintil. iii. 8, 53), or (2), for more advanced pupils, *controversiae*, in which legal questions were handled. The advice which young Juvenal in his theme gave to Sulla was that he should purchase sleep by resigning his dictatorship.

Altum. This accusative is often called "adverbial," and is well translated by an adverb in English ; but it is best regarded as a *cognate* accusative, *altum dormiret* being equivalent to *altum somnum dormiret*. So *indoctum canere, magnum tonare, torvum clamat, dulce loquentem, perfidum ridens.*

17. Ubique. "In the forum and in the bath, standing, sitting, running, in the *thermae* and in the swimming-bath." So Mayor, from references in classical writers.

18. Vatibus, *bards ;* here used satirically. In the time of Ennius *vates* was used contemptuously of those poets who adhered to the old Saturnian measure, while those who adopted the more artistic measures and style of the Greeks were called *poetae*. From the time of Virgil and Horace, however, *vates* was the nobler term, like our *bard* as compared with *poet*.

Periturae. The paper is sure to perish, any way ; somebody else will scribble on it, if I do not.

19. Hoc decurrere campo, *to run my course in this field* (i. e. the field of satire). The metaphor here, and in equos flexit, is taken from the race-course. Weidner, citing Tac. *Ann.* ii. **7, says** that *decurrere* is the proper term for military exercises and parades.

20. Auruncae alumnus. C. Lucilius, the father of Roman satire, who was born at Suessa Aurunca (now Sessa), in the southern part of Latium, and is said to have lived from B. C. 148 to B. C. 103. He belonged to the brilliant literary circle of which the younger Scipio was the centre. "The satires of Lucilius, whereof more than eight hundred fragments remain, were satires indeed, a medley of politics, manners, literature, grammar, chiefly in hexameters, partly in iambics and trochaics; his main function was to scourge the corruption of the times."

21. Placidi rationem admittitis, i. e., if you lend a kindly ear to the reason. Some take *placidi* as the gen. sing., instead of the nom. pl., in the sense, "If you will listen to one who is perfectly calm;" to which Lewis well objects that "the poet is not perfectly calm. He tells us, a few lines on (30, 31), that he cannot contain himself."

22. Mevia stands here for any woman of rank. Fighting with wild beasts at the circus and amphitheatres, and engaging in gladiatorial combats, were permitted to women by Nero, but at length forbidden by Severus A. D. 200.

Tuscum. Cf. Stat. Silv. iv. 6, 10: Tuscus aper generosior Umbro. Mart. xii. 14: si te delectant animosa pericula, . . . Tuscis insidiemur apris.

23. Nuda mamma. She was in the hunting costume of Diana and the Amazons. (How does the quantity of final *a*, shown by the metre, determine the *case* of the adjective?)

24. Omnis. Accusative plural.

Unus, *one single man.* Possibly Cinnamus, a barber, "dominae munere factus eques" (Mart. vii. 64).

25. Who used to be my barber. **Gravis,** *heavy,* i. e. thick and luxuriant. Others, "that had grown incommodious to me," "my superfluous beard."

26. Pars, appositive to Crispinus.

Verna Canopi, a slave born-and-bred at Canopus (or Canobus), a dissolute seaport fifteen miles S.E. of Alexandria. — **Verna** "connotes the gay impudence" of house-bred slaves.

27. Crispinus, after coming from Egypt to Rome, dealt in saltfish, but afterwards rose to riches and honors under Nero and Domitian, becoming *princeps equitum* and member of Domitian's privy council. Martial, with his accustomed servility to the Emperor, flatters his favorite.

Tyrias. The expensiveness of Tyrian purple denotes his luxury. The color of the true Tyrian dye was that of "clotted blood, varying with the light in which it was seen."

Umero. *Umerus* is the original spelling of *humerus.*

Revocante, "*hitching up;* the mantle floats on the wind" (Mayor). "Which falling off his shoulders still **revoke**" (Stapylton). Some explain the motion of the shoulders as a foppish effort to display the fine texture of the mantle; "while he gathers now, now flings his purple open" (Gifford). The plural (*lacernas*) indicates the frequent repetition of the movement. Lacernae are light and fine mantles or cloaks, often of costly dye and material, worn usually over the toga.

28 sq. Effeminate luxury reaches its height in this picture of a dandy who has a lighter set of rings in summer than for winter.

Ventilet, etc. "He airs his summer-ring, waving his hand to display it;" or he fans himself with his hand, and thus his glittering ring plays in the sunlight.

29. Pondera. The plural is either ironical, *the heavy weight,* or generalizes the expression.

30 sq. Iniquae tam patiens urbis, *so tolerant of the town's iniquities.* Macleane.

32. Causidicus is a title that Cicero uses with more or less contempt. The proper words for an "advocate" are *orator* and *patronus.* Macleane.

Lectica. A sedan or palankeen.

Matho, a pettifogging lawyer, is again spoken of as a bankrupt (vii. 129) and as a wind-bag (xi. 34). He makes a display of wealth to give a notion of success and attract clients.

33. Plena ipso, "crammed with himself" or "filled by his lordship." The *lectica* had room for two persons of ordinary size.

Delator. The reference is probably to any notorious informer.

34 sq. Cito — superest, *about to clutch, ere long, all that remains of the devoured nobility.* — **Nobilitas** = *nobiles.* "So *levis armatura, juventus, mortalitas, peregrinitas, senectus.*" — **Comesa,** i. e. whose goods have been devoured, both by the exactions of the emperor and the rewards or blackmail of the informers. See the citations in Heinrich and Mayor.

35 sq. Massa, according to the scholiast, was a favorite mountebank of Nero's, and **Carus a dwarf.** But it is more probable that the reference is to the notorious informers Baebius Massa (Tacit. *Hist.* iv. 50; *Agric.* 45) and Carus Mettius (*Agric.* 45). Their fear of Juvenal's *delator* depicts him as one of those *quos timent etiam qui timentur* (Sidon. *Ep.* v. 57).

Latinus, a mime-player under Domitian, and himself a notorious spy, propitiates the more powerful informer by secretly sending him the actress Thymele.

46. Gregibus comitum. Crowds of attendants, as clients and slaves, incommoding the people in the streets.

46 sq. Hic spoliator — prostantis, *this plunderer of his ward,* (who is in consequence) *living in shame.*

47 sqq. Et hic (*another*), i. e. **Marius,** damnatus inani judicio, etc. **Marius Priscus,** who had been proconsul in Africa, was accused of cruelty and extortion by the Afri A. D. 99. Pliny and Tacitus were ordered to prosecute. The case was heard in the senate, Jan. 100, before Trajan, then consul. Marius was condemned to pay 700,000 sesterces (about $27,000) into the treasury, and exiled; yet he retained the greater part of his spoils, and lived in luxury. — The judicium was inane (empty, idle, *ineffectual*), because it left him gorged with his ill-gotten wealth.

48. Salvis nummis. Ablative absolute.

Infamia. "By the *lex Julia repetundarum* passed by Caesar in his first consulship, B. C. 59, the penalties for extortion were a fourfold fine, expulsion from the senate, exile in graver cases, and the degree of *infamia* called *intestabilitas,* which excluded the condemned from giving evidence, prosecuting, or sitting as *judices.*" Mayor.

49. Exul, (though) in exile.

Ab octava (sc. *hora*), i. e. two o'clock. The usual hour for dining was the ninth (three o'clock); sometimes as late as the tenth or later. An early dinner was luxurious, as breaking into the working day. Cf. Horat. *Carm.* i. 1, 20; *Sat.* ii. 3, 8. — Bibit here connotes excess. M.

Fruitur dis iratis, *enjoys* (makes himself only the more comfortable under) *the anger of the gods.* "A parody of Sen. *Herc. Fur.* 33, 34, where Juno says of Hercules *superat et crescit malis, iraque nostra fruitur.*"

50. Victrix. A forensic term, of one victorious in a suit.

51. Credam, agitem. Questions of appeal.

Venusina lacerna, *the Venusian lamp,* the midnight (or early morning) lamp of Horace, who was born at Venusia: i. e. "lucubrations in the style of" the Venusian satirist. Cf. Horat. *Epist.* ii. 1, 112 sq., i. 2, 34 sq. "There is also an allusion" (Mayor says) "to the scorching heat of satire, and its fierce glare (cf. the lantern of Diogenes, *seeking a man*)."

52. Agitem, *pursue*, handle (these themes).

Quid magis, sc. *agitem.*

Heracléas, Diomédéas, Heracléïds, Diomedéïds ; epics on the adventures of Hercules or Diomedes. The form is the same as in *Odyssea.*

54. Puero (i. e. Icaro). Best taken as ablative of instrument, "as it is the boy's dead weight" (well says Mayor) "that strikes the sea." See note on verse 13 *supra.* Simcox considers *puero* as dative of disadvantage (wrongly called dative of the agent), "the sea which the boy found he had struck."

Fabrum, *joiner;* a term applied in sarcastic depreciation to this consummate artist Daedalus.

55 sq. "By the *lex* Voconia (B. C. 169) no citizen of the first class (*classicus*), i. e. whose estate was assessed at 100,000 *asses* or more, could make a woman his heir. But the law might be *evaded* by bequeathing the estate to a third party *in trust* for the woman." Here the pander husband, wittolly conniving at his wife's guilt, "is the *heres fiduciarius* of the rich adulterer; and may himself claim, for his risk as trustee, the fourth part of the inheritance."

Capiendi, of receiving the inheritance.

56. Spectare lacunar. As if wrapt in thought. Or the beauty of the ceiling, gilt and inlaid with ivory, might be an excuse for distraction. Sometimes the panels in the ceiling shifted, and displayed scene after scene to the guests. Mayor.

57. Ad calicem, *over his cup.* Cf. Cic. *pro Coel.* 28, 67 : nonnumquam etiam ad vinum diserti sint. Ov. *Trist.* v. 3, 4 : ad tua vina.

59 sq. Caret . . . censu, *has lost all his family estate* (of a senator or knight), squandering it on his stables; and hence seeks a military command for his maintenance. On *caret* cf. Cic. *Tusc.* i. 36 : *Triste enim est nomen ipsum* carendi, *quia subjicitur haec vis : habuit, non habet; desiderat, requirit, indiget.*

61. Flaminiam (viam). The Flaminian Way was the great northern road from Rome, extending to Ariminum. It was begun in the censorship of C. Flaminius, Hannibal's unfortunate opponent. Skirting the Campus Martius (where it is now the *Corso*) it left the city by the *porta Flaminia* (now *porta del popolo*). It was much frequented.

Puer Automedon, (*like a*) *young Automedon.* As we might say, *the young Jehu.* Automedon was the charioteer of Achilles.

9 — Juv.

61, 62. Nam — amicae. Himself his own page, he shows himself off to his brazen-faced mistress, who wears a man's cloak, — his " Bloomer mistress" Mayor calls her.

63. Nonne libet, *does not one feel inclined.*

Ceras. "Pugillares" or *tablets,* which were thin pieces of wood usually of an oblong shape, covered over with wax on the inner sides. They were fastened together at the back by means of wires (for hinges), so that they opened and shut like our books; and to prevent the wax of one tablet rubbing against the wax of the other, there was a raised margin around each. The wax was written on by means of the *stilus.* Dict. Antiq.

64. Sexta cervice = *sex cervicibus.* The chair is carried on the shoulders of six slaves. — The subject of feratur is signator (67).

65. Patens, exposed (to view).

In what case is **nuda cathedra** ? (Scan the line.) — Nuda paene, almost uncovered or unveiled, i. e. with the curtains drawn. — The cathedra was used chiefly by women. "In the *sella* (line 124) you sat, in the *lectica* (32) you reclined, and in the *cathedra* you were able to loll."

66. Reminding you strongly of the way in which Mæcenas used to sprawl. Simcox. Mæcenas was notorious for his luxury and effeminacy. **Referens,** *recalling.*

67 sq. A friend, called in at the mortal agony to give validity by his signature to the will, takes that opportunity to deceive the testator. Mayor.

Signator falso, *the signer and sealer of a forged will.* With our punctuation (which is both the traditional one and adopted by all the recent editors except Mayor), the syntax of falso cannot be explained without some difficulty. It has been regarded (1) as an adverb, qualifying the noun like an adjective (see Nägelsbach's Stylistik § 75) ; (2) as an ablative, and (3) as a dative: in the last two cases *instrumento* (J. F. Gronovius) or *signo* (Heinrich) being supplied, or **falsum** being taken as a substantive in the sense of *a forgery* (as the term is used in the Roman law; cf. Plin. *Ep.* ii. 20, 12) or *a forged instrument.* Mayor follows Turnebus and Ruperti in punctuating *signator, falso,* etc., which punctuation Madvig approves in case his own conjecture *signato falso* be not adopted. With Mayor's pointing, *falso* would be translated *by forgery.* The best *conjectural* readings are *signator falsus* and *signator falsi.*

Lautum, "genteel ;" *a gentleman.* — **Beatum,** *rich.*

68. His high respectability and wealth cost him two little tablets, on which he writes the **forged will**, — ("it would be enough to say (Gaius ii. 117) *Titius heres esto* or *Titium heredem esse jubeo*"), — and the trouble **of moistening his ring** to get a clean impression in attaching his signet.

69. Occurrit, sc. *mihi.* — **Matrona potens,** *some* powerful matron ; or *the* powerful matron, for dramatic individualization. There were many instances of the infamous crime here described among women of high rank in Rome.

Ribbeck places the four verses 69–72 between verses 76 and 77.

70. Viro sitiente. Generally explained as abl. absolute: a rare construction, where the noun in the abl., in the parenthetical clause, might have been expected to stand in the *main* clause (here in the dat., after *porrectura*). Weidner feels constrained by the position of the words to take *viro* as dat. and supply *eo* with *sitiente*. But a dative is unnecessary here, or at least can be left to be supplied in the mind (e. g. *ei*). Translate: *who, about to offer mild Calenian, when her husband is thirsty, mixes with it the bramble-toad.*

71. Melior, an *improvement on*. Lucusta was a professional poisoner, employed by Agrippina to poison Claudius, and by Nero to poison Britannicus. **Galba ordered her** to be executed.

73. Aud' aliquid. Notice the elision of the long syllable in the first thesis. See L. **Müller, de re metr. 286 sqq. Aliquid, the** reading of the MSS.(Pω) is stronger than the *aliquis* of many editors. Cf. Cic. *in Caecil.* 48 : ut tu tum aliquid esse videare. Plin. *Ep.* i. **23, 2** : erraverim fortasse qui me aliquid putavi. Plat. *Apol.* ad fin. ἐὰν δοκῶσί τι εἶναι μηδὲν ὄντες.

Gyaros, a small rocky island among the Cyclades, was used as a place of deportation of the worst criminals.

76. Stantem, standing out *in* bold *relief.*

78. Praetextatus, i. e. "in his teens."

80. Cluvienus. Some obscure poetaster, **otherwise unknown.**

81. Ex quo, *from the time when.*

83. Mollia. Cf. Ov. *Met.* i. 400 sqq. Proleptic. Remember, however, in translation, that our own language admits of prolepsis.

84. Pyrra = Pyrrha. The wife of Deucalion. Ov. *Met.* i. 260 sqq.

86. Discursus, *restless pursuits,* men's uneasy runnings to and fro, or runnings and chasings, after wealth **and honor,** or even lower objects. In this meaning it is a word of the silver age. Cf. Sen. *ad Ser. de ot.* 6, 5 : discursus et sudor. *Brev. vit.* 3, 2 : officiosa **per** urbem discursatio.

Est follows the number of the predicate *farrago,* as it commonly does when the predicate is a substantive and the copula follows immediately upon it.

87. **Et** often begins an indignant question. Hand *Turs.* ii. p. 492.

87 sq. **Quando** — sinus, i. e. When were the sails of avarice more widely spread? Three other translations have been proposed: viz.: (1) When did a larger haven lie open to avarice? (2) When did the gulf of avarice yawn wider? (3) When did the toga fold of avarice open wider (i. e. to pocket her gains)?

Alea . . . animos. Supply *habuit.* — **Hos** = *tales.*

89 sq. Men do not go to the gaming-table with their purses only, but they stake their money-chests. Tabulae, sc. *aleatoriae.* Loculi (in this sense *plurale tantum masculinum*) were small coffers, of wood or ivory, in which money, jewels, or other valuables were kept; here distinguished from the large *arca,* a "strong-box" or money-chest, bound with iron.

91 sq. The cashier or steward is the arms-bearer, the arms in this battle being coins. "The word *dispensator,* like *dispendium, pensio,* pound, *stipendium,* recalls the time when money was weighed for every payment." Mayor.

93. **Reddere,** here, as often, means to give as in duty bound; to give one what is his due.

94. **Quis avus.**

Fercula septem. Augustus contented himself with three courses, or, when he had guests, with six at most. Suet. 74.

95. **Secreto.** Contrary to the advice of Epicurus: "Choose your company first, and then your provision. For it is a lion's life or a wolf's to gorge without a friend." Sen. *Ep.* 19, 10.

Sportula. "In the days of Roman freedom, clients were in the habit of testifying respect for their patron by thronging his atrium at an early hour, and escorting him to places of public resort when he went abroad. As an acknowledgment of these courtesies, some of the number were usually invited to partake of the evening meal. After the extinction of liberty, the presence of such guests, who had now lost all political importance, was soon regarded as irksome, while at the same time many of the noble and wealthy were unwilling to sacrifice the pompous display of a numerous body of retainers. Hence the practice, under the empire, of bestowing upon each client, when he presented himself for his morning visit, a certain portion of food as a substitute for the occasional invitation to a regular supper (*cena recta*), and this dole, being carried off in a little basket provided for the purpose, received the name of *sportula.* For the sake of convenience, it became common to give an equivalent in money, the sum established by general usage being a hundred quadrantes. In the atrium, the *servus nomenclator* handed the money over at the morning visit of salutation, at which the clients were obliged to appear in the *toga*. The donation in money, however, did not entirely supersede the sportula given in kind. (See Satire iii. 249 sq.)"

97. **Ille.** The patron.

Inspicit, *scrutinizes*, pries into, examines searchingly.

99. The *nomenclator*, or slave who calls out the names of the people, is here called ironically praeco, "his lordship's *crier*."

100. **Trojugenas.** "The older families claimed a mythical descent from the Trojan Aeneas and his companions; as the Julia gens from Iulus, the Sergia gens from Sergius, the Memmii from Mnestheus."

Vexant, "infest."

101. **Da,** etc. The words of the master to the *dispensator*.

104. **Fenestrae,** holes (for ear-rings).

105 sq. **Quinque . . . parant,** *my five shops bring me in an income of four hundred thousand sesterces,* which was a knight's estate. With *quadringenta* supply *sestertia*. Another interpretation of *quinque tabernae*, based upon Livy xxvi. 27, is given by Heinrich after Dusaulx, and meets with much favor among recent editors: viz., *the five banking-houses* bring me in, etc., — alluding to the man's transactions on 'change. This last translation, however, is rejected by Becker (i. 297) and by Mayor.

106. **Purpura major,** i. e. the *latus clavus* or laticlave. See Lex. s. vv. *clavus* and *laticlavius*.

108. **Corvinus** was a cognomen of the Messalae, who were a branch of the gens Valeria, one of the oldest families in Rome.

Custodit conductas oves, keeps sheep for hire (i. e. as a hired laborer).

109. **Pallas,** brother of the procurator Felix before whom Paul preached, was a freedman of Claudius, and was worth over two millions sterling.

Licinis. Generic plural. Licinus was a Gaul, a prisoner of Julius Caesar who emancipated him and made him his *dispensator*. Under Augustus he amassed great wealth as procurator of Gallia.

110. **Sacro honori,** etc., i. e. let him not give place to (make way for) the inviolable tribune, whose person was *sacrosanctus*. Abstract for concrete.

111. **Pedibus albis.** Slaves newly imported are said to have had their feet chalked or marked with gypsum when exposed for sale.

116. *And Concord, who clatters when her nest is hailed.* The temple of Concord (perhaps the one in the Carinae which was built by Camillus after the expulsion of the Gauls) had become inhabited by storks. The noise of the birds clapping their bills is attributed to the goddess.

117. Summus honor. Another instance of the use of the abstract for the concrete.

118. "Juvenal is alone in representing the rich and noble of both sexes as actually receiving the dole. Martial speaks only (xii. 26) of their going the round of morning visits."

119. Comites, *his followers,* the poor clients.

120 sq. Densissima lectica, *a great crowd of litters.* Cf. *multo delatore* (iv. 47), *plurimus aeger* (iii. 232), and the use of συχνός in Greek.

122. Praegnas = *praegnans.*

123. Petit, sc. sportulam. Absenti, sc. uxori.

Nota jam callidus arte, by this time an adept in the profession which he has mastered. See the Lexicons s. v. *callidus.* Mayor.

126. Quiescet, *she'll be asleep;* you'll find that she's asleep. K. Fr. Hermann, cited by Mayor, compares Terent. *Phorm.* 801-2: CH. cognatam comperi esse nobis. DE. quid? deliras. CH. sic e r i t; non temere dico. Many editors, however, give *quiescit,* although P has the future.

127. Rerum, *of engagements.*

128. Juris peritus Apollo. In the forum of Augustus, where courts were held daily, there was a statue of Apollo. Having stood there so long listening to lawsuits, Juvenal calls him *learned in the law.*

129. Triumphales, sc. *statuas.* The forum of Augustus formed two semicircles, one on each side of the temple of Mars Ultor, and in these two *porticus* Augustus set up statues "triumphali effigie" of all the great Roman conquerors.

130. Nescio quis. Contemptuous. "Un je ne sais quoi."

Arabarches. As eastern Egypt from the Nile to the Red Sea bore the name of Arabia, the governor of Thebais (one of the three presidencies into which Egypt was divided) was also called Arabarches on the analogy of Asiarch. The *Egyptian upstart and Arabarch* here meant is probably Tiberius Alexander (son of Alexander Lysimachus), an Egyptian Jew turned pagan, who was made procurator of Judaea circa 46 A. D., prefect of Egypt 66 or 67 A. D., was the first to proclaim Vespasian emperor, 1 July, 69, and was general-in-chief under Titus at the siege of Jerusalem.

131. Non tantum (*not only*), etc. One may, without sacrilege, commit more than one kind of nuisance. Lewis. *Non tantum fas est* = you may do more than —.

132 sq. The vestibulum was an empty space before the door of the house, through which there was an approach from the street (Aul. Gell. xvi. 5). Although they had received their *dole* in the morning, the clients, after following their patron about during the whole day and escorting him home, still hoped for an invitation to a *recta cena*.

136. Rex, the great man, their patron. — Tantum, *all alone*.

137 sq. In these lines the selfish luxury is satirized of men who, while having many large round tables, of costly wood and antique workmanship, which would serve for many guests, set out but one, from which they eat alone, and yet with the most lavish expense.

139. Jam, *soon*.

141. Ponit, *serves up*.

141. Con-vivia. Cic. *Cat. Maj.* 45 : bene enim majores accubitionem epularem amicorum, quia vitae conjunctionem haberet, convivium nominaverunt.

143. P. reads *crudus.* — **144. Intestata.** The friends would receive no legacy, and hence be angry.

145. Another reading (pω), is *it nova*, etc. The best recent editors read *et* with P.

149. In praecipiti stetit, stands at its highest point, has reached the highest pitch. The perfect emphasizes the fact that this highest point *has already* been reached.

Utere. The poet addresses himself.

151. Materiae unde. Observe the hiatus, a liberty not uncommon in Juvenal's hexameters. Cf. iii. 70, v. 158, viii. 105.

Priorum, of our forefathers.

153. Simplicitas. Independence, frankness, openness, *bold freedom* ; παρρησία.

Cujus — **an non ?** The quotation is from Lucilius (*supra* note on verse 20); but with some modification, inasmuch as Lucilius could not have used *audeo* as a dactyl, its final syllable being in his age always long (L. Müller de re metr. 336 sq.).

154. Quid refert, *what matters it ?* what difference does it make?
Dictis, jests, sarcasms.

Mucius is the great jurist, P. Mucius Scaevola, cos. B. C. 133. He was an enemy to Scipio Nasica and Scipio Africanus the younger, the friends of Lucilius.

155. Pone, *portray;* attempt to sketch.

Tigellinus. The cruel and wanton favorite of Nero, and his accomplice in the burning of Rome.

Pone : lucebis, etc. (Satirize Tigellinus, and you'll fare as the
Christians did.) This is an elegant construction, equivalent to *si
pones, lucebis.* "In such cases Cicero never inserts *et* before the
apodosis. Later writers insert or omit it indifferently."

Taeda — harena, *you will shine in those pine-fagots, in which
standing* victims *burn and smoke with their breasts fastened to a
stake, and you draw a wide furrow* (after you) *in the midst of the
sand.* Various translations have been given of this doubtful passage.
Next to the above, I should prefer that which translates *taeda in
illa* "in that torch" or "those torches;" reference being made to
Nero's execution of the Christians (whom he falsely charged with
setting fire to Rome, to avert the odium of the crime from himself
and his favorite), by covering their bodies with tar and setting fire to
them, "that they might serve for torches and give light to the spectators, they being so fastened that they could not bend their bodies."
A similar meaning has been brought out by translating *taeda* "a
pitched shirt," *tunica molesta* (viii. 235); but it would be hard to
find authority for the use of the word *taeda* in that sense.

In deducis we have the lively use of the present for the future,
picturing the scene as if now going on. The allusion is to the drag-
ging away of bodies through the arena, either living, for execution,
or after death. The MSS. vary between this reading and *deducit*
and *diducit.* In P. the last letter is erased or illegible. *Deducis* is
adopted by Heinrich, Jahn, Hermann, Ribbeck, Macleane; Mayor
and Madvig (opusc. ii. 177) read *deducit,* supplying in thought the
relative *quae* referring to *taeda.* Various emendations have been
proposed, the neatest of which (offered in the Porson tracts) is *quae
ducit.*

158. Ergo, etc. *What, then,* is an infamous poisoner to be borne
aloft in luxury and look down on honest men?

Vehatur. An indignant question of appeal.

159. Despiciat. So Heinrich, Ribbeck, Macleane, Mayor, after
some MSS. Jahn and Hermann, with P., *despiciet.*

Pensilibus plumis means a lectica with soft feather-bed and cushions, raised aloft on men's shoulders. Macleane.

160. "Cum with the future, future perfect, or universal present, is
often almost equivalent to si." G. 584.

Veniet contra, *he shall meet you.* Contra = obviam.

Compesce, etc., *padlock your lip with your finger.* Gildersleeve.

161. Even to say the single word " That 's he !" would be dangerous. His guilty conscience would see in you an accuser, and **contrive**
severe punishment for **you.**

162–4. Write of the dead and gone, if you would be safe.

Licet committas, *you may match,* set fighting together, pit
together.

Rutulum. I. e. Turnus.

Hylas was the armor-bearer of Hercules; " drawing water at a
well he was dragged in by the nymphs, and Hercules sought him
long, sorrowing and calling upon his name, and set the people of the
country (Mysia) to seek him."

165. Lucilius. See note on verse 20. Cf. Horat. *Sat.* ii. 1, 62 sqq.;
Pers. *Sat.* i. 114 sq.

Infremuit, *has growled,* or has roared.

Frigida is used of the chill which the sense of guilt sends to the
heart.

167. Tacita culpa, *" with concealed guilt."* A cold sweat coming
over the heart through the power of conscience and the fear of exposure is a forcible description.

169. Animo. Another reading is *anime.* But the vocative seems
the less likely in so masculine and unsentimental a writer as
Juvenal.

Ante tubas. Before the battle is begun. The trumpets give the
signal both for the charge and the retreat.

Galeatum. The man who has once put on his helmet. On the
march, the helmet hung on the left breast, being suspended by a
strap over the right shoulder. Soldiers are so represented on Trajan's
pillar.

Duelli. In the old form *duellum* for *bellum* the derivation from
duo is evident.

171. Flaminia atque Latina, sc. *via.* " The chief roads leading
out from Rome were lined for several miles with the tombs of the
wealthier citizens, burial within the walls of the city being forbidden
by the twelve tables."

M 2

SATIRE III.

———◦◦✕◦◦———

ARGUMENT,

1-9. ALTHOUGH I am distressed at the departure of my old friend Umbricius, I commend him for preferring a quiet home in Campania to the fires and falling buildings and the thousand perils and the reciting poets of Rome.

10-20. While his family and goods were all being packed into a single cart, Umbricius halted at the Capenian gate. Here we stepped down into Egeria's vale and grottoes — how all unlike the true! How far more manifest were the divinity of the stream, if grass edged its waves with green, and no marble profaned the native tufa!

21-57. "Since," says my friend, "there is no room for honest industry at Rome, I will find a home elsewhere, while I have yet vigor to go. They who can make black white, and are willing to stoop to the meanest and most dishonest occupations, may stay here and thrive. Such men can give the people shows, and then go back to their low trades. And why should they not thus shift about, since they only imitate Fortune, who has raised them? What is there for me to do at Rome? I cannot flatter, nor be an instrument of crime, nor privy to the crimes of the great. Not for all the gold of the Tagus should you be willing to forego your peace of mind by harboring a guilty secret.

58-80. "I'll tell you in whom our rich men most delight, and whom I most avoid: 'tis Greeks, and worse, 'tis Syrians: for Syria has poured her refuse into Rome, — her language, customs, harps, and drums, and harlots. From every town the Greeks swarm and creep into rich houses — Jacks of all trades, clever, abandoned, impudent, prompt, fluent. All arts, all sciences, are familiar to the starveling Greek; and bid him fly to the skies, he'll do it; for Daedalus was a Greek, and born at Athens. **81-108.** Shall I not avoid their purple robes? Shall that man, blown to Rome by the same wind as figs and damsons, rank before me, whose infancy breathed the air of Rome? They can flatter most grossly, and yet be believed. What player on the stage can surpass them? Not even Antiochus or Haemus would seem wonderful among the Greeks, for the whole nation are actors in daily life. **114-125.** Pass on to a graver crime.

138

Think of that Stoic who killed his friend and pupil, that old wretch born at Tarsus. There is no place for a Roman here ; these Greeks have got sole possession. By a few drops of the poison of calumny the oldest and most faithful clients are driven away, nor is their loss felt.

126-167. " What are a poor man's services, when praetors rush before them to do their homage to rich childless ladies ? The first question at Rome is ' What is a man's wealth ? ' the last, ' What is his moral character ? ' Poverty is always laughed at — the hardest thing to bear in the poor man's lot. The poor man's tattered clothes, and his ejection from the front rows in the theatre, to make room for a crier's foppish son or a gladiator's, are a jest to his patron. What poor man gets a wife, or an inheritance, or the humblest office ? All Romans true should long ago have joined to fly their country. 'Tis hard to rise where virtue is kept down by poverty ; but hardest of all at Rome, where food and lodging are so dear.

168-189. " Here a man 's ashamed to dine off earthenware ; not so when he goes into the country. In the country both great and small appear in public in their undress tunics; in town the client must wear the costly toga. Here men live beyond their means. How much will you give to call on this grandee, or for a glance from that one ? When a patron offers to some god the locks of a handsome page, and the house is full of sacrificial cakes, poor clients must fee the slaves, or they are not admitted to a share.

190-222. " In the country who fears falling houses ? Rome is shored up with buttresses. I 'd rather live where there are no fires nor midnight terrors. The poor man's house burns, he loses his little all, and no one will help him ; the rich man receives contributions which more than replace his losses. **223-231.** You may buy a house and a little garden in the country for the annual rent of a garret in Rome. **232-238.** The poor cannot sleep at Rome, for the noise of the crowded streets.

239-267. " The rich man is borne through the streets in a litter, where he may read or sleep at ease; the poor is hustled by crowds, bumped by logs of timber, trampled on by a soldier's hob-nailed boots. A client, returning home with his slave bearing his dinner in a chafing-dish, is crushed to death under a wagon-load of marble. His household is making ready to receive him ; but he the while cowers on the shores of Styx, without a farthing for the ferryman.

268-277. " The night has other dangers,— such as pots from lofty windows ; count yourself happy if you get no more than their contents. A wise man makes his will before he walks abroad at night. **278-301.** A drunken rioter meets you, who sleeps not till he kills his man. Though 'flown with insolence and wine,' he knows how to avoid the rich man's train and torches, but I am his victim, who go forth by the light of a candle or the moon. With insulting speech he picks a quarrel, if that be quarrel where one gives, the other does but take the blows. Whether you answer or not, it 's all the same ; he knocks you down, then (as if he were the aggrieved party binds you over to appear in court. This is the poor man's license when he 's beaten, to pray he may be suffered to carry home a few teeth in his head,

302-314. "Then when your doors are closed and barred, the robber breaks in and robs or murders you. For thieves come to Rome as their preserve. Their fetters soon will leave no iron for our tools. Happy our ancestors, for whose need one prison was enough!

315-322. "But I must go: the horses and the driver are impatient, and the sun is setting. Farewell, remember me; and when you go to Aquinum send for me, and I'll come help you write another satire." — MAYOR and MACLEANE, *with modifications.*

---

1. Confusus, *distressed.* Cf. Plin. *Paneg.* 86 : quam ego audio confusionem tuam fuisse, cum digredientem prosequereris!

Amici. Juvenal calls the name of his friend Umbricius (vs. 20). We have no reason to suppose that any real person is meant.

2. Vacuis, empty, *unfrequented.*

3. Quod . . . destinet. *Quod* with the subjunctive is used when we state both the reason and the assertion by another party that the fact is so. (M. 357.) *Because,* as he tells me, *etc.* The *infinitive* after *destinare* is found in Caesar, Nepos, Livy, and Ovid, but becomes more frequent in the silver age.

Sibylla. The Cumaean Sibyl was supposed to dwell in a large artificial cave; modern travellers are shown what may be some remains of it. Justin Martyr (*cohort.* 37) saw at Cumae a great basilica, hewn out of the rock, with three baths in which the Sibyl bathed. After her bath, she retired into an inner shrine, also hewn, like the baths, out of the rock, where, sitting on a lofty tribunal and seat, she gave her oracles. Mayor.

4. Janua Baiarum. The Via Domitiana, a branch of the Via Appia from Sinuessa, led to Cumae, whence travellers took an older road that led to Baiae and the principal towns on the bay as far as Surrentum, all of which were favorite resorts of the wealthy Romans. "This *gratum litus* was so thickly studded with houses that, according to Strabo, they looked like one town."

Amoeni secessus. Genitive of quality : *affording* an agreeable retreat. "Un lieu d'un très agréable séjour."

5. Prochyta (now Procida) is a small island near Cape Misenum.

Subura (or Suburra) was the name of a low street leading from the Esquiline to the Viminal,—the noisiest and most disreputable part of Rome.

7, 8. The many stories of the Roman houses, of which the upper (*tabulata, contignationes*) were of wood, the narrowness of the streets,

and the wooden outhouses, all increased the risks of fire. **Conflagra-**
tions were frequent and extensive. Owing to the dearness of land
and cost of lodging, speculators carried their buildings to a great
height, and employed very frail materials; earthquakes and inunda-
tions often undermined even more solidly **built houses.** Mayor.

10. **Dum componitur, substitit.** When *dum* denotes what happens *while* something else happens, it is usually constructed with the
present, although the action be past and the perfect be used in the
leading proposition. M. 336, obs. 2.

Domus, his household.

Reda. "A Gallic vehicle, much used at this time by the Romans.
It was four-wheeled, drawn by two or four horses,— a family, and
later a stage-coach, constructed to carry passengers and goods."

11. **Arcus.** An aqueduct was carried on arches over the porta Capena, and the gate was called in the time of the scholiast "the dripping
arch." From the **porta Capena,** one of the principal gates in the
wall of Servius, the Appian way led to Capua. The discovery of the
first milestone on the Appian way has fixed the position of the gate
at the foot of *mons Caelius.* It is fifteen hundred yards within the
porta Appia of the wall of Aurelian, now called *Porta San Sebas-*
tiano.

12. **Hic,** *here.* **Ubi,** etc. I. e. in the *lucus Camenarum* (or grove
of the four Latin prophetic divinities, Antevorta, Postvorta, Car-
menta, and Egeria), directly before the porta Capena, on the left
hand as one passed out of the city. As the grove was filled with
poor Jews, Umbricius leads Juvenal farther aside into the quiet
valley of Egeria, whence they could still see the Appian way. This
grove, which had a fountain in it (Liv. i. 21), the poet represents as
the scene of the meetings of Numa and Egeria. From the strange
notion that these meetings must have been in the valley of Egeria,
Jahn and Ribbeck place the five lines 12–16 after line 20, and H. A.
J. Munro, while retaining the old order of the verses, offers his friend
Mayor an ingenious but strained interpretation of the passage.

Amicae. Egeria, one of the four Camenae; a prophetic muse, not
a nymph. (Dion. Hal. ii. 60, 364.) Juvenal chooses to give a
satirical turn to the tradition of Numa's interviews with this
goddess.

14. The large wicker *basket* and the *hay*, which constituted the
scanty furniture of the Jews to whom the grove and the aedes Camenarum had been let, were used, the first for a receptacle for their
provisions and for alms, the second for a bed.

15. Mercedem, a rent. **Populo,** to the Roman people.

16. The wood itself is said to go a begging, as its occupants beg.

17. Notice the asyndeton. As the Muses' grove is now so uninviting, we go down *at once* into Egeria's valley.

Speluncas. "Juvenal speaks of artificial grottoes, but does not" necessarily "mean more than one."

18. Veris, *natural* ones. But translate, *unlike the true.*

Praesentius. How much *nearer to us* would the goddess of the spring seem to be! Another reading is *praestantius.*

19. Cluderet = *clauderet.*

20. Ingenuum, native, natural, plain, unsophisticated.

Nec . . . violarent, *and . . . did not wrong* (spoil).

23. Res, *my property,* my means.

Here was the form commonly used in Juvenal's time. The pronunciation of the final letter was intermediate between *e* and *i.* (Quintil. i. 4, 8.) Augustus wrote *heri.*

23 sqq. Eadem — aliquid, "and will again to-morrow wear away something from its small remainder."

Proponimus. Plural for the singular.

Illuc . . . ubi Daedalus, etc. To Cumae. Cf. Verg. *Aen.* vi. 14 sqq.

27. In the Greek conception of the Μοῖραι, who according to Hesiod were three — Clotho, Lachesis, and Atropos — it was Clotho's business to spin the thread of human life. Lachesis determined the duration and condition of it, [and Atropos, "the inflexible," held the shears, and at Clotho's command cut the thread.] But, as in Horace, the three sisters are sometimes represented as spinning, and here Clotho's functions are usurped by Lachesis. Macleane.

29 sq. Artorius et Catulus. "Any two scoundrels." Strauch thinks that Juvenal chooses names which will include both nobles (Catulus) and plebeians (Artorius).

30. Qui vertunt. The indicative emphasizes the action as an actual fact.

31. Quis = *quibus.*

31–33. Who are willing (as *redemptores, mancipes,* or *conductores*) to *undertake* the building or repair of temples, the dredging or embanking of rivers, the construction or clearing of harbors, the draining of the sewers, the carrying out the dead to burial; and, having made the most of their contracts, to embezzle the money, and when that is safe become bankrupt. Mayor. Some understand *flumina* and *portus* of the farming of the public revenues, and *eluviem siccandam* of the draining of marshes, or even of salt-making (Tac. 13, 57).

33. *And to offer themselves to be sold up, under the spear, the symbol of lawful ownership;* i. e., to go into bankruptcy. Juvenal might have said *praebere se venales.* The expression "he is sold up" is used for "his goods are sold." The State, as creditor, had the right to put itself in possession of the goods of the bankrupt (*creditor in bona debitoris mittebatur*), and they were sold at auction *sub hasta* (signo justi dominii, Gaius iv. 16). The fraudulent debtor became *infamis,* and the *infamia* entailed the loss of *status* (Walter, § 788, p. 455). Mayor; Schömann Jahrb. 99, 765–7. Others interpret this verse of contracting for the sale of slaves by auction. The custom of setting up a spear at auctions is said to have been derived from the practice followed in old times of selling prisoners and booty on the field of battle under this symbol.

36. Munera, sc. *gladiatoria.*

Verso pollice. Those who wished the death of a conquered gladiator turned (*vertebant, convertebant*) their thumbs towards their breasts, as a signal to his opponent to stab him ; those who wished him to be spared, turned their thumbs downwards (*premebant*), as a signal for dropping the sword. Mayor.

37. Populariter. "To win good will."

38. After giving the people shows, they go back to their trade, which condescends to low gains (Macleane). They farm the *cabinets d'aisance;* and why should they not contract for anything?

42. Poscere. I. e. to ask for a copy, to read carefully at home.

Motus astrorum, etc. I am no astrologer, to promise a wicked expectant heir the speedy death of his father.

44. Ranarum viscera, etc. I have never, as an haruspex, inspected the entrails of frogs. "The superstitious consulted the entrails of animals not commonly used for the purpose."

47. Nulli comes exeo. Since I will bear no part in extortions, no governor takes me with him in his *cohors* into a province. That *fur* and *comes* are to be thus explained, appears from the mention of Verres (53). Mayor; and so Weidner and Lewis. Macleane says that "*comes* means *comes exterior,* the great man's walking companion."

48. Exstinctae corpus non utile dextrae, *a useless trunk, with right hand destroyed.* "Exstinctae dextrae" is the genitive of quality or description.

49. Conscius, *an accomplice.*

Cŭĭ. Here a dissyllable. Cf. vii. 211.

55. The Tagus was one of those rivers which were supposed to have gold in their sands.

56. Ut somno careas, etc. That for it you *should be willing to* forego your peace of mind by harboring a guilty secret.

Ponenda = *deponenda.* The gifts and honors must sometime be parted with, at least at death.

57. **Tristis,** like *somno careas,* implies the absence of true happiness which always accompanies an unquiet conscience.

61. **Quamvis,** *and yet.* Used like *quamquam* (Aen. v. 195) in correcting one's self. — **Quota portio faecis Achaei?** Best translated in English as an exclamation: *how small a portion of our dregs are Greeks!* Lewis says, "I cannot understand how Heinrich and Macleane" (he might have added "and all the leading editors") "put a note of interrogation after *Achaei.*" They could do nothing else. **Quotus** is an interrogative adjective pronoun, and *quota portio* means properly, in the words of Mayor, "one part amongst how many?" or "how many parts, each equal to this, go to make up the whole?" Macleane explains himself very well when he says that "*Whath part?*" would express *quota pars,* if we could coin an interrogative adjective after the analogy of the *seventh* part, *eighth,* etc. He refers to Key's Latin Gram., ₴ 248 and note.

63 sq. Chordas obliquas, triangular harps. The *sambuca* is referred to.

Gentilia tympana, *the tambourines of the nation;* chiefly used in the worship of Cybele. "They correspond," Macleane says, "to the Indian tom-tom, and are beaten with no perceptible reference to time . . . . The Orientals have little or no ear for music; and on lower ground than Umbricius takes, he might have run away from the music of Eastern flageolets, harps, and drums. They were probably such as are still in use all over Asia, and no discord is comparable to that which is there listened to with satisfaction."

65. **Circum.** The Circus Maximus.

66. **Ite,** *hie thither!* Ruperti says "ite in malam rem;" which to be sure is the same thing.

Picta. Find by scanning the verse the quantity of the final *a.* In what case is *picta,* accordingly, and with what other word only in this line can it agree?

Mitra. A species of light turban, worn by Asiatic women of bad fame.

67. **Rusticus ille tuus,** *thy old-time rustic;* "that son of thine, the rustic of old."

Trechedipna. A Greek word of obvious derivation. (See the Lexicons.) Of the two meanings given by the Scholiast, "vestimenta parasitica, vel galliculas Grecas currentium **ad caenam,**" **Freund** adopts the first, a *garment* worn by parasites running **to a supper;** recent editors incline rather to the second, a kind of *dress-shoes* worn as above. Simply for *translation*, we need not solve the difficulty. Anthon remarks that " Juvenal means to lash not only the introduction of effeminate Grecian manners and costume, but also the accompanying inroad of Greek terms into the Roman tongue;" and he purposely retains the word in his translation, "puts on the trechedipna."

68. Ceroma was a mixture of oil, wax, and earth, with which the athletes rubbed themselves before wrestling.

Niceteria, prizes of victory, such as collars, chains of gold, rings, and (as perhaps here) wreaths or garlands.

69. Alta Sicyone. " Old Sicyon lay in the plain near the sea, but Demetrius Poliorcetes razed the walls **and** houses, and removed the inhabitants to the Acropolis."

Amydon was on the banks of the Axius **in Macedonia.**

70. Notice the hiatus in a Greek word before the principal caesura.

71. What hill of Rome is here spoken of as deriving its name from the osiers that grew on it? (Varro, however, says (v. 51), *Viminalis a Jove Vimino, quoi ibi arae;* but adds *sunt qui quod ibi vimineta fuerint.*)

72. Viscera, *the vitals,* the heart; " bosom-friends."

73. Ingenium — perdita, *" their wit is quick, their impudence desperate."*

74. Isaeo torrentior = *torrentior quam sermo Isaei.* " The ablative **of the person,** instead of **the** ablative (*sermone*), of that which belongs to him." M. 280, obs. 2; Z. 767 *in fine.*

Isaeus was a Greek rhetorician of distinction, who came to Rome about A. D. 97, being then upwards of sixty years of age. Pliny the younger (*Epp.* ii. 3) speaks in the highest terms of his ready eloquence.

75. Quem vis hominem, *any character you choose.*

76. Geometres is here a trisyllable, the ĕ and ō being contracted into one syllable by synaeresis.

Aliptes. The slave who anointed his master in the bath.

78. Graeculus, *the Greekling.* The contemptuous use of the diminutive.

Jusseris = *si jusseris.* Strictly, a hortatory subjunctive.

79. In summa, *in short, in a word,* denique. In the golden age, this expression was used only to denote the whole as opposed to the

single parts: cf. Cic. *ad Quint. fr.* ii., 16, 3 : Drusus erat de prae-
varicatione a tribunis aerariis absolutus, in summa quattuor sententiis, cum senatores et equites damnassent; where *in summa* means
in the whole number of the judges : quoad judices universos, vicit
quattuor sententiis. *Ad summam* would be the Ciceronian expression in our passage, and so some editors, after ρω, have read; so also
Freund and other lexicographers. Our reading is that of P. and S.,
adopted by Jahn, Hermann, Ribbeck, Weidner. The later Latin
used both *in summa* and *ad summam* in the sense of *denique.*

80. Mediis natus Athenis. The reference is to Daedalus.

81. Horum. Notice the passage, in lively discourse, from the
generic singular to the plural.

Conchylia. I. e. purple robes.

82. Signabit. I. e. as witness, e. g. to a marriage-deed (x. 336) or
will (i. 67).—**Recumbit,** *etc.* I. e. be ranked higher at table.

83. Pruna et cottona, *plums* (of Damascus, whence our "damsons," originally "Damascenes"), and small Syrian *figs.* Other
readings are *cottana* (and so Hesychius) and *coctana.*

84. Usque adeo nihil est, *is it so utterly nothing?* is it so entirely
to go for nothing?

85. Baca (bacca) **Sabina,** the Sabine olive.

86. Quid quod, *why add that?*

91. Ille . . . . quo . . . . marito = *ille maritus* (i. e. gallus), *quo.*
Attraction of the antecedent substantive into the relative clause.
M. 319, obs.—**Ille,** i. e. vox illius. Cf. verse 74.—**Quo marito.**
See note on i. 13 : *adsiduo lectore.*

93 sqq. Is the comedian, when he plays Thais, etc., a better actor
(than the Greek is in private life)? So do the Greeks excel in flattery and deception, that actors maintaining the most difficult parts,
even men personating women so as to be mistaken for them, do not
surpass their art. So Madvig, *Opusc.* i. 51.

Thais. A courtesan, e. g. in the *Eunuchus* of Terence.

94. Doris. A name of a servant-girl. Madvig, *Opusc.* i. 53.

Nullo cultam palliolo, *clad in no mantle;* not having a *palliolum*
(or *pallium*), the outer dress of the lower order of women, but clad
in the chitōn alone. So K. F. Hermann, Madvig, Mayor, and others.
Macleane wrongly accepts the definition of *palliolum* as " a small
square cloth worn over the head to protect it from the weather, or to
hide the face."—For nullo Jahn adopts Büchner's conjecture pullo.

97. Tenui — rima, parted by a narrow cleft.

98, 99. The names here given are those of four distinguished
actors in Rome, all of them Greeks.

Nec tamen. *Still, neither* Antiochus, etc. "It is true that the actor personates a woman to the very life; still the best actors do no more than what *every* Greek can do."

Illic. I. e. in their own country.

Molli. Delicate and graceful, in tone and gesture.

102. **Nec**, *and yet not.* Plin. *Epp.* v. 6, 36: ita occulte temperatur, ut impleat nec redundet. Mayor.

103. **Endromidem.** A thick woollen rug thrown over the body after violent exercise.

Here Gifford quotes Hamlet's dialogue with Osric:

Osr. I thank your lordship, 't is very hot.
Ham. No, believe me, 't is very cold: the wind is northerly.
Osr. It is indifferent cold, my lord, indeed.
Ham. But yet, methinks, it is very sultry, and hot for my complexion.
Osr. Exceedingly, my lord; it is very sultry, — as 't were, — I cannot tell how. — *Hamlet*, v. 2.

Cf. Gnatho in Ter. *Eun.* ii. 2, 19.

105 sq. Aliena — facie, to assume an expression of countenance from another's face. "According to Athenaeus, one Kleisophus used to make a wry face whenever Philip tasted any pungent dish. Plutarch compares such a flatterer to a polypus, or to a mirror which reflects all images from without."

106. **Jactare manus,** *to throw up his hands* in admiration and astonishment. Another (but inferior) reading in the preceding clause is *alienum sumere vultum,* which requires the words *a facie jactare manus* to be taken together, and translated *to fling kisses.*

Laudare paratus. Juvenal is fond of this construction of the infinitive after adjectives. A. & G. 57, 8, *f*, 3; G. 424, 4; H. 552, 3.

108. Weidner understands *trulla aurea* of a *golden ladle* with which wine was dipped from the wine-jar. The patron has drained the jar and turned it upside down (inverso fundo), and then asks his Greek parasite to dip him some wine. The parasite eagerly hastens to obey, and strikes the bottom of the jar with his ladle, so that it rings, before he perceives that it has been inverted. Instead of being offended at the poor joke played upon him, he laughs aloud and applauds his master's wit. With this explanation, the verse is rendered, *if the golden ladle has rung on the bottom of the wine-jar.*

An interpretation more commonly adopted explains *trulla* as a *drinking-cup;* the verse would then be translated, *if, when its bottom is turned upwards, the golden goblet has given a gurgling sound.* So Stapylton:

> Or if, the bottom o' th' gilt bowl turn'd up,
> He fetcht the froth off with a gallant sup.

Others still, less plausibly, understand that he dashes the heel-taps of his goblet into a basin or upon the floor, as if playing the *cottabos*.

The examples given by Forcellini sufficiently prove that *trulla* may mean either a *ladle* or a *drinking-cup*. Some suppose that its meaning here is *scaphium* or *matella*, and that *fundus* in this passage is equivalent to *anus*. Heinrich argues ingeniously in favor of the scholiast's first explanation, *si pepederit*, taking *trulla aurea* as *venter divitis*. The second interpretation of the scholiast has little probability: si calix aureus crepitum dederit cadens e manu divitis.

114. Transi, *pass by;* say nothing of. Others take it as equivalent to *transi ad.*

115. Gymnasia, *their training-schools.* "Quit the playgrounds of vice."

Facinus majoris abollae, *a crime of the larger robe;* i. e. a crime committed by a man of high position.

116. Servilius Barea Soranus was proconsul of Asia in the reign of Claudius, and a man of high character. He fell under the displeasure of Nero, and was charged with treasonable practices, and his daughter Servilia with aiding him. They were condemned to death. The chief witness against them was P. Egnatius Celer, a Stoic philosopher, grave of garb and mien, but treacherous, crafty, avaricious, and lustful. Egnatius was rewarded with riches and honors: afterwards, however (A. D. 69), he was exiled.

117 sq. Nutritus, etc. Egnatius is said to have been born at Berytus; but he was educated at Tarsus, if the interpretation usually given to verses 117, 118, is the correct one. The *Gorgoneus caballus* (caballus, *nag* or *hack*, contemptuously; like Persius's *fonte caballino* of Hippocrene) is Pegasus, who sprang from the blood of the Gorgon Medusa when Perseus struck off her head at Tartessus in Spain. According to the legend, he lost a wing (ταρσός) at Tarsus, on the banks of the Cydnus in Cilicia, whence the city had its name. Strabo (xiv. 673 sq.) says of Tarsus in his day, "with such zeal do the inhabitants study philosophy and literature, that they surpass Athens, Alexandria, and all other schools of learning. . . . Rome knows well how many men of letters issue from this city, for her streets swarm with them." "The apostle Paul, Apollonius of Tyana and the Stoics Nestor, the teacher of Tiberius, and Athenodorus,

with others," are mentioned by Mayor as having received instruction
in this city.

120. Notorious parasites.

123. Naturae, *of his own* (i. e. the parasite's) *disposition.*

Patriae, *of his country,* i. e. of Greece.

Veneno, *venom.*

124. Perierunt, have been wasted ; have gone for naught.

125. "My long slavery" is the client's bitter expression for his
attentions and civilities to his patron.

Nusquam — clientis, *nowhere do they make less of pitching a client
overboard.* "The word *cliens,*" says Macleane, "is used to express
a totally different relation between patron and dependant from what
it expressed in the earlier times of the republic. At this time it did
not involve a legal and political distinction, and meant no more than
an humble friend, a dependant who looked to another for support,
counsel, and so forth."

126. Officium, *service.*

Ne nobis blandiar, *not to flatter ourselves;* to tell the plain truth.

127 sq. Si — currere, *if he take the pains to run while it is yet
night in his toga.* The toga, the "dress-coat" of the Romans, was
always worn in calls of civility and other *officia.*

128. *While the praetor treads on the heels of his lictor,* etc. "The
poor man stands no chance of being noticed, when even the higher
magistrates are hastening on the same errand." The praetor at
this time had two lictors when within the city, and six without.
Impellat implies *hitting against,* in whatever manner. Cf. Sen. *de
Tranq. An.* 12, 2: impellunt obvios et se aliosque praecipitant.
Heinrich understands *manu,* and translates *pokes the lictor in the
ribs.*

129. Dudum vigilantibus orbis, *the childless ladies having been
awake* (i. e. up and ready for their reception) *for a long time.*

130. The names represent two rich and childless matrons.

137 sq. Hospes numinis Idaei. Livy (xxix. 10, 11) relates that
when in 205 B. C. the Sibylline books were consulted, it was found
that Rome might be secured against all invaders, if only the Idaean
Mother were brought from Pessinus to Rome. The Delphic oracle
directed that the best man in the city should receive her with a
proper welcome ; and the senate (B. C. 204) selected P. Cornelius
Scipio Nasica, a young man who had not yet been quaestor, for that
honor (Liv. xxix. 14). He received the image at Ostia from the ship
that had conveyed it, and then delivered it to the charge of the

matrons.   This image which the priests of Pessinus presented to the
Romans as the veritable Mother Cybele was a rude field-stone.

Numa was the most pious of kings.

138 sq. Qui — Minervam.   L. Caecilius Metellus, twice consul,
when pontifex maximus (B. C. 241), saved the Palladium from the
burning temple of Vesta.   In this act of courageous devotion he lost
his sight from the effect of the flames.

140. Ad, *in regard to,* with reference to, as regards.   Cf. Cic. *de
Fin.* ii. 20, 63 : non timidus ad mortem ; *in Cat.* i. 5, 12 : ad severi-
tatem lenius.   **Moribus,** *his character.*

Seneca (*Epp.* xix. 6, 14) translates from an old Greek tragedian as
follows :

> Sine me vocari pessimum, ut dives vocer ;
> "An dives" omnes quaerimus, nemo "an bonus ;"
> Non "qua re et unde," "quid" habeas, tantum rogant.

144. Samothracum.   The most secret mysteries known to the
ancients were connected with the worship of the Cabiri : deities
worshipped nowhere else so solemnly as in Samothrace.   Macleane.

149. Sordidula, *a trifle soiled.*

151. Non una cicatrix, " more than one seam" or patch.

153. Inquit, sc. *designator,* the usher.   *Inquit* is often used without a subject expressed.   The scene is now in the theatre or amphitheatre.

154. Pulvino equestri.   The orchestra was appropriated to the
senators ; the fourteen front rows of the *cavea,* which were cushioned,
were reserved for the knights.   Any one might take his place there
who had the equestrian census of 400,000 sesterces.   The tribune L.
Roscius Otho (verse 159) proposed this law B. C. 67.   Having grad-
ually fallen into disuse, it was revived by Domitian.

158. A pinnirapus, or *crest-snatcher,* was a gladiator matched with
a Samnite.   The Samnite gladiators wore a crest on their helmets ;
the *pinnirapus* sought to snatch away this crest, or a feather from it.
Gladiators were not allowed to sit in the knights' benches : it appears
that the restriction did not extend to their sons.   Praecones too were
of low social position, and not eligible to the rank of *decuriones* so
long as they followed their calling.

160 sq. Censu — impar, *inferior in estate, and not a match for the
young lady in his money-bags.*   The last clause may also be translated,
not a match for the young lady's money-bags.   Others render *sarcinulis,* "dowry ;" others still "trousseau ;" others refer it to such

things as the woman fancied she wanted after marriage, the poor man
being described as unable to keep his wife in " trinkets and finery."
Censu may refer to the equestrian estate, "or *censu minor* may be
taken generally for a man of small means."

162. When is a poor man an "assessor" (i. e. a legal adviser) even
to the police? The aediles were at this time police-officers.

163. Olim, *long ago ;* a meaning which this word often has in
writers of the silver age.

164. Haut = *haud.* Johnson's vigorous version of this sentence
was inspired by his own experience :

"Slow rises worth by poverty depress'd."

166. Magno, sc. constat.

167. Servorum ventres. "Petron. 57 : viginti ventres pasco."
"Horace, who lived as plainly as any man could do, and was a
bachelor, could not sit down to his dinner of leeks and fritters without three slaves, which he considered the height of independence
(Sat. i. 6, 116). Umbricius was married, and had children, and the
customary number of slaves in every household had grown enormously
since the days of Horace."

168. Negabis is a conjecture of Valesius, adopted by Jahn, Ribbeck, Weidner. The MSS. *negavit;* but *b* and *v* are often interchanged in manuscripts. Grangaeus conjectured *negabit,* which
Hermann adopts.

170. The cucullus was a sort of cape, worn over the *lacerna.* It
was provided with a hood, which could be drawn over the head
either to disguise the wearer or to defend him from the weather.
Venetus, sea-green; sometimes blue, or shifting between blue and
green; sometimes of ferruginous color (Lyd. *de mens.* iv. 25).

172. After death, the body of a free person was always clad in a
toga, such as accorded with his rank. Augustus forbade the citizens
to appear without the toga in the forum or circus. But the toga was
costly and inconvenient, and hence gladly laid aside on informal
occasions. Pliny mentions among the charms of his Tuscan villa,
nulla necessitas togae (Epp. v. 6, 45).

172-4. Order: Si quando ipsa dierum festorum majestas ("*the
solemn holidays*") colitur herboso theatro.

Tandem, after a long interval.

175. Exodium, a merry *farce ;* originally an *interlude* (Liv. vii. 2).
Personae, etc. In the farces grotesque masks were used, " having
the mouth wide open, representing broad laughter or grinning."

Lucian *de Salt.* 27, quoted by Mayor, speaks of an "actor with a mask that towers above his head, and a great mouth gaping wide, as if to swallow up the audience."

177-9. "In the rustic crowd there is no distinction of *latus clavus* or *angustus clavus,* nor any *praetexta;* even the municipal senate (*decuriones*), who occupy the *orchestra,* as the senators do at Rome, are dressed like the rest of the spectators in tunics;" and a *white* tunic is sufficient to mark the dignity of the "great aediles," the common people appearing in dark-colored tunics. *Clari honoris* and *summis* are used humorously, like Horace's *magni* quo *pueri, magnis e centurionibus orti.*

180. Habitus. Genitive. The use of this word in the sense of *dress,* as here and in line 177, is rare before the post-Augustan writers.

182. Ambitiosa, ostentatious, pretentious.

184. Quid das. I. e. to Cossus's servants.

Cossus. "A noble," says the scholiast. Probably an informer and accuser like Veiento.

185. A. Fabricius Veiento, praetor B. C. 55 (when he ran dogs instead of horses in the games), was banished from Italy B. C. 62 for libelling senators and priests, and for selling various offices, and was afterwards consul under Domitian, and a notorious informer. He was a friend also of Nerva's. Cf. Plin. *Epp.* iv. 22, 4: Cenabat Nerva cum paucis. Veiento proximus atque etiam in sinu recumbebat. *Dixi omnia, cum hominem nominavi.* Mayor.

Clauso labello. Without deigning to open his lips.

186 sq. Ille, hic. Any other patrons.

Deponit, *cuts,* i. e. causes to be cut.

"When a youth first shaved, it was a holiday, and the young down was sometimes offered to some god, with the long hair worn in boyhood but cut off when the 'toga virilis' was put on. This ceremony was observed by certain masters with their favorite slaves." In each of the cases here supposed, the house is immediately full of sacrificial cakes provided by the master. These cakes are offered by the slaves to the clients, in expectation of a *douceur.*

187 sq. Accipe — habe: Tàke the cake (says Umbricius), and keep it as something to stir your bile, that *praestare cogimur,* etc.

189. Cultis, foppish, dandified; or pampered.

190. Praeneste. Feminine, as in Verg. *Aen.* viii. 561. It is generally neuter. "Declined like *caepe, gausape, Reate, Arelate, Bibracte.*"

194. Sic. I. e. for it is in this way that. It is "by such crazy props and shores" that.

Labentibus. Sc. *aedificiis,* implied in *urbem.* Others, "the falling inmates."

195. Vilicus = *insularius,* an *agent* or steward who lets lodgings in town. Mayor after K. F. Hermann.

196. Securos, sc. *nos.*

198. Poscit aquam. Tantamount to *cries fire!* Cf. Quintil. *Decl.* xii. 6 : ut "arma" bello, ut "*aqua*" *incendio inclamari publice solent.*

199. Ucalegon. I. e. your neighbor. An allusion to Verg. *Aen.* ii. 311 : proximus ardet Ucalegon. "Here, a richer tenant who rents a lower story of the high lodging-house (*insula*), the third story of which, immediately below the tiling, is let to the poor client, who sleeps through all the confusion."

Tibi. Ethical dative. Or more strongly, dative of disadvantage.

203. Procula was the name of a dwarf well-known at Rome. Some commentators think that in this passage it is only an expression for "his short wife."

Minor, *too short for.*

204. The abacus was a slab, sometimes of silver or gold, but sometimes as here of marble (see verse 205), used as a *sideboard* on which plate was exhibited.

205. Chiron. A figure of Chiron the centaur, who was renowned as a musician.

206. Jam vetus, *old by this time.*

207. Opici is here used in the sense of "ignorant," *barbarian.* "Goths of mice." "Cat. ap. Plin. xxix. 7 (1) : nos quoque dictitant [Graeci] barbaros, et spurcius nos quam alios *opicos* appellatione foedant." "The Opicans were the same as the *Oscans,* and perhaps as the Ausonians, whose settlements were in Campania, and whose language was widely spread and survived the nation."

210. Cumulus. Fr. *comble.* His "sorrow's *crown* of sorrow."

212. Asturicus. A name representing some nobleman of a conquering family, coined from the Astures, a people in Spain, after the analogy of Creticus, Numidicus, Macedonicus. So Persicus (221).

Cecidit. I. e. burns to the ground. — **Horrida mater.** The matrons go *with dishevelled hair,* in sign of mourning.

213. Differt vadimonia. Adjourns his court. Literally, "puts off the *vadimonia,* which was the word for the engagement entered into by a defendant to appear on a given day. Cf. Horat. *Sat.* i. 9, 36." In modern legal phrase, "enlarges the defendant's recognizances."

214. Gemimus. Some MSS., including P., read *geminus*, which is a manifest error, although adopted by Heinrich and Weidner.

215. Ardet. Impersonal; or supply *domus*.

Qui donet, qui conferat. Relative pronoun with the subjunctive, denoting purpose.

217. Euphranor was a very distinguished statuary and painter, born at Corinth, but pursuing his calling at Athens, in the times of Philip and Alexander of Macedon. — The elder Polycleitus is probably the one here meant. He was a contemporary of Pericles, and an artist of the very highest rank; a statuary in bronze, a sculptor in marble, an architect, and an artist in toreutic. He is classed by Socrates (Xen. *Mem.* 14, 3) with Homer, Sophocles, and Zeuxis.

218. Phaecasiatorum — **deorum,** *antique ornaments of white-shoed gods*. The right reading of this verse can hardly be asserted with confidence. Most of the MSS. have *phaecasianorum* or *fecasianorum;* P., S., followed by Hermann, Ribbeck, Macleane, Weidner, *haec Asianorum;* Jahn takes the liberty to alter the gender of the pronoun, and reads *hic Asianorum.* I follow Mayor in adopting Roth's conjecture based on the prevailing MS. reading. Professor H. A. J. Munro gives Mayor a note, opposing Jahn's *hic Asianorum*, in which he says, " I cannot help suspecting that *phaecasia* in some form or other should come in, as this word is not uncommon in Latin to express apparently some luxurious kind of shoe."

219. Forulos mediamque Minervam, *book-cases, and, among the books, a statue of Minerva.* Macleane wrongly translates "and a bust of Minerva;" as K. Fr. Hermann has shown, *medius* is used as equivalent to *dimidius* "only in the Scrip. r. r. and hist. Aug. Cas. ad Jul. Capitol. p. 109."

220. Reponit. He replaces his losses with *etc.*

221. Persicus is the occupant of the "house of Asturicus" (verse 212), which may have been so called from a former owner.

Orborum lautissimus, *the most sumptuous of childless men.* It was because he was *orbus*, that the *captatores* paid him court.

223. The Ludi Circenses or **Magni** were celebrated annually, and consisted of horse-, chariot-, and foot-races, sham fights (both land and water), wrestling, boxing, and fighting with beasts, as well as feats of horsemanship. Macleane.

223-4. Three small towns in Latium are here named.

226. Hic. I. e. in the country. (In the places *I am speaking about.*)

227. Tenuis. Accusative plural.

229. The Pythagoreans were forbidden animal food.

231. A humorous extenuation of the pleasures of ownership, especially of owning landed property. Many words have been wasted on the interpretation of this verse, by commentators from the scholiast down. It means just what it says; but the being master of a lizard involves being master of the ground it makes its home.

232. **Plurimus,** *many a one.*—**Hic** in this verse is of course in Rome. —**Vigilando.** The *o* is short. There are two examples in Seneca, which, with this, are the earliest instances of short *o* in the ablative. Juvenal has also *octŏ, ergŏ,* and often *ŏ* in the present indicative of verbs.

233. **Inperfectus.** I. e. undigested.

234. **Meritoria,** *hired lodgings.*

236. **Redarum.** Either private carriages or *stage-coaches.* As a rule, carriages were not allowed to be used in the streets of Rome in the daytime, and travellers were obliged to set out from, arrive at, or pass through the city in the night. Cf. Friedland *Sittengesch,* i. 45 sq.

237. **Convicia** (*con* and vec, a form of **voc** the root of *vox;* Sanscrit vak), "any *confused din;*" here including "both the drovers' abuse and the lowing of the herds."

Mandra is a cattle-pen, or sheep-fold, here used by metonymy for the animals themselves; *the standing cattle* = the horses, mules, or other animals stopped in the street. Hermann thinks that *flocks of sheep* are meant, disturbing slumber by their bleating.

238. The Emperor Tiberius Claudius Drusus was notorious for his addiction to sleep. Pliny says of seals *nullum animal graviore somno premitur.*

239. **Officium** is here used for the man's attendance on the great or rich. Macleane.

240. **Ingenti Liburno,** *borne by huge Liburnians.* Literally, "Liburnian;" Hermann compares Ovid. *Fast.* iii. 29: *principis corpora;* and *Heroid.* xvi. 366: *innumerus miles.* For the ablative, see note on Sat. i. 13. Macleane takes it as dative of reference, after *super ora.* Our reading is that of Pω, followed by Hermann, Ribbeck, Macleane, and H. A. J. Munro (note in Mayor's edition). Jahn, Weidner, Mayor, read *liburna* after S (where the reading is corrupt and doubtful) and *h;* understanding the word of *a large litter* (octophoron) borne by Liburnian slaves, and humorously called *liburna* or "swift-sailer," as we might say "clipper."

242. The **fenestra** is simply the opening in the curtains.

243. Ante. I. e. "before poor people who are bent on the same errand."

Tamen, *yet ;* nevertheless. (Although he takes things so easily.)

244 sq. The throngs of people before and behind hinder our passage. On *unda* cf. Verg. *Georg.* ii. 461–2 :

> Si non ingentem foribus domus alta superbis
> *Mane salutantum* totis vomit aedibus *undam.*

248. Clavus, *hob-nail.* "The common soldiers and inferior officers wore heavy shoes, *caligae,* studded with hob-nails." Cf. Sat. xvi. 24.

249. Quanto celebretur **sportula fumo.** *With what clouds of smoke they crowd around the sportula.* The dole appears to have been sometimes taken away in the afternoon, although the clients' salutation to the great man was paid in the morning. So Hermann and most commentators. Weidner follows Buttmann (in Seebodes Biblioth. 1821, 1, 396) in supposing that a *cena collaticia* or "picnic," δεῖπνον ἀπὸ σπυρίδος, is here referred to. The smoke, with either explanation, comes from the charcoal in the *foculi gestabiles* or *culinae.*

250. Convivae. Ironical. "They ought to be the great man's guests, and he puts them off with a mess of meat."

Culina. A kind of *brazier* or portable kitchen which kept things carried in it warm.

251. Cn. Domitius Corbulo, a Roman general, is described by Tacitus (*Ann.* xiii. 8) as *corpore ingens.* His name may have become a synonyme for any strong man.

254. Sartae modo, *that have just been patched.*

255. Quintilian (viii. 3, 21) calls serracum a "sordidum nomen" for *plaustrum.*

257. Saxa Ligustica. Marbles from the quarries of Luna (near the modern Carrara) and Pisa, much used in Rome both for sculpture and building.

261. More animae, *like his breath.* Some translate "like his soul" or "like his life."

Domus, *his household.*

Secura. (Notice, in the Lexicons, the exact meaning of this word.)

262. (Find, by scanning the verse, whether bucca is nominative or ablative.)

Sonat, clatters, rings.

263. Striglibus *= strigilibus.* Many forms thus shortened passed into the Romance languages, e. g. *frigdus,* froid ; *caldus,* chaud ; *anglus,* angle. Translate, *flesh-scrapers.* They were curved instruments of metal, bone, or wood, used for removing oil and perspiration from the body after bathing. **Gutus** (or **guttus**), *oil-flask*, was a flask with a long thin neck, often made of horn, used here for dropping oil over the body. The lintea are towels. The servants are making these preparations for their master, as it was the custom to bathe before taking the *cena*.

264. Pueros, *the slaves*. **Ille** is, of course, the master.

265. Ripa. I. e. of the Styx.

266. Porthmea. I. e. Charon; "portitor" in Virgil.

Alnum. I. e. Charon's *boat*. That these fables were not generally believed in, appears from Sat. ii. 149 sqq.:

> Esse aliquos manes et subterranea regna,
> Cocytum et Stygio ranas in gurgite nigras,
> Atque una transire vadum tot milia cumba,
> Nec pueri credunt, nisi qui nondum aere lavantur.

(The words *nondum aere lavantur* refer to the fact that children under four years of age were admitted to the public baths gratuitously.) Cf. Cic. *Tusc. Disp.* i. 5, 6.

267. Trientem. A copper coin, the third of an as, used here to represent the *obol*, which was placed in the mouths of the dead among the Greeks as Charon's fare.

269. Quod spatium tectis sublimibus, *what a distance* there is *from the lofty roofs* to the street. **Augustus** limited the height of houses to seventy feet; Trajan afterwards to sixty.

269-271. The interrogative adjective pronoun, quod, and the interrogative adverb quotiens and adj. quanto, depend upon respice.

270. Testa, *a tile*.

Fenestra, French *fenêtre*, German *Fenster*.

272. Silicem. I. e. the pavement.

273. Notice the spondee in the fifth foot in conjunction with the monosyllabic ending of the verse.

274 sq. Adeo, etc., *so true is it :* or, *so surely is it the case* that as many fatal chances await you as there are wakeful windows open on that night, *etc.* "Wakeful windows" are, of course, the windows of chambers whose occupants are still awake. The windows ("winddoors") opened, like doors, on hinges; as so often now in Europe.

276, 277. Of the two wretched alternatives, you can only hope that they will empty the foul contents of their basins upon you, rather than endanger your life by dropping the vessels themselves upon your head.

279. Dat poenas, *suffers tortures*. There is something very humorous, as Lewis says, in this comparison between this insolent fellow, who has *not* found any one to pummel, and Achilles, who has lost his friend Patroclus (Hom. *Il.* xxiv. 9–11). "He longs to thump some innocent passer-by, as Achilles longed to kill Hector." We can fancy him complaining, like Mercury in the *Amphitryon* of Molière (cited by Lemaire):

> "Depuis plus d'une semaine
> Je n'ai trouvé personne à qui rompre les os;
> La vigueur de mon bras se perd dans le repos;
> Et je cherche quelque dos
> Pour me remettre en haleine."

281 sq. *Can he not sleep, then, without all this,* you will ask. No; *some men can sleep only after a broil.* Ribbeck, Heinecke, and Ruperti regard line 281 as spurious. Gifford cites here Proverbs iv. 15.—Ergō. The ō, also in ix. 82; elsewhere in Juvenal, ŏ.

282. Improbus, *insolent,* impudent, saucy, hot-headed.

282 sqq. The wanton Mohock, "flushed as he is with folly, youth, and wine," confines his "prudent insults" to the poor. (So Johnson's paraphrase.)

283. The scarlet laena, thick and warm, which was worn by the rich, was dyed with the "coccum" or cochineal.

285. Aenea. Of Corinthian bronze and costly workmanship.

287. Candelae were cheap candles or torches of rope dipped in wax, tallow, or pitch. Sometimes the wick was of rush.—Dispenso et tempero. I. e. I husband and check from burning too fast. (Mayor.)

288. Cognosce, *hear me tell.*

292. Aceto, sour wine; or vinegar mixed with water (*posca*), which was a usual drink of the soldiers and common people.

293. "Porrum, *leek,* was either *sectile* or *capitatum.* When intended to be *sectile* it was sown thickly, and the blades were cut (*secabantur*) as they shot up, like asparagus. The reveller abuses his victim for his foul breath."

296. *Tell me, where is your stand?* (whether for begging or for selling.) *In what Jewish oratory am I to look for you?*

Quaero. Present, where we should expect the future. This is more striking than the inceptive present, which denotes the beginning of an act, and even than the *conative* present, to which, however, it is allied. As Key says (Lat. Gram. 457), the present in Latin is sometimes used when "the mind alone" is as yet employed upon the action, "or the matter at best is only in preparation; as 'uxorem ducit,' *he is going to be married.*"

298. Vadimonia faciunt. *They bind you over to appear in court;* as though they were the aggrieved parties, they threaten they will have the law on you. (Cf. v. 213.) " Les battus paient l'amende."

303. Derit. Ribbeck, Weidner, Mayor give this contracted form for *deerit.*

304. "Shops and houses were barred at night, and the bar secured by a chain."

Compago, fastening, " the fittings of the folding-doors." From *com* and *pango* (root PAG), to fasten, fix.

305. Grassator, a street-robber, footpad.

Agit rem, goes to work, *plies his trade.*

306 sqq. The Pontine marsh, and the Gallinarian wood (of pine trees, on the coast of Campania, near Cumae: cf. Cic. *ad fam.* ix. 23) were well adapted for robbers. When they were effectively held by soldiers, the robbers, beaten out of their accustomed haunts, flocked to Rome "as a gentleman goes to his preserves to shoot."

> "Les voleurs à l'instant s'emparent de la ville :
> Le bois le plus funeste et le moins fréquenté
> Est, au prix de Paris, un lieu de sûreté."
> (Boileau's paraphrase, cited by Lemaire.)

309. The negative belongs with *quo fornace* as well as *qua incude.* The regular order would have been *qua fornace, qua incude, non* conficiuntur *graves catenae?*

313. Sub tribunis. I. e. in the republic.

314. Uno carcere. The Mamertine prison.

315. Poteram. This is the imperfect of unfulfilled action ; I *could,* but do not (on account of want of time). Cf. Key's Lat. Gram. 1257; Gildersleeve, 246, R. 2; Madvig 348, 1.

317. Jandudum. So Jahn after P ; p, *iam dudum.*

319. Refici reddet. The prose construction would be reddet *reficiendum* or *ut reficiaris.*

320. Ceres and Diana were both worshipped at Aquinum, a *municipium* (Cic. *Phil.* ii. 106) or colony (Plin. *H. N.* iii. 9) in Latium on the via Latina, near the river Melpis. No satisfactory explanation has been given of the epithet *Helvina* here applied to Ceres.

321 seq. If your satires are not ashamed of me, I will put on my hob-nailed shoes, and come for their help to your cool fields. — Macleane is probably right in rejecting "the notion of the commentators about Umbricius's going to Juvenal dressed like a soldier," (the *caligae* being worn by soldiers,) " to do service in the ranks and help him attack the follies of the age."

SATIRE IV.

ARGUMENT.

1-36. CRISPINUS here again! and I must often bring him on the stage, a monster with no virtue by which to ransom himself from the vices which enslave him. What avails all his wealth and pomp? No wicked man is happy, least of all one so utterly impure. But now of smaller matters. He bought a mullet of six pounds for as many sestertia : not as a present, for some crafty end, but for himself. He, the Egyptian slave! a fish that cost more than the man that caught it, or than an estate in the provinces or Apulia. When so costly a dainty was but a side-dish on the table of this upstart, who used to cry stale fish from his native country, what must we not look for in the emperor? Begin, Calliope! nay, keep your seat; you need not stand up to sing; tell a true tale, ye Muses chaste and young; and since I call you so, give me your favor.

37-71. In Domitian's reign, the huge bulk of a *rhombus*, large as the Byzantine, fell into a fisherman's net off Ancona. The captor, making a merit of necessity, destines it for the chief pontiff, — for the shores were full of informers, — and hurries with it to the Alban villa. Here a crowd admiring stops him; when it parts the doors fly open; the senate waits without. Brought to the great man, he begs him accept the fish as one reserved for his times and eager for the honor of being served up at his table. What flattery could be grosser? and yet Domitian's feathers rise. **72-129.** But where find a dish capacious enough to contain the fish? This is a point for a council of state to determine. A council is summoned. First comes Pegasus, the city's bailiff — for what else then were prefects? — an upright judge, but much too merciful for the times he lived in. Pleasant old Crispus next, whose heart was like his speech, a man of gentle temper; an excellent companion for the world's master, if he might speak his honest mind. But who dare so speak to such a tyrant, when on every trivial sentence hung one's life? Crispus was not the man to swim against the stream, and risk his life for truth : and so he lived in safety eighty years. Then comes Acilius, with his son, who is one day to fall a victim to the tyrant's jealousy (for nobility and great age have long been strangers), which he in vain endeavors

160

to lull by devoting himself to sports unworthy of his birth.   Next,
and, though not marked out by noble birth for Domitian's hatred,
not less alarmed, comes Rubrius, guilty of a foul offence, but impudent as the catamite who writes satires.   Then come Montanus with
his belly huge, and the scented fop Crispinus reeking with perfumes;
the informer Pompeius too, whose softest whisper was a dagger; and
Fuscus, who dreamt of wars in his marble villa, and kept his vitals
for the Dacian vultures.   Crafty Veiento then, and Catullus, whose
blindness preserved him not from lust — a conspicuous monster even
for our times, whose ready adulation might qualify him to gain his
living as a beggar: none admires the fish so much as he, though
indeed he turns to the left to admire, while the creature lies on his
right; — in the same way he is wont to praise the fighters and the
stage-tricks in the theatre.   Veiento finds in the capture of the foreign
fish an omen of triumph over some foreign king; and he can almost
tell the animal's country and its age.   **130–149.** " Well, now," says
the Sire, " what think ye? is it to be cut?"   " Nay," says Montanus,
" far be such disgrace!   Let's get a noble dish to put it in, Prometheus too to make it: haste, clay and wheel!   henceforth, O Caesar,
potters must attend your court."   His motion, worthy of a palate
trained at Nero's table, was adopted; no one has beat him in my
time in gastronomic lore.   He'd tell you at a taste where an oyster
came from, and declare at sight an echinus' native coast.   The council
is dismissed, having been convoked in as headlong haste as though
some war had broken out.   **150–154.** And would that, engrossed with
such fooleries, Domitian had wanted time for the murder of Rome's
nobles, whom he slew with impunity until the rabble began to fear
him. — MAYOR and MACLEANE, *in part.*

---

1. **Crispinus.** See i. 27, note.

2. **Ad partes** (sustinendas), *to play his part.*   " I must often bring
him on the stage."

4. **Deliciae,** " *a rake* " (Mayor); or, with more sarcasm, *the pretty
darling; the jackanape.*   The reading here given is the best supported.

Viduas, unmarried women; " women without husbands, whether
they had ever had one or not."

Tantum (*only,* alone) modifies *viduas.*

Spernatur. From the deponent *spernor,* a very rare form.   Another
reading is *aspernatur.*

6. The rich built private porticoes (i. e. covered walks or colon-
nades), under whose shelter they took drives in bad weather.
" **Fatiget** is a poetical word in this connection.   Cf. Verg. *Aen.* i.
316."

11 — Juv.   O 2

Vectetur. " Is carried about in his lectica or sella."

7. Supply *vicinas foro* with *aedes.* So Jahn and others.

9 sq. Incest was committed either with *virgines sacratae* or *propinquae sanguine* (Isidor. *Orig.* v. 26, 24, cited by Mayor). " Of such incest (with a vestal virgin) Crispinus had been guilty, but was screened from punishment by Domitian. Unchaste Vestals were carried out on a litter to the Colline gate, and there immured in a chamber under ground, no sacrifices being offered."

12. Idem refers to the *leviora facta.*

Caderet sub judice morum = *damnaretur a censore* (S.). Cf. Nägelsbach's *Stilistik* 127, 1. Domitian took upon himself the censorship for life; being the first of the emperors who assumed that office.

13. (Lucius) Titius and (Gaius) Seius were the " John Doe and Richard Roe " of the Roman law-books; German "Hinz und Kunz."

14. **Quid agas,** etc. *What are you to do* when you have to represent a character whose crimes beggar all description? (Mayor.) The indefinite second person. (See the Grammars.)

15. **Crimine,** accusation, charge.

Sex milibus, for six thousand sesterces, or *six sestertia;* about $230 in our gold.

16. The pounds in the mullet equalled the *sestertia* paid; i. e. it weighed six pounds. The mullet was esteemed in proportion to its size. The ordinary weight was two, or at most four, pounds.

Sane, *it is true.* " Said ironically, as though in excuse."

18. **Artificis,** the crafty contriver; the artful fellow.

19. **Praecipuam in tabulis ceram,** *the chief place in the will.* Cf. Hor. *Sat.* ii. 5, 53. " A will was usually contained in three tablets (prima, secunda, and ima cera or tabula), in the first two of which were entered the names of the heredes, and in the third those of the ' substitute,' who took in the event of any heres being disqualified."

20. **Est ratio ulterior,** there is a motive which goes still further,—a motive beyond that. He hopes to gain something through the *influence* of the " *magna* amica," as well as from herself.

21. **Cluso** (P, ς) = *clauso* (ω).

Specularibus. Windows of *lapis specularis* (mica or talc). Glass too was known to the ancients; " panes of glass having been found at Herculaneum, Pompeii, Velleia."

Antro. " Her closed up den " is her *sella.*

23. **Apicius,** called here in bitterly ironical comparison with Cris-

pinus "*sordid and niggardly*," "poor frugal man," was a notoriously extravagant gourmand in the reigns of Augustus and Tiberius. Hoc, *pretio* (**25**).

24. Crispinus had been a slave in Egypt (Sat. i. 26) ; hence **patria**. Cheap clothing was sometimes made of the coarser kind of **papyrus**. Plin. *H. N.* xiii. 22 (11) : **ex** ipso quidem papyro navigia **texunt**; et e libro vela tegetesque *nec non et vestem*, etiam stragulam ac funes. "In such coarse garments, tucked up as the manner of slaves was (Hor. *Sat.* ii. 8, 10), Crispinus used to appear in former days." Ruperti, citing **Anacreon** iv. 4 sq., understands *papyro* not of the tunic, but of a *cord*, passing round the neck, by which the tunic was held up when the wearer was *succinctus*.

25. **Hoc pretio squamam**, sc. *emisti*. This reading (*Valla*, *Cramerus ad schol.*) is adopted by Jahn and by most of the recent editors. Pω read *hoc pretio squamae*, and so Lewis. Macleane, after a few MSS., *hoc pretium squamae*. H. A. J. Munro, in a note furnished Mayor, asks, "Is it certain that the MS. reading (23, 25) will not do? *hoc tu!* . . . . *hoc pretio squamae!* i. e. *hoc tu fecisti! hoc pretio squamae emptae sunt!*" — Notice the humorous exaggeration in saying *a fish-scale* for *a fish*.

26 sq. In the provinces you may buy an estate for the money, but a still larger one in Apulia. (Land in Apulia brought a low price.) Notice the use of **sed** in the sense of *and moreover* or *yes, and*. But why do I say "the provinces" in general, when in Apulia, where land is cheap, you could get a lordly domain for that sum? Cf. Ov. *Met.* viii. 283 : misit aprum, quanto maiores herbida tauros non habet Epiros, *sed* habent Sicula arva minores. **Mart. ix.** 42, **3** : scelus est, mihi crede, *sed* ingens. **Plaut.** *Rud.* 799 : DAE. duas clavas. LA. clavas? DAE. *set* probas. So often *mais* in **French**. Cf. Molière *L'Avare* iii. 9 : vous êtes un astre, *mais* un astre le plus bel astre qui soit dans le pays des astres.

28. **Putamus.** Notice the indicative. There is no doubt implied in the question, and no deliberation is needed for its answer.

29. Juvenal uses the archaic and dignified form **induperator**, for *imperator*, with mock gravity.

30. **De margine.** As we say, *from the side-dishes ;* as opposed to the *caput caenae*, or principal dish (at large dinners commonly a wild boar), in the middle of the board.

31. **Purpureus.** Cf. Sat. i. 27.

Palati. "The palace which the successive emperors occupied was on the Palatine hill."

32. Princeps equitum, i. e. *praefectus praetorio.* Cf. Vell. ii. 127, 47 ; Suet. *Galb.* 14, Casaub. (Mayor.)

33. Municipes fracta de merce siluros, *the sheat-fish of his town-ship from his damaged wares.* For **fracta** Ribbeck (after C. Barth) reads **farcta,** understanding it of cured-fish *closely packed.* Various unnecessary emendations have been proposed.

34 sq. You need not rise, as you would for poetry and song ; I only ask a plain narrative of facts.

37. Jam (*by this time*) limits *semianimum* (pronounced here " semyanimum ").

Flavius. The full name of Domitian was Titus Flavius Domi-tianus Caesar Augustus. He was the third Flavius. Though he was the last emperor who had borne the gentilician name of Flavius when this satire was written, all the Constantines were Flavii. Macleane.

38. Calvo. Domitian was very sensitive about his baldness. Juve-nal calls him a Nero, to intimate that he was as bad a man as that tyrant. With still greater sarcasm Tertullian (*De Pall.* 4) calls him *Subnero.*

39. Incidit. "Sinus" is the object of this verb as well as of *implevit :* " incidit in sinus retis eosque implevit," *fell into the meshy folds and filled them.* See Nägelsbach, 90, 3.

Adriaci spatium admirabile rhombi. This is like *Crispi jucunda senectus* (81) ; *mite Thaletis ingenium* (xiii. 184). "The *rhombus* is usually supposed to have been a turbot, but it is uncertain ; it was a flat fish."

40. Ancon, the modern Ancona, was founded by refugees from Syracuse, which was a Dorian city. Here was a temple of Venus, the tutelar deity of the place, built probably upon a height, whence **sustinet,** *holds up.*

41. Haeserat (sc. *sinubus*), *had been caught.*

Illis, sc. *rhombis.* Ablative.

42, 43. "The turbots of the Black Sea were supposed to get fat and big by hibernating." — **Torrentis** (S), *rapid, streaming,* is un-questionably the true reading. So Madvig and the best editors. The MSS. *torpentis.*

46. The office of **pontifex maximus** was always borne by the emperors from Augustus downwards for about four centuries. Juve-nal uses just this title here partly in scorn, and partly perhaps be-cause the pontifical dinners were proverbial for luxury.

Proponere, *to offer for sale.*

48-52. Delatore. There were informers all along the coast, who poked into the very weeds for something to tell about, and they would soon call the poor fisherman to account, and would be ready to swear they knew the fish by sight, and that it had got away from the emperor's preserves, and must be sent back to its old master. (Macleane.)

Agerent cum, *would take the law of.*

53. Palfurius and Armillatus were jurists and notorious informers.

55. Fisci, of the imperial treasury.

Donabitur, sc. *piscis.*

56. Ne pereat, *lest it should be lost ;* lest the captor should lose all profit from it. — **Letifero.** In autumn the pestilential south-wind (auster) prevailed.

57. Quartanam sperantibus aegris. The patients hope that their disease will assume a milder form as the cold weather comes on. Cic. *ad Fam.* xvi. 11, 1 : cum in *quartanam* conversa vis est morbi, ... spero te, diligentia adhibita, etiam firmiorem fore.

58. Recentem, *fresh,* untainted. So kept by the cold.

59. Hic, "our man ; " the fisherman.

60. Lacus. The plural either means "the broad bosom of the lake " — (the Alban lake *lies* directly *under* the site of Domitian's villa) — or comprehends the lake of Nemi also, if not other lakes now dry. See Orelli on Horat. *Carm.* iv. 1, 19. It should be remarked, however, that Pliny speaks of the *Vallericcia* (which had been a lake in ancient times, and was again in the Middle Ages) as dry in his day.

Diruta, etc. Alba was destroyed by Tullus Hostilius, but the temples were spared.

61. Minorem. *The lesser* as compared with the great temple at Rome.

63. Cessit, sc. turba miratrix.

64. Patres. Domitian used to convene the senate at his Alban house.

65. Atriden. A sarcastic assimilation of Domitian to Agamemnon, —a model in the Roman poets of the *dominus superbissimus*, on account of his sacrificing Iphigenia, and his arrogance towards Achilles.

Picens. Ancon was in Picenum.

66. Majora, *things too great for.*

Genialis, etc., *let this day be celebrated to your Genius.* "The genius is the divine element which is born with a man, and when he dies becomes a *lar*, if he is good; if he is wicked, a *larva*, or a *lemur*. Departed *genii* were called *manes* — 'good fellows' — doubtless with a view to propitiation." (Gildersleeve, on Pers. ii. 3.) See note on Hor. *Ep.* ii. 2, 187. To give one's self to feasting and personal indulgence was called *genio indulgere* or *obsequi*, *genium curare* or *placare*, while the opposite was *genium defraudare*.

67. Stomachum laxare saginans, "'*to let your stomach out by cramming it*,' 'give yourself a good blow-out.'" H. A. J. Munro, who joins with Mayor in giving this text: "as *saginam* and *saginas* are the best attested readings, *saginans* may be right." Jahn gives (also from conjecture) *saginae*, with the sense "relieve your stomach (by means of emetics) for a good meal."

69 sq. Quid apertius? (what flattery could be more glaring?) et tamen illi surgebant cristae. Raoul gives the sense thus:

"Quelle dérision! le despote crédule
En conçoit cependant un orgueil ridicule."

71. Domitian caused all letters to his procuratores to begin with "Dominus et Deus noster sic fieri jubet." **Dis aequa** = deorum potestati aequa. This comparison of some *quality* of one person directly with another *person* or persons is a frequent usage. Cf. iii. 74. M. 280, 2; Z. 767.

72. Mensura, i. e. the proper, *corresponding* size. On the omission of such adjectives see Nägelsbach 76, 2.

74. Pallor, etc. The very friendship of the tyrant, wretched no less than distinguished, is fraught with danger.

75. Liburno, sc. *servo*; the servus admissionis.

76. Rapta = *correpta*.

77. Pegasus was a jurist of eminence in this and the preceding reigns.

Attonitae. The city under the tyrant was mazed with horror, stupefied, *semianima* (37).

Modo, lately; but just now.

Vilicus (villicus). Juvenal calls the *praefectus* urbi a steward or bailiff, as though the city were the emperor's private estate and the people his slaves.

78 sqq. Optimus . . . . **sanctissimus** (*most conscientious*), etc. Referring still to Pegasus.

81. Crispi jucunda senectus, *the cheerful* (pleasant, jovial) *old man Crispus*. He was an orator famed for the pleasant, easy flow of his eloquence.

82 sq. Mite ingenium, "a gentle nature."

84. Clade et peste. Applied to Domitian : abstract for concrete.

85. Si liceret (ei), *if he had been allowed.* The *imperfect* is used in the Latin, because in affirmative narration we should have *licebat consilium adferre,* the imperfect of a continued state or customary action.

86. Violentius, *more irritable,* more touchy.

88. Pendebat, "hung suspended in the balance."

93. Armis, *armor.*

94. Ejusdem aevi, *of the same age* (as Crispus). *Homo* is often omitted in the poets before such genitives of quality or description.

94 sq. Acilius . . . . juvene. M'. Acilius Glabrio, father and son, both senators, the son also consul. Domitian caused him to be executed on a charge of treason, after he had fought with lions (λέοντα Dio Cass. lxvii. 14) at the Alban villa, and come off uninjured.

96. Domini, *of the Sire ;* strictly "of the lord." Domitian insisted on receiving this title, which Augustus and Tiberius declined. The early Christians refused to give it. See note on verse 71.

Olim est, *has long been.* This use of *olim* is characteristic of the silver age. Cf. iii. 163. Cicero would say *jamdudum,* and the Greeks πάλαι.

98. Fraterculus gigantis, *a giant's little brother,* means a man of obscure birth. Such men were called popularly *terrae filii* (Tertul. *Apol.* 10), and the giants were sons of Earth.

101. Artes patricias. "The various arts the patricians had recourse to to save themselves. Glabrio's was that of degrading himself into a *venator.*"

103. Such a trick as that of Brutus, who passed himself off for a fool, might go down with Tarquinius Superbus, a king of the old days when they wore beards, but was not likely to impose upon modern tyrants. (Macleane.)

104. Melior vultu, more cheerful. Mart. iv. 1, 4 : semper et hoc vultu vel meliore nite.

105. Rubrius Gallus, who is said to have corrupted Julia the daughter of Titus, and to have feared that her uncle would punish him for the crime.

106. Inprobrior, more impudent, more shameless in abusing others, than a pathic who should turn satirist, *in aliis sua vitia reprehendens.*

107. And now the big, unwieldy belly of Montanus waddles into the hall. This *may* be the Curtius Montanus mentioned by Tacitus, but it is uncertain.

108. Amomo. A perfume prepared from the leaves of a shrub, supposed to be the *cissus vitiginea*, which grew in India, Armenia, Media, and Pontus. To go perfumed in the morning was an extravagance.

109. "A corpse was thoroughly smeared with ointment; burning censers were carried in the funeral procession, and perfumes of all sorts, and flowers, were thrown upon the funeral pile."

110. Pompeius. An unknown *delator*.

Saevior aperire. M. 419. The use of the infinitive after the adjective corresponds to its poetical use after the cognate verb *saevio*.

112. Cornelius Fuscus was employed by Vespasian in high commands, and by Domitian as "praefectus" of the praetorian troops. He was sent by him on an expedition against the Dacians, and was killed, together with the greater part of his army, by that people. Retirement and the degrading life of a Roman senator of that day did not suit him, and he thought of battles even in his marble villa. (Macleane.)

113. For *the crafty* Fabricius *Veiento*, see note on iii. 185.

Catullus Messalinus, blind (or nearly so) and cruel, was *mortifer* as an informer. He lusted after a woman he had no eyes to see.

116. Dirusque a ponte satelles is generally interpreted as meaning "he was brought from begging at the bridges, where beggars commonly stood, to be Domitian's savage servant." Emendations of the text have been attempted, without satisfactory success. Lewis suggests that *a ponte satelles* may mean "a satellite such as one might pick up at one of the bridges," "a beggarly flatterer."

117. The Arician hill, on the Appian way, swarmed with beggars. Aricia was about sixteen miles from Rome.

118. Devexae. As it goes down hill.

119. Rhombum stupuit. M. 223, c; R. 1123; Z. 383 *in fin.*; A. & G. 52, 1, *a*; G. 329, Rem. 1; H. 371, 3; A. & S. 232, (2); B. 716.

121. Cilicis. A gladiator of the time. Cf. Threx and Syrus, Hor. *Sat.* ii. 6, 44. Cilician gladiators were common.

Ictus. His cuts and thrusts, i. e. his swordsmanship. (Lewis.)

122. Pegma, the stage-machine. The "pegmata" were great wooden structures, of two or more stories, which let up and down by machinery, or parted or came together. Here, by some ingenious contrivance, a boy is suddenly carried up to the awnings from the pegma, for the amusement of the spectators, and the blind flatterer pretends to admire a thing he cannot see.

123. Non cedit. Veiento will not be outdone by Messalinus.

127. Arviragus. No British prince of this name is recorded by any writer.

128. Sudes, properly *stakes*, here *fins.* "The beast is foreign, and behaves himself rebelliously; lo, how he seems armed for resistance, rebel-like!" (Holyday, cited by Mayor.)

129. Fabricio. Veiento (line 113).

130. Domitian, in all form, calls on his council of state for their opinion. Cf. Liv. i. 32: "dic," inquit ei, quem primum sententiam rogabat, "quid censes?"

Conciditur, *is it to be cut up?* Is that in your minds? For the tense, see note on iii. 296, *quaero.* Cf. Madvig *Opusc.* ii. 40 sq. The emperor thinks there is no possibility that such a question should be entertained.

132. Colligat, may contain.

Orbem, *circumference* (of the fish).

133. Prometheus. I. e. a potter.

135. Castra, "sc. domestica." But Juvenal introduces the word in sarcasm against the emperor, who was cowardly and unwarlike, although vain of his military titles and pretended prowess.

136. Vicit, carried the day; prevailed. The proper technical word. Cf. Liv. ii. 4: cum in senatu vicisset sententia, quae censebat reddenda bona.

137 sq. Noctes Neronis jam medias, Nero's revels prolonged even till midnight.

Aliam famem. Either the second appetite which follows hard drinking (as the scholiast has it), or that caused by the use of emetics.

Pulmo. Lewis says that this word must be taken of "the inside" generally. But Juvenal may use a popular mode of speech, although famous physicians had pointed out the error of Alcaeus and Plato in speaking of wine as passing into the lungs.

139. Usus, *experience.*

141. Saxum. I. e. rocky coast.

Rutupino. Rutupiae, the modern Richborough, was a haven of the Cantii in the south of Britain. The ordinary route to England was from Bononia (*Boulogne*) to Rutupiae.

142. Depraendere = deprendere (deprehendere).

143. Echini. The sea-urchin was esteemed by epicures as one of the best of shell-fish.

145. Albanam in arcem = Albanam in villam. Cf. Tac. *Agric.* 45. "For this place under the Alban mount, from which it received its

name, he chose out as a kind of citadel (ἀκρόπολιν)." Dio Cassius
lxvii. 1.

146. Attonitos, *awe-stricken.*

149. Anxia pinna. Probably simply " on hurried wing ; " although
the scholiast and others assert that as a laurel was inserted in letters
of victory, so a feather in letters announcing ill-tidings ; or that the
messengers in the first instance bore a spear entwined with laurel, in
the second a feather on the spear-point or in their caps.

153 sq. "Domitian had murdered the noblest citizens with impunity, but when he began to practise upon the vulgar, they got rid
of him. He was murdered A. D. 96 by certain conspirators whom he
had resolved to put to death."

Cerdonibus, "by the Hobs and Dicks." Conington (in a note
furnished to Munro) says, " I should print Cerdo as a [plebeian]
proper name, answering to *Lamiarum,* and in viii. 182 to *Volesos
Brutumque.* From Jahn's note on Persius iv. 51, and addendum, I
have little doubt that it stands on the same footing as Dama, meaning a slave, and Manius, meaning a beggar ; a name used generically,
but not to be confounded with an ordinary substantive. It is like
the *Hob* and *Dick* of Shakspeare's Coriolanus."

Lamiarum. Domitian took away from the Aelius Lamia of his day
his wife, married her, and afterwards put Lamia to death. Horace
has two odes addressed to his friend Aelius Lamia of this family.

SATIRE V.

———◦◦◦◦◦———

ARGUMENT.

1-11. IF you are not yet ashamed, Trebius, of the life you have chosen, submitting to anything for a dinner, I would not believe you on your oath. The stomach wants but little; but suppose you have not that little, why can't you beg? **11-23.** For, first, when you 've had your dinner, you 've got your full reward; though it comes but seldom, your patron, Virro, puts it down to your account. Once in two months he has a vacant place at his table, and says, "Come and dine:" the height of your ambition! the reward for which you are ready to break your rest, in order to anticipate your brother parasites in the *officium salutandi* at uncouth hours of the morning! **24-79.** And what kind of a dinner is it? The wine is such that wool refuses it. If it gets into your head, Virro's freedmen are ready to pick a quarrel with you for his amusement. The host, meanwhile, is drinking the choicest, oldest wines. Virro's cups are jewelled, yours of cracked glass; or if a jewelled cup is set before you, a slave stands by to guard the treasure. The master gets his water iced, not you. On you an ill-favored Moorish runner waits; on him a fair youth of Ionia, who would scorn to obey your orders. You must gnaw a crust of black, mouldy bread; if you venture to touch Virro's loaf, the slaves are at hand to make you restore it. "Then 't was for *this*," you mutter to yourself, "that I so often left my bed before dawn, and braved cold and hail in my zeal to do honor to my lord!" **80-106.** See that great lobster, looking down scornfully upon the guests as it is borne along,—that goes to the master; *you* get a scanty crab with half an egg. He oils his fish with fine Venafran, while your poor cabbage stinks of the lantern. Before Virro the most costly foreign fish are set; before you the poorest, fed upon the garbage of the sewers.

107-113. But now a word with the rich man himself. Nobody asks of you the bounties which good rich men of old would send to their poor friends. We only beg you 'll dine as a fellow-citizen with his equals; then spend your money as you please.

114-124. See before the host is a fat goose's liver, and a fowl as big as a goose, a wild boar, and truffles if 't is spring. ("Keep your

171

grain, Libya," the glutton cries, " but send us truffles!") To make
one angry as can be, you see the carver flourishing his knife and
dancing till he goes through all his lesson. 'T is of the first importance with what gestures hares and fowls are carved! 125-131.
You 'll be dragged by the heels, and put out of the door, if you
venture to open your mouth, as if you were a freeman. Do you suppose the great man will ever drink to you? Is any of you so bold as
to pass him the cup and say " Drink"? There are many things a
man dare not say with holes in his coat. 132-145. But if the gods or
some good man gave you a fortune, what a friend you would soon
become of Virro's! " Here, help Trebius; put it before Trebius:
allow me, my dear brother, to help you from the loin." It is the
money that is "dear brother." But if, as a rich man, you want to be
the patron's lord and master, you must be childless. Now that you
are poor, however, your wife may have three children at a birth, and
yet Virro will not be estranged from you, but amused rather by the
prattle of the baby parasites.

146-155. Suspicious mushrooms are for the poor friends, boletus for
the master. Phaeacian apples, stolen you 'd think from the Hesperides, are for the host and favored guests; you eat such scabby fruit
as the monkey gnaws on the goat's back learning his drill.

156-173. Perhaps you think 't is stinginess in Virro. No, he sets
himself deliberately at work to tantalize his guests. What fun so
great as a disappointed belly? He wants to see you cry with rage
and gnash your teeth. You think yourself a freeman and the rich
man's guest: he thinks the smell of the kitchen draws you, and he 's
right. What freeman is so poor that he would bear such treatment
twice? You 're cheated with false hopes of a good dinner. You sit
in silent expectation, ready for the scraps that do not come. He
serves you right. If you can bear all sorts of treatment, you ought
to bear it. Some day you 'll come upon the stage to be flogged, you,
so worthy of such feasts and such a friend. — MACLEANE and MAYOR,
in part.

---

1. Propositi, purpose; purposed course of life.

2. Bona summa. More often *summum bonum.* The plural is used
in humorous exaggeration. "You think that *all* the highest bless-
ings are summed up in this."

Aliena **vivere quadra,** i. e. " to live on the crumbs of another man's
table." *Quadra* is used of a fragment (a square morsel), as in Sen.
de Ben. iv. 29, 2: *quadram panis;* Mart. ix. 91, 18: secta plurima
quadra de placenta; xii. 32, 18: quadra casei; Verg. *Moret.* 49.
" Some flat round loaves, scored into four or eight parts, have been
discovered at Herculaneum." Some take *quadra* for *table.*

3. Sarmentus. A parasite in the time of **Augustus.**

Iniquas, *ill-sorted;* where prince and parasite feast together. (Mayor.)

4. Gabba. Another parasite, servile and wittol, though a wit.

5. Jurato, *on oath.* (See M. 110, obs. 3.)

6. Frugalius, "more easily satisfied."

8. Crepido, the steps of a public building, a raised foot-path, the wall of a quay at the river-side, or other conspicuous position, frequented, as were also the bridges, by beggars.

Vacat, sc. ad mendicandum.

Tegetis .... brevior, *and a piece of matting* (for a bed) *too short by half.*

9. Tantine injuria cenae? *Do you prize so highly the insolence of a dinner?* Cenae is epexegetic genitive.

10 sq. Is your hunger so ravenous, when it might more honorably at the street-side or on the bridge (illic) even stand shivering and gnawing dirty bits of dog-biscuit?

12. Fige. Similar to *pone,* but stronger.

Jussus, *invited,* bidden. Cf. Verg. *Aen.* i. 708 : toris *jussi* discumbere pictis.

13. Mercedem solidam, *payment in full.*

14. Inputat, *charges to your account,* claims gratitude for. Cf. Tac. *Germ.* 21. This use of the word is post-Augustan.

Rex. The *vox propria* for *patronus.*

17. "Of the three couches in a triclinium, the *summus* lay to the left, and the *imus* to the right of the *medius.* The *medius lectus* was the most honorable post, then the *summus.* It was not usual for more than three to recline on each couch. Between the guests were placed pillows (*culcitae*), on which they rested their left elbows."

19. Trebius. The parasite.

20. Dimittere, to leave unfastened.

21. Alarmed lest his rivals should already have gone the round of their patrons. (Mayor.)

22. Dubiis, "fading from sight," in the early dawn. The other time (illo tempore) is earlier, when the wagon of Bootes is seen slowly wheeling around.

23. Frigida. Because Bootes is a northern constellation.

24. Sucida (succida) lana is wool lately cut but not yet cleaned. Wool in this state was used, drenched with oil, or wine, or vinegar, for healing applications. But this wine the very wool would reject. (Macleane.)

25. Corybanta. I. e. frantic as the priests of Cybele.

Videbis. The subject is general; but the *tu* of **torques (26)** refers to Trebius.

27. **Rubra.** Bloody.

29. **Saguntina commissa lagona,** waged with Saguntine pitchers. "The *lagona* (λάγυνος) was an earthenware jug with a handle."

30. **Ipse.** The great man himself.

Diffusum (*bottled*), sc. *vinum.* "*Diffusum* is the word for transferring from the *dolium*, the large vessel in which the wine fermented, to the *amphora* or *cadus* in which it was kept."

Capillato consule. Under some consul with long hair; an exaggeration, as the Romans are said to have left off beards and long hair 300 years before Christ.

31. **Bellis socialibus.** The war waged by the Italian allies, with the Marsi at their head (cf. Hor. *Carm.* iii. 14, 18), in order to secure the enjoyment of the *civitas* which had been promised them by Livius Drusus.

32. **Cardiaco.** Plin. *H. N.* xxiii. 25, 1 : cardiacorum morbo unicam spem in vino esse certum est.

Cyathum. A ladle, holding the twelfth of a pint, with which the wine was drawn from the *crater* (tureen, punch-bowl), into the cups.

33 sq. "The **Alban** wine (famed for its excellence in modern times also) was inferior only to the Falernian, in the opinion of Dionysius of Halicarnassus (though ranked by Pliny as only third-rate). But in the days of Juvenal, the **Setine**, a Campanian wine, had come to be the favorite vintage."

34. **Titulum,** *l'étiquette.* The name of the consul in whose year the wine was made, and also the name of the vineyard, were painted on the amphorae or written on *tickets.*

35. **Fuligine.** When the natural process of ripening was to be hastened by exposure to *smoke,* it was customary to place the wine in bins erected in such a manner as to receive the hot air and smoke of the bath-furnaces.

36 sq. P. Thrasea Paetus was put to death by Nero, and his son-in-law, Helvidius Priscus, by Vespasian. They were stoics, and free in thought and speech. "They are here represented as drinking to their heroes' memory in the choicest wine, with crowns of flowers upon their heads, which was from the earliest times the common practice at dinner, especially on important occasions."

38. L. Müller remarks that this is the only verse in Juvenal that ends with three spondees.

38 sq. **Heliadum crustas et inaequales berullo phialas,** *cups in-*

crusted with (lit. *incrustations of*) the **tears of** *the Heliades* (i. e. *with amber*) *and paterae* ("saucers") *all rough with the beryl.* "The *crustae* were exquisitely wrought in relief, and fastened upon the surface of the vessels they were intended to adorn."

41. **Ungues observet acutos.** To watch your sharp nails, **lest you** should pluck any of the gems away.

42. Excuse him; there is a splendid jasper on that cup which is much admired. Some commentators give these words to the servant: "Excuse me; but that cup has a fine stone on it."

44. **Quas.** I. e. such as.

45. **Juvenis.** Aeneas. Cf. Verg. *Aen.* iv. 261.
Iarbae. Cf. Verg. *Aen.* iv. 36, 198.

46. *The cobbler of Beneventum* is Vatinius, one of the vilest creatures of Nero's court, who rose to wealth and power first **as** a buffoon, and then as an unscrupulous accuser. His name was given **to** a drinking-cup with "nozzles" (*nasibus*) or spouts, — perhaps from the length of his **nose.**

47. **Nasorum quattuor. Genitive** of quality.

48. **Rupto . . . . vitro,** *and calling for sulphur* (i. e. brimstone cement) *for the broken glass.* **Others,** *in exchange for* the broken glass.

50. **Decocta.** Boiled water cooled down **with snow.** Nero is said to have introduced the custom.

52. **Aliam.** A different water: i. e. neither boiled nor **iced.**

52, 56. **The poorer guests** are served by **a** Moorish out-runner, the patron by an Ionian page.

54. It was a bad omen to meet anything black in the night.

55. Cf. i. 171, note. 57. Take **pugnacis** with **Tulli.**

59 sq. The Moor is *your* "Ganymede," — a name often given to minions, such as this *flos Asiae.*

61. **Miscere.** To mix the wine and **water.**
Puer. Virro's page, "flos Asiae."
Sed — sed = *at — at.*

62. **Digna supercilio.** Justify his disdain.

63. "The guests at Roman feasts were served with either hot or cold water, as they preferred. A favorite drink was warm water **mixed** with wine and spiced."

64. **Quippe.** You must know. (Mayor.)

65. **Quod** with the subjunctive gives the reason in the mind **of the slave spoken of,** who is the agent in the main proposition (*indignatur,* etc.).

67. Murmure, *grumbling.*

68. Vix fractum (sc. *mola*). (Made of meal) *hardly ground.* A very coarse bread, with the grains almost entire. Otherwise understood of "bread too hard to be cut, which has with difficulty been broken into rough lumps."

Jam mucida. Mouldy by this time.

69. Quae agitent. *Quae = talia ut.* Anthon makes the subjunctive here one of purpose : "intended to."

72. Artoptae, of the bread-mould (distinguishing the master's fine bread from yours).

73. Inprobulum, a trifle audacious.

Superest illic, there is one standing over you there.

74. Vis tu, *will you?* exactly in our sense, "will you keep quiet?" (Lewis.) *Voulez-vous bien.* Perhaps we more often say, *will you not?* It is a formula of bidding or exhortation. (Gronovius on Sen. *de Ira* iii. 38 ; Bentley on Hor. *Sat.* ii. 6, 92.)

75. Impleri, *fill yourself.* Middle.

76 sqq. It was for this, *it seems* (**scilicet**), mutters Trebius to himself, that I so often left my bed before dawn, and braved cold and hail, in my zeal to pay my respects to my patron.

Fuerat. "This end I *had* proposed to myself." Cf. Ramshorn, p. 602.

77 sq. Per — Esquilias. Hendiadys. "Up the hill which had to be faced, the cold Esquiline." Under the empire, this hill had become a fashionable place of residence.

79. The paenula was a heavy, sleeveless cloak.

80-90. *First course.* A fine lobster with asparagus for the patron ; a little crab with half an egg for the client.

80. Distinguat, *adorns,* sets off, marks. Some editors read *distendat,* after inferior manuscripts.

81. Squilla. Here a *lobster* or a *sea-crab;* sometimes prawn or shrimp.

82. Asparagus is generally used in the plural : *heads* or *stalks* of asparagus, or young shoots of similar plants.

84. Dimidio constrictus ovo, garnished (lit. hemmed in) with half an egg. Some suppose the egg sliced ; others the fish covered with a thin batter.

Cammarus. A common crab or crayfish.

85. Feralis cena, *a funereal supper.* At the *feriae novemdiales* or *novemdialia* a very simple meal was laid on the grave nine days after burial.

86. Venafrano, sc. *oleo.* The best oil in Italy.

87. Pallidus, withered, sickly.

88. Olebit lanternam. M. 223, c, obs. 2; R. 1123; Z. 383 (second paragraph); A. & G. 52, 1, *c; G.* 329, Rem. 1 *in fin.;* H. 371, 3, (2); A. & S. 232, (2); B. 716.

Illud, sc. *oleum.*

Alveolis, small *dishes,* saucer-shaped. Lewis translates "sauce-boats," wrongly.

89. Canna, a canoe of cane. "Probus exponit, cannam navem esse quae gandeia (ganleia *Jac. Gronovius*) dicatur."

Micipsarum, *of the Micipsas,* although only one Micipsa is known; i. e., of the Numidians. Generic plural.

Subvexit, *has brought up* (the Tiber to Rome). (Mayor.)

90, 91. Numidian or African oil was so fetid that the natives besmeared with it had nothing to fear from snakes, who got out of the way to avoid the smell, and no Roman would bathe with them.

Boccare (or Bocchare). Poetic individualization for any African.

91. This line is omitted in some of the best MSS.

92–106. *Second course.* A costly barbel and a lamprey for the patron; for the client an eel or a pike from the Tiber fattened in the sewers.

93. Rupes. Sen. *N. Q.* iii. 18, 4: audiebamus nihil esse melius *saxatili* mullo.

Peractum, gone through, "ransacked."

96. Proxima. Sc. maria ac flumina.

98. Laenas, a legacy-hunter. Aurelia, the rich lady fished after, sells as much of her presents as she does not want. — "Observe the chiasmus in this line." Laenas is circumflexed on the last syllable. Prisc. v. 22.

101. Carcere. An allusion to Verg. *Aen.* i. 51.

102. Contemnunt, *brave.*

104. Tiberinus. Sc. *lupus* (pike). Cf. Horat. *Sat.* ii. 2, 31.

Et ipse. It too (as well as the eel).

106. Cryptam, drain, sewer. "The **Subura** lay in the hollow formed by the junction of three valleys: (i) that between the Quirinal and Viminal; (ii) that between the Viminal and Esquiline; (iii) that which separates the northerly portion of the Esquiline from the chief mass of the hill. The cloaca under the Subura [connected with the Cloaca Maxima, and] was directly accessible from the Tiber." "To penetrate so far, the fish must swim nearly a mile, through all the filth of the town."

12 — Juv.

107. Ipsi. The host, *ut passim*. **Pauca,** sc. *dicere.*

108. Modicis, *humble,* poor.

109. The younger Seneca, Nero's teacher, and C. Piso, a conspirator against Nero, were noted for their wealth and liberality.

Bonus, liberal, munificent.

Cotta. Perhaps Aurelius Cotta, who lived in Nero's time.

112. Civiliter, like a fellow-citizen, acknowledging that your guests have rights as well as yourself. Hence *civilly,* with civility; or *socially.*

113. Dives tibi, pauper amicis. Selfishly using your wealth only for *your own* enjoyment.

114–124. *Third course.* "Foie gras," a fat capon, and a wild boar for the patron, followed by truffles. The client looks on.

117. It was thought that frequent thunder-storms produced truffles.

118. Alledius. Any epicure.

119. Dum = dummodo. M. 351, b, obs. 2 ; A. & G. 61, 3, note ; G. 575.

120. The **structor** *arranged* the dishes on the tray in which they were served up. (Verg. *Aen.* i. 704: penum struere.) Another part of his duty was to *carve* the dishes, which he did with artistic flourishes.

121. Chironomunta, the Greek participle in Roman letters (χειρονομοῦντα), gesticulating, flourishing his knife about.

122. Dictata, the lessons. There were regular professors of the art of carving.

127. Hiscere, to open your mouth.

Nomina. "Most freeborn Romans had a *praenomen,* as Publius, which denoted the individual ; a *nomen,* as Cornelius, which denoted his *gens ;* and a *cognomen,* as Scipio, which denoted his *familia* or *stirps.* To these was sometimes added an honorary name, called *agnomen,* as Africanus. Freedmen also assumed the praenomen and nomen of their liberator, generally before their own name."

128. In drinking healths, it was a complimentary way to first take a draught, saying "bene te" or "bene tibi," and then pass the cup to the person saluted, with the word "bibe!"

129. Usque adeo, to such an extreme; so utterly.

130. Perditus, (so) *reckless.* — **Regi,** the patron.

131. Pertusa. With holes in it.

132. Quadringenta, sc. *milia sestertium.* The census equester. See iii. 154, note.

133. Homuncio. "In amusing contrast to *deus.* Some good little man, like to the gods, and kinder than the fates."

135. Pone ad. Set (the dish) *before.* Cf. *ad pedes, ad manum;* and on *pono* Aen. i. 706: pocula ponunt.

Frater. Horat. *Epp.* i. 6, 54: frater, pater, adde; ut cuique est aetas, ita quemque facetus adopta.

136. Ilia = *lumbus.* " Would n't you like a nice slice off the loin (of the boar) ? "

137 sq. If, as a rich man, you would be your patron's lord and master, you must be childless, that he may court you for a legacy.

141. Nunc, *as it is;* now (that you are poor).

Mygale. Your wife.

143. Viridem thoraca, *a green doublet.* Green was a favorite color for the dress of children and women.

146–155. *The desert.* The finest mushrooms and fragrant apples for the patron and the other grandees, doubtful funguses for the client, and scabby apples, such as monkeys munch.

147. Set (sed) **quales,** *aye, and such as.* See note on iv. 26 sq. The emperor Claudius was very fond of mushrooms. His wife Agrippina poisoned him with one A. D. 54.

151. Homer (*Odys.* vii.) represents the gardens of Alcinous, king of the Phæacians, as filled with perpetual fruits.

152. Sororibus Afris. The Hesperides.

153. In aggere. On the rampart of Servius Tullius.

154 sq. A *monkey* is here represented, dressed up in regimentals and sitting on a goat, munching an apple in the intervals of throwing a dart for the amusement of spectators [and perhaps his master's gain]. So at last Mayor. *Ab capella* in the sense of *from the back of* a goat is justified by *ab equo* in Propert. iii. 11, 13, and Ovid. A. A. i. 210.

157. Hoc agit, this is his aim; he is bent upon this. Cf. v. 157 ; vii. 20, 48.

159. Si nescis. " Elegans formula pro *ut hoc scias, ne hoc ignores.*"

163-5 Who that wore in his boyhood the golden *bulla,* or even the leathern *bulla* of the freedman's son, would so degrade himself as twice to submit to the insults of such a host? (Mayor.) The *bulla,* worn by children born free and rich, was hollow, and of two parts, globular or heart-shaped. It was suspended from the neck, and rested on the breast. The practice was of Etruscan origin. A leather strap with a knot at the end of it answered the same purpose with the poor. — Signum, i. e. signum libertatis.

166. Jam, *presently.*

168. Minor, too small for my lord. (Mayor.) Others take it as equivalent to *semesa.*

168 sq. Inde — tacetis. Thence it is that (or, in hope of this) you all sit in silent expectation, with the bread you have extorted from the slaves uneaten and grasped in your hands like a drawn sword ready for action.

171. The *morio* or *stupidus* was a standing character in comedy and mime. He is introduced with shaven crown, and cuffed and knocked about. Parasites sometimes suffered similar treatment at feasts. Cf. Ter. *Eun.* 243 sq.: at ego infelix neque ridiculus esse neque *plagas pati* possum. Plaut. *Capt.* 86 sq., 469.

SATIRE VII.

―――◦◦◦◦―――

ARGUMENT.

1–16. THE hope and motive of our studies is in Caesar only. He only cares for the Muses in these times when poets leave the vales of Helicon and live by baths, by baking, or by auctioneering. For if Pierian woods won't give you bread, you must e'en ply the crier's trade. And this is better than to rise to wealth by the base art of lying in the courts, though Asiatic and Cappadocian and Bithynian knights may do it. **17–35.** Henceforth, however, no poet shall be degraded to do dirty work. Up and bestir yourselves! the prince is seeking whom he may reward. If you are looking for encouragement from any other quarter, burn your poems or leave them to the worms; go break your pens and wipe out all your lines; the rich men but admire and praise, as children do a peacock. But the useful years of life are passing, and when old age comes on, weary and poor though eloquent, it hates itself and its own Muse. **36–52.** But hear their arts. To avoid giving poets their due, the rich man will be a brother poet (equal to Homer save in years), and free of the guild; at most, he will (which he can do without expense) lend a dusty room for recitation and freedmen to applaud; but he'll not give as much as the benches cost to hire. Still the poetic frenzy is not cured by all this neglect.

53–97. But a rare bard, none of your common sort, is made so by a mind free from care and free from all bitterness, loving the woods and Muses' springs. 'T is not for poverty to sing. Horace was full when he cried Euhoe! What room for genius if other cares than for his verse disturb the poet's breast? If Virgil had not had a servant and a tolerable house, the snakes had dropped from his Fury's head, her trumpet had been dumb. We expect forsooth that our poor playwright should rise to the old cothurnus, who to produce his play must pawn his dishes and his cloak. Numitor, poor man, has nothing for his friend, but plenty for his mistress and his lion — of course the brute eats less than a poet. Lucan may lie in his fine gardens content with his great fame, but what is fame to poor Serranus and Saleius, suppose they get it? Statius delights the town who crowd to hear him; but after all he starves if Paris does not buy his play.

Paris procures honors for the poet, a player what the great should do. Yet will you pay your court to those noble people? Praefects and tribunes come of plays; but you'd not envy him who gets his living by the stage. Where will you find me now any of those Maecenases of old, in whose days many found it worth their while to pale their cheek with study and keep from wine through all December's holidays?

98-104. Next to speak of historians,— are their labors more productive? History demands more time and pains than poetry. Yet vast as the field is, how scanty a crop does it yield! **105-149.** "But historians are an idle herd." Well, what do the lawyers get for all their roaring? However (to deceive creditors or allure clients) they magnify their gains, the patrimonies of a hundred of them are counterbalanced by that of one driver in the circus. The court have taken their seats; pale Ajax rises to plead for a man's liberty with a clown for judex. What is your pay? A little quarter of rusty pork, or a jar of thunnies, or old roots, black slaves' rations, or five jars of bad wine. If, after four pleadings, you get a gold-piece, the attorneys must have a part according to agreement. Aemilius is a rich nobleman, and has a statue and triumphal chariot, and so he gets the largest fee allowed by the laws, and yet we can conduct a case better than he can. 'T is this that brought Pedo to bankruptcy, and Matho too; this was Tongilius's ruin, whose broad purples got him credit. And yet these fine clothes are of use; it's policy to make a noise and wear the look of wealth. Trust we our eloquence? Why Cicero would get nothing now unless he wore a great ring on his finger. No man employs you till he hears how many slaves you keep. So Paulus hired a ring and got more fees than Basilus or Cossus. Eloquence in rags is rare. What chance has Basilus of being heard? Go off to Gaul or Africa and practise if you have set a value on your tongue.

150-214. Do you teach rhetoric? O nerves of steel, when your whole class is slaying savage tyrants! They sit and read, and then get up and say it word for word from first to last,—the same old cabbage served again, killing the wretched teacher. All would learn rhetoric, but none will pay. "Your fee? what have I learnt?" "Of course it's the teacher's fault that the boy is a blockhead, whose 'Hannibal' has stunned me week by week. Ask what you will I'll give it, if you can make his father listen as often as I have listened to his nonsense." Nor is Vettius a singular instance of a rhetorician who must leave his school-declamations for *real* strife in the courts, to sue his pupils for payment. Since then it is so small a pittance that the *rhetor* earns, not amounting at best to more than the cost of a ticket for bread, and since even for that he must go to law, I would advise him rather to follow any other profession. See how much the music-master gets, and you'll tear up your "Elements of Rhetoric." He builds him costly baths, and porticoes to ride in when it rains. What, must he wait till the sky clears, and go splash in the mud? And then a dining-room on marble pillars. Whatever his house costs, he has his butlers and his cooks besides. Meantime Quintilian gets his two sestertia, and that a splendid fee! There's nothing a father will not pay more for than for his son. How then is Quintilian so rich? He is a lucky man; and *your lucky man* is everything that's great and good and wise and eloquent. It makes a great difference under what star you were born. Fortune can make a rhetorician consul, and if she please a consul rhetorician. What was Ventidius, what Tullius? what but a star and influence of hidden destiny? Fate can give a slave a kingdom and a prisoner triumphs. But Quintilian is a lucky rhetorician, rare as a white raven. Many grow weary of the fruitless teacher's chair — witness Carrinas and Thrasymachus; he too was poor to whom Athens could give nothing but cold hemlock. Light lie the earth and fragrant be the flowers above the worthies of old time who held the teacher in the place of parent! Achilles on his father's hills learnt singing, and reverenced the rod when now grown up, unable to laugh even at the tail of his master the Centaur. But Rufus and the rest are flogged by their own pupils.

215–229. Who pays the grammar-master what his toil deserves? E'en from his little fee the pedagogue nibbles part, and the paymaster will take his slice. Bear with the fraud, and bate a little of your just demand, like retailers selling blankets, provided only you do not utterly lose the trifle for which you've sat from midnight till the dawn, where a blacksmith or a weaver would not sit, and smelt the lamps whose smoke stains Horace and blackens Virgil. But fees are few which can be recovered without a trial before the tribune.

229–241. But lay strict terms upon them, that the teacher speak grammatically, and know all history and all authors as well as the nails on his hand; so that at any moment he can tell who was Anchises' nurse, who and whence Archemorus' stepmother, how long Acestes lived, and how much wine he gave the Phrygians. Require that he shall mould his pupils' morals as a man makes a face of wax; require that he be their father, and keep them from vice. "This do," they say, "and when the year comes round you'll have a gold-piece, as much as a jockey earns in a single race." — MACLEANE and MAYOR.

---

1. Ratio, *motive;* "the *raison-d'être.*"

Studiorum, as here, in the sense of *studies,* without an addition such as *artium liberalium,* is post-classical.

Caesare. Probably Hadrian.

4. Gabiis. For any small country town, in which but little custom could be expected. Cf. iii. 192.

Furnos, ovens; *bake-houses.*

6. Praecones, *criers.* They got persons to attend auctions, in which they called out the biddings, and stimulated the purchasers, while the *magister auctionis* knocked the lots down. They kept silence in public assemblies, like "ushers of the court." Their calling was profitable, but despised ; and so long as they followed it, they were not eligible to the rank of *decuriones.*

7. Atria, sc. *auctionaria.*

8. Pieria. The grove of the Muses on Mount Helicon, between the fountains Aganippe and Hippocrene, is here called *Pierian* by the conventional name of the Muses, although the historical Pieria lay north of Olympus.

9. Ames. Used like the Greek ἀγαπᾶν, στέργειν, *to be content with.*
Machaerae. Some *praeco* of the day.

10. Commissa auctio, *the auction's contest,* " ubi licitantes utrinque pretio pugnant; translate a gladiatoribus." (Grangaeus, Mayor.) " Cf. committere proelium, ludos, spectaculum." Otherwise explained as the *auction entrusted* to the praeco, or as *an auction of forfeited goods* (bonorum commissorum).

11. Oenophorum, a wine-jar (with handles). Marquardt v. 2, 425.
Armaria, cupboards, cabinets, or cases, standing against the walls; French, *armoires.*

12. Paccius and **Faustus,** tragic poets of the day. Alcithoe, daughter of Minyas, for her refusal to share in the worship of Dionysos, was changed into a bat. **Thebes** furnished many a subject for the stage. **Tereus** was the subject of tragedies by Sophocles, Philocles, Carcinus the younger, and Attius.

13. Sub judice = *apud judicem.*

14 sqq. Faciant, etc. Although slaves from Asia who have been raised to knighthood do so (i. e. give false testimony).

15. The MSS. read *equitesque.* The first syllable of *Bithyni* is elsewhere long (Juv. x. 162; xv. 1). In the omission of *-que,* and in punctuation, I follow (with Mayor) H. A. J. Munro (note in Mayor's second edition), who has relieved the difficulties of a much vexed passage. The recent editors very generally have considered this verse as spurious. Retaining it, **Asiani** must (according to Munro) be limited to the people of the *province* Asia; "thus Catullus, writing in Bithynia, says *ad claras* Asiae *volemus urbes,*" and verse 16 may be explained by the fact that " Bithynia and Gallatia had got very much mixed up together."

16. Altera Gallia, *New Gaul,* i. e. Galatia ; so named from the Gallic tribes, which, separating from the main body of Gauls under Brennus, were invited into Asia B. C. 278 by Nicomedes of Bithynia, and were confined to the district which bore their name by Attalus I. cir. B. C. 230. (Mayor.)
Nudo talo. Cf. *pedibus albis,* i. 111.

Traducit, *sends across the sea.* Some render it "puts forward to view."

18. Posthac. Now that the emperor favors genuine poets.

20. Hoc agite, make this your earnest pursuit; *set about it.* Cf. verse 48, and v. 157.

21. Ducis. I. e. of the emperor.

22. Si qua aliunde, *if from any other quarter.*

23 sq. Crocea membrana tabella impletur, *the parchment is filled by its yellow page:* "by means of its yellow page; i. e., one page getting filled after another, the quaternion or whatever it may be of parchment is filled." (H. A. J. Munro.) Some understand *crocea tabella* of a wooden case or covers.

Crocea. Cf. Ov. *Trist.* iii. 1, 13 : cedro flavus.

25. Dona Veneris marito. Give to the flames.

Telesinus. We are not to suppose that any particular person is referred to under this name.

26. Clude (P, S, *f, g.*) = *claude* (ω). Shut up your books in the cases (*in scriniis* or *in capsis*), and let the worms eat holes in them.

28 sq. Compare Ben Jonson's lines, at the end of *the Poetaster :*

> "I, that spend half my nights, and half my days,
> Here in a cell, to get a dark, pale face,
> *To come forth worth the ivy or the bays,*
> And in this age can hope no other grace."

Cf. also Boileau, *Ars. Poet.* iv. :

> "Aux plus savans auteurs, comme aux plus grands guerriers,
> Apollon ne promet qu'un nom et des lauriers."

Venias = *prodeas ;* Jonson's *come forth.*

Hederis. Notice the plural, *the ivies,* "ivy wreaths.". "The ivy, being sacred to Bacchus, formed the wreath of victors in scenic contests; thence transferred to poets generally."

Imagine macra. "A poor lean bust, such as a half-starved poet's would be. There were put up in the library of Apollo on the Palatine, and in other public and private libraries, busts of distinguished literary men." (Macleane.)

32. Juno's bird is the peacock.

32–35. " But the useful years of life are passing, in which success might be gained in other occupations, and a weary old age comes on, in which the poor poet has nothing to look to."

36. Artes. Madvig (*Opusc.* ii. 176) introduced the period here,

and the comma in place of a period after *relicta* (37). He is followed
by Jahn, Ribbeck, Weidner. **Artes,** *the tricks, the artful con-
trivances* of the rich, to excuse their neglect of poor poets.

Iste (the demonstrative of the second person), *that* patron *of yours.*

37. Poems were often recited in the porticos attached to the
temples; but our poet reserves his verses for his patron's ear. The
temple of Apollo is that on the Palatine (Horat. *Carm.* i. 31), in
which Becker infers from Mart. xii. 3, 7–8, that statues of the Muses
also stood. There was a temple called Herculis Musarum, built by
Fulvius Nobilior. Weidner interprets *Musarum et Apollinis aede
relicta* of giving up independent, disinterested composition.

38 sq. He acknowledges Homer as his superior only because he
wrote a thousand years ago.

40. Maculosas (= *sordidas*). Heinrich's conjecture. P, macu-
lonis; ω, maculonus. Weidner reads *maculonsas,* which orthography
may account for these MS. readings.

41. Longe = *diu.* See Forcellini.

Servire. To serve your purpose.

42. Sollicitas. Because beleaguered.

Notice the distinction between **janua** and **porta.**

43 sq. There are two kinds of *claquers:* the more intelligent freedmen, sitting at the ends of the rows, give the cue, and poor clients
(*comites*), scattered about the room, obediently shout their bravos.

45 sqq. Subsellia, the seats on the ground floor. Quae — tigillo,
the rising-seats of hired plank that hang in the air (cf. "hanging-
gardens," *pendentes hortuli Semiramidos*). The orchestra, or the
foremost rows, devoted to persons of distinction, *is set* out (posita est)
with luxurious chairs. **Reportandis,** because hired.

48. Hoc agimus, we pursue this purpose; we are engrossed with
this. Cf. Cic. *Tusc.* i. 20, 46.

48, 49. Tenui — aratro. Proverbial expressions for labor thrown
away.

50. Si discedas, if you try to get away. The subjunctive means,
in any instance, at any time. We have here the second person
singular for a general indefinite subject.

Ambitiosi. Jahn (followed by Ribbeck), wrongly deeming line 51
an interpolation, reads *ambitiosum,* to agree with *cacoethes.*

53. Publica, ordinary, *common,* commonplace.

54. Expositum, *trite.*

Deducere, *to spin out.*

55. Coius a trivial poem of the common stamp.

57 sq. Acerbi impatiens, ἄγευστος πικροῦ, free from the suffering of bitterness, which is that of poverty, disappointment, mortification, and self-contempt. (Macleane.)

58. Aptusque. The reading of the MSS.—Jahn and Weidner have *avidusque*, found in the Scholiast, where, however, it may be only a gloss on *cupidus*. Weidner moreover changes *bibendis* into *bibendi*.

60. Thyrsum. "Bacchus and the Muses are always close companions."

64. Dominis. For the ablative, see i. 13, note.

Cirra (Cirrha) was the port of Delphi; its lord was *Apollo*. Nysa is the name of many places connected with *Bacchus*, — the original one being generally placed in the Punjaub; here probably a village on Mount Helicon, which claimed to have been the home of the god in his boyhood.

Feruntur, *are carried away*, borne headlong (in inspiration).

66. Juvenal uses attonitae for *perplexed*, as the word belongs to inspiration. Cf. Hor. *Carm.* iii. 19, 13. (Macleane.)

67, 68. I. e. to write like Virgil.

Rutulum. I. e. Turnus.

69. Desset = deesset. The use of the imperfect here and in the apodosis is lively, and has the same effect as the use of the historical present. Cf. M. 347, b, note 2; Z. 525; Verg. Aen. iii. 187 ; Prop. iii. 6, 43 sq.

70, 71. Cf. Verg. *Aen.* vii. 447, 513 sqq.

72. Rubrenus Lappa. Some small play-writer, who was obliged to pawn his dishes and his cloak while writing his tragedy of Atreus.

Cothurno. A symbol for *tragedy*. (Why?) On the ablative, cf. iii. 74, note.

74 sqq. Numitor. Some great noble. The name is humorously taken to imply ancient descent. This great man — poor fellow — has nothing to send to his friend the poet, but plenty to give to his mistress, and enough to buy meat for his tame lion. (Macleane.)

78. Nimirum, *no doubt*. Ironical.

79. Jaceat. On the *lectus*.

Lucanus. The author of the *Pharsalia*. He inherited a large fortune from his father.

Hortis marmoreis. I. e. in the gardens attached to his marble villa, themselves adorned with statues and surrounded with porticos.

80. Serranus. Ranked by Quintilian (x. 1, 89) among epic poets; deep in debt, if he is the same as the person spoken of by Martial (iv. 37, 2 sqq.).

Tenui, poor ; of slender estate.

Saleius Bassus. An epic poet praised by Tacitus and Quintilian.

81. Tantum, only; alone. (How is this meaning derived from the original meaning of the word?)

82 sqq. P. Papinius Statius, author of the Thebais, and patronized by Domitian, recited portions of that epic from time to time during the twelve years in which he was composing it. It would appear that he had an agreeable voice.

Diem. A day for reciting.

86. Fregit subsellia. Cf. i. 13. "He has broken down the benches by his poem, i. e. by the loudness and energy with which he recites it."

87. Intactam — Agaven, *unless he sell his virgin "Agave" to Paris.* Paris, a native of Egypt, was a pantomime of great celebrity in Domitian's reign. Martial (xi. 13) wrote his epitaph:

> quisquis Flaminiam teris, viator,
> noli nobile praeterire marmor.
> urbis deliciae, salesque Nili,
> ars et gratia, lusus et voluptas,
> Romani decus et dolor theatri,
> atque omnes Veneres Cupidinesque,
> hoc sunt condita quo Paris sepulcro.

Intactam, i. e. new, not as yet exhibited.

Agave, the sister of Semele.

88. Ille et. He does more for the poets than buy their plays; he gets them military honors and the knights' gold ring.

Largitus. So Jahn and Mayor, after some MSS. Pω *targitur.*

89. Semenstri **auro,** with the six-months' gold, i. e. *the six-months' ring.* This means the ring (which was a badge of equestrian rank) won by six months' service. "The tribune of a legion became, as a matter of course, an *eques.* On account of this advancement in rank the office was conferred by the emperors on persons who did not intend to follow the military profession, but after six months' service, *tribunatus semestris,* retired as *equites* into private life." Mayor.

90 sq. Tu — curas. Young men sought to gain the favor of the great and influential, as an aid to their own advancement. Camerinus was the name of a good old family of the patrician gens Sulpicia. (Cf. viii. 38.) On **Barea** see note on iii. 116. — **Atria.** The *atrium* was the reception-room in the houses of the great.

92. The two plays here named, like the **Agave,** were probably the *cantica* or texts for pantomimic representation.

94, 95. Proculeius is celebrated by Horace (*Carm.* ii. 2, 5–6) for his generosity to his brothers. Paulus **Fabius** Maximus, consul B. C. 11, was a steady friend of Ovid. Cotta Messalinus (or Cotta Maximus), son of the great M. Valerius Messalla Corvinus, was also one of Ovid's patrons. Lentulus is perhaps the consul P. Cornelius Lentulus Spinther, who procured Cicero's recall from exile, B. C. 57.

97. The Saturnalia, with its attendant festivals (at one of which little figures were sold as toys or presents), occupied seven days in the month of December. Indeed the whole month was sacred to Saturn, and was a month of feasting and revelry.

100. **Modo,** *limit.* — Our reading *nullo quippe modo* is given by Jahn, and the best editors generally, after P, Serv. ad Aen. iv. 98, and Schol. Lucani i. 334. Macleane reads with inferior MSS. *namque oblita modi.* — **Surgit,** springs up, begins.

101. **Omnibus,** sc. *historicis.* — **Damnosa,** *to their loss.* Cf. Hor. *Sat.* ii. 8, 34. Papyrus was costly ; parchment, of course, still more so.

102. **Rerum,** of topics ; things to be mentioned. — **Operum lex,** the conditions or law to which writers of such works are bound.

104. **Acta,** *the newspaper.*

105. **Lecto,** the couch.

106 sq. **Civilia officia,** *services to their fellow-citizens ;* legal services, for the protection of lives and fortunes. — **Praestent,** "bring them in." — **Magno** — libelli, the big bundle of documents (briefs, depositions, extracts from laws, etc.) with which they are accompanied.

108–114. Madvig (*Opusc.* ii. 179, 180), followed by Mayor, rightly explains this passage as follows : " The lawyers themselves talk very grandly, and boast that they receive great fees ; but when do they so talk ? particularly when persons are listening whom it is for their interest to impress with the belief that their practice brings them in a large income. And who are such persons? In the first place, a creditor of their own, who is to be convinced that his claim is safe ; secondly, some rich litigant, more eager even than the creditor, who comes to employ the advocate in a doubtful case, and will be the more ready to pay him a large fee if he believes that he is generally paid more than the average of lawyers. Then, indeed, their bellows blow enormous lies : then the lawyers make such assertions of prosperity, that, to avert the wrath of the gods provoked by proud words, in accordance with an ancient superstitious practice, they spit in their bosoms. But their *real* income is so different from this false boasting that a single charioteer in the circus is richer than a hundred lawyers." This suits better with the context (" quid praestent officia.") and the antithesis to their lying boasts, "*veram* depraendere messem," than the interpretation more generally adopted, which is thus stated by Macleane : " They talk very big of their own accord (ipsi), but still more if the creditor is listening for whom they are acting ; or louder still if the client is eager and nudges his ' causidicus,' being afraid of losing his money. Then truly do they puff their lies like bellows, spluttering all their breast."

109. Tetigit latus. I. e. has spurred the lawyer on to lie. So Madvig, *l. c.* p. 180, foot-note.

Acrior. Ribbeck reads *aegrior*, so interpreting aecrior (p) and ae*rior (P).

110. Grandi codice. The large size of the ledger indicates (says Madvig) a rich litigant.

Nomen, *a debt.* See Lexicon, and Dict. Antiq. s. v. Fenus. Weidner translates it "debtor" (which meaning it also bears), and understands it of the lawyer himself.

111. Cf. Pers. v. 10 ; Horat. *Sat.* i. 4, 19.

112. Mayor's citations sufficiently prove that spitting three times in the bosom was an ancient superstitious practice to avert the wrath of the gods and to break spells. In this sense we should rather expect to find *despuitur* (see examples s. v. in Forcellini), but the use of *conspuere* does not exclude Madvig's interpretation. One may follow Madvig, however, in all other points in this passage (108–114), and still take *conspuitur sinus* as meaning simply that the eager, mouthing speaker "splutters his froth all over the folds of his toga."

Depraendere (= deprehendere, deprendere). With Jahn I follow P.

114. Russati. " The drivers in the chariot-races were divided into four parties, called *factiones*, and distinguished by the color of their dress ; there was the white, *alba*, red, *russata*, blue (but see note on iii. 170), *veneta*, and dark-green, *prasina*." — Lacerna is (the scholiast says) an *auriga abjectus* of " the red."

115 sqq. A scene in court, the first line parodied from Ov. *Met.* xiii. 1, 2, where the contest between Ajax and Ulysses for Achilles' armor is described :

> consedere duces ; et vulgi stante corona
> surgit ad hos clypei dominus septemplicis Ajax.

"The chiefs" have taken their seats ; the lawyer rises, a pale " Ajax," to plead the cause of one who is claimed as a slave, with a neatherd as *judex*.

116. Dubia. I. e., which is disputed. The action was a *vindicatio.*

Bubulco judice. The office of *judex*, after the changes introduced by Augustus, was no longer an honor, but a burden. Any free male adult, who had not been condemned for a criminal offence, might, it would seem, now sit as judex. Mayor.

117. Jecur. The supposed seat of the passions.

118. After a forensic victory, lawyers used to hang palm branches over their doors. The supposed advocate in this case lives in hired lodgings in a garret, and can only decorate his stair-case.

119. Quod = *quale*. Interrogative adjective pronoun.

Siccus petasunculus, *a rusty little quarter of pork.* The *petaso* was eaten fresh; the *perna* (or *ham*) was a part of the *petaso* (Athen. xiv. p. 657 e), and was smoked or salted.

120. Maurorum epimenia, *the monthly rations of Moorish slaves.* **Maurorum** (P *a c*) is adopted by Jahn and recent critical editors generally, except Macleane, who reads *Afrorum* (ω).

121. Wines *brought down the Tiber,* such as the Sabine and Veientane, were very inferior to the Campanian and foreign wines, which came up the river.

Lagonae = *lagenae.* Macleane places a comma after "lagenae" and a period after "egisti" in the next verse. All other recent critical editors punctuate as I have done.

122. Si quater egisti = si causam perorasti. The process required four pleadings.

Why is **contigit** the right word here, and not **accidit**?

Aureus. The gold-piece was now worth 25 denarii, or about $4.

123. *The attorneys' percentage is deducted from it, by agreement.*

124. The Aemilia was one of the noblest of the patrician families.

Quantum licet (P and best editors. Other readings are *petet, petit, libet*), *as much as the law allows.* "In B. C. 204, a *plebiscitum* was passed, prohibiting any person from taking a fee for pleading a cause. This was confirmed by a *senatus consultum* in the time of Augustus; but was relaxed in that of Claudius, after which time a man might take ten sestertia for a fee," — i. e. one hundred "gold-pieces," one of which was thought enough for our poor *causidicus.*

Et, *and yet.* Cf. xiii. 91: hic putat esse deos et pejerat. Tac. *An.* i. 38: reduxit in hiberna turbidos et nihil ausos.

125-128. In Aemilius's porch stands the triumphal statue of an ancestor in a *quadriga;* also his own equestrian statue, aiming a shaft which bends and quivers as it is poised for the throw, for certainty of aim one eye being closed (*lusca*).

129. Sic. By imitating this display of wealth. — **Pedo.** An unknowp lawyer. — **Conturbat** (sc. *rationes*), becomes a fraudulent bankrupt (confusing his accounts). — **Matho**. See Sat. i. 32. — **Deficit**, "*fails*" as in English.

130 sqq. Tongilius may be the one alluded to in Martial (ii. 40). To show his consequence, he goes to bathe with a dirty crowd of retainers, and is borne through the forum in his *lectica* with a long pole, making fine purchases.

130. Rhinocerote. An oil-flask (*gutus*) of rhinoceros horn.

131. Vexat, *mobs.*

132. His bearers are **Maedi**, Thracians from the west bank of the Strymon, from whom the northern district of Macedonia, between the Axius and Strymon, was called Maedica.

133. Murrina. "Porcelain" is a good modern analogue, but not the right translation of this word. The murrina were probably *bowls of agate*, of great cost, fragments of which are now often turned up in the soil of Rome. See Mayor, who cites *inter alios* C. W. King (Nat. Hist. of Precious Stones and Gems, pp. 237–245). Fr. Thiersch (Abh. der Münchn. Akad. i. 439 sq.) contends that the *murrina* were made of fluor-spar.

134. Spondet (lit. gives security for him), *procures him credit.* Mayor.

Tyrio stlattaria (stlataria) **purpura filo,** *broad purple* (i. e. his purple robe) *of Tyrian web.* Etymologists concur (Curtius, Corssen, Vaniçek) in deriving **stlataria** from the root star- (*to strew, spread, extend*), whence στορ-έ-ννυ-μι, ster-n-o, (stra-vi, stra-tu-s). As in the Slavic languages the root occurs sometimes with *l* and sometimes with *r*, so here stla-ta is identical with stra-ta. This is also the root of *lâtu-s*, where *st* has fallen away entirely before *l*. "Stlata," says Festus (Paul. Diac., p. 312, Festus, p. 313), "is a kind of ship *broad* (latum) rather than long, and so named from its breadth (a latitudine), but in the same way as men used to say stlocum for locum and stlitem for litem." *Navis stlata* is therefore a vessel built broad for merchandise ; *navis longa*, one long and narrow for war. O. Müller (on Festus *l. c.*) understands *stlataria purpura* of purple cloths imported on such *stlatae*, and hence genuine Tyrian merchandise. So the lexicographers generally, rendering *stlataria* "sea-borne." An old scholiast asserts that Probus explains *stlataria* as meaning *illecebrosa*, and so Heinrich, in an elaborate note (*ad schol.*, pp. 396–399), renders it *seductive, decoying, alluring, enticing,* understanding *stlata* (after Flavius Caper and others) of a *pirate vessel*, quae, (to cite Heinrich,) "in hostium naves lenocinia, insidias, fraudes, ludificationes, illectamenta" exercet. It is perhaps safe to go back, with **Corssen** (*Kr. Beiträge*, 462, 463) to the etymology of the word, and render it as I have at the beginning of this note.

136. Convenit = utile est, prodest.

137. **Strepitu et facie.** The genitive (*mojoris census*) supplies the place of an adjective, so that we can have the modal ablative without *cum*.

138. This verse is bracketed by many editors as out of place.

142. **Togati.** Clients (iii. 127).

143-5. Three poor lawyers are named.

146. It was a custom in Rome, as well as in Greece, to introduce in the epilogue relations (as mothers, wives, sisters, children), sometimes in mourning garments and in tears, to work on the jurors' feelings.

148 sq. **Gallia** abounded in men of eloquence; under the empire rhetoric flourished in **Africa.**

149. *To put a price on your tongue;* i. e. (if you want) to make money. On this meaning of ponere cf. Hor. *Sat.* ii. 3, 23: callidus huic signo ponebam milia centum. Inferior MSS. read *imponere.*

150. **Declamare** is a general term for rhetorical exercises. — **Ferrea,** I. e. patient, enduring, apathetic. — **Vettius** Valens was the founder of a new school of rhetoricians. His name here represents the class of rhetoricians in general.

151. The class declaim invectives against tyrants or laudations of tyrannicides.

152. The class read their declamations sitting, and standing up repeat them again (perferet) from beginning to end. (Macleane.)— **Cantabit,** *will drone,* in a hum-drum, sing-sing tone. — **Versus** applies to the *lines* in prose as well as in poetry. Cf. Hor. *Sat.* ii. 5, 54.

154. There was an old proverb, δὶς κράμβη θάνατος. Mayor cites Quintil. ii. 4, 29 : necesse est . . . . fastidium moveant velut frigidi et repositi cibi.

155. **Color.** We must retain the metaphor in translation : "what may be the color to be given to the case." Mayor says that "color" denotes the varnish, gloss, or color by which the accused endeavors to palliate, the accuser to aggravate, the allowed facts of the case. **Summa,** *main.*

156. **Quae — sagittae,** *what shafts* (a metaphor for arguments) *may chance to come from the opposite side.* **Diversae,** belonging to the opposing side; from the enemy. Inferior MSS. read *diversa parte sagittae.*

13 — Juv.   R

158. Quid enim scio ? *Why, what have I learnt?* **Enim** like γάρ.
(" You surely cannot expect a fee? *For* what do I know ? ")

159 sq. The ancient Romans placed the seat of the intellect in
the heart. Cf. Cic. *Tusc.* i. 9. — The **Arcadians** were proverbially
dull; their country was famed for its asses, both literally and meta-
phorically.

161. Dirus Hannibal. Cf. x. 166 sq.

162 sq. Urbem. Of course Rome. — **An . . . . an.** Not a double
question, but two separate questions. The occasions are different,
the second being B. C. 211, five years after the battle of Cannae,
when Hannibal retired from the walls of Rome in consequence of a
great storm repeated on two successive days (Liv. xxvi. 11).

164. Circumagat, wheel, wheel round. — **A,** from, *away* from.

165. Our reading (p ω) gives the simplest construction. Munro
(note in Mayor's edition) thinks that *quid* (P, *Priscian*) "may,
perhaps, be right:" *quantum vis stipulare, et protinus accipe* —
" *quid?*" *do ut totiens,* etc. "Receive what?" says the one to
whom the offer is made; then the other replies, "Why, I give it on
condition that," etc. Hermann (who edited *quod do,* "ne Pithoe-
anum *quid do* tironum oculos offenderet,") suspects a corruption of
the text, but proposes no emendation. Ribbeck makes the happy
conjecture *qui* (i. e. qua conditione) *do ;* Mommsen proposed *quin do*
(and so Weidner), Lachmann *qui dum?*

Quod do, what I offer.

166. Ut, *on condition that.* — **Totiens,** as many times as I have
(heard him). On fathers' coming to hear their sons recite, cf. Pers.
iii. 45–47.

Alii. Many other teachers make the same complaint as Vettius.

167. Sophistae here = *rhetores* or *grammatici.* On the use of the
term see Grote's famous chapter, with " Cope's criticisms in Journ.
of Class. and Sacr. Philol. i.–iii."

168-170. The rhetoricians *pursue real lawsuits* to get their fees,
leaving their fictitious disputations on stock-themes, as "*the
ravisher,*" "*outpoured poisons,*" "*the wicked and ungrateful husband,*" " *eye-salves,*" and the like. — We may refer these topics of
declamation to the stories of Paris, Medea, Jason, and old Pelias, or
to such fictitious legal cases as those described in Quintil. *Decl.* 247,
Senec. *Exc.* 7, 8, p. 420 (B), Quintil. *Decl.* 17, Senec. *Contr.* ii. 13,
p. 156 (B), *Exc. Contr.* ii. 5, p. 354.

170. Veteres caecos, *men who have been long blind.* Cf. Juv. ix.
16 : macies aegri veteris.

171. Ergo. Notice the short *o*.

Sibi dabit ipse rudem, *will give himself his own discharge.* The *rudis* was a wooden sword with which the gladiators practised, and which (with the *pileus*) they received as a symbol of their discharge. On the metaphorical use of the phrase cf. Hor. *Epp.* i. 1, 2 sq.

173. Pugnam = *veras lites* (verse 168). — **Descendit.** Perfect tense. — **Rhetorica ab umbra,** *from his scholastic shade;* from the retirement in which he has practised the rhetorician's art.

174. The **tessera** was a round or square tally of metal or wood, entitling the possessor to a share of grain in the monthly distribution to the poorer citizens. The ticket could be sold or bequeathed. It is here sold by one whose name is on the list to our rhetorician, who, probably as not being a citizen (for most of the rhetoricians were Greeks), has no title to the privilege. The ticket is "vilis," as the amount of grain received was small.

Venit is in the present tense. From what verb? (Notice the quantity.)

176. Two music-masters are named.

177. Artem scindes Theodori. You'll tear up your old rhetoric book. — **Ars,** like τέχνη, is used of an elementary work, — here, "Elements of Rhetoric," as Theodorus was a rhetorician. — The MSS. read *scindens; scindes* is Jahn's correction, approved by Hermann, Ribbeck, Weidner, Mayor. If *scindens* be retained, it must agree with the subject of *tempta,* as Madvig shows, — the caesura after *pueros* separating the interposed clause from connection with this.

178–188. The rich spend immense sums on their houses and establishments, but offer only a pittance for the education of their sons.

178. Sescentis, sc. milibus nummûm; 600,000 sestertii.

179. Gestetur, sc. *vehiculo.* Cf. verse 180.

181. Hic, i. e. in the porticus. — Mules were in great request by the wealthy Romans.

182. Parte alia. "His baths here, his covered drives there, his dining-room elsewhere." — The *tall columns of the Numidians* are pillars of the yellow Numidian marble.

183. Algentem solem, i. e. the sun in winter.

184 sq. Quanticumque domus, sc. *sit.* However expensive the house, money will be forthcoming for the purchase of a *structor* (cf. v. 120) and a *pulmentarius.*

185. Pulmentaria, *dainties.*

Condiat (dissyllable) is Lachmann's emendation, adopted by Jahn. Most MSS. *condit,* some *condat.*

186. Quintiliano. The celebrated author of the Institutio Oratoria. — **Sestertia duo.** Two thousand sestertii.

187. Ut multum. As we say, *at most.* — **Sufficient.** Gnomic future. Cf. verses 201, 219, and Pers. ii. 5.

189. Saltus, pasture lands among the forests on the hills. — Juvenal exaggerates Quintilian's wealth. " He was rich among poor men, and poor among the rich." Cf. Plin. *Epp.* vi. 32.

Exempla novorum fatorum, *instances of rare good fortune.*

Transi, *pass by ;* do not take into account. Cf. iii. 114.

190. Felix, *the lucky man* (εὐδαίμων, the man favored by Fortune), is both beautiful and brave.

191. Sapiens, nobilis, and **generosus**, are used appositively : the lucky man, *as* both wise and noble and high-born, sews (subtexit), etc.

192. Becomes senator. The shoes of the senators came higher up the leg than ordinary *calcei*, and bore in front a crescent. The sub in **subtexit** is not *under the shoe,* but simply *below.*

193. Jaculator. He excels in the games of the Campus Martius. Others translate " a debater," hurling arguments against his opponent.

194. Perfrixit (from *perfrigescere*), *he has a cold.*

197 sq. Quintilian received the *ornamenta consularia,* which, while they did not necessarily admit into the senate, facilitated such admittance, and conferred a high *dignitas.* Pliny (*Epp.* iv. 11) speaks of Valerius Licianus who had become a teacher in Sicily : " Praetorius hic modo inter eloquentissimos causarum actores habebatur, nunc eo decidit, ut exul de senatore, rhetor de oratore fieret. Itaque ipse in praefatione dixit dolenter et graviter : quos tibi, Fortuna, ludos facis! facis enim ex professoribus senatores, ex senatoribus professores! "

199. P. Ventidius Bassus, a native of Picenum, in the Social War was carried captive with his mother to Rome, and appeared in the triumphal procession of Cn. Pompeius Strabo, B. C. 89. When he grew up he gained his livelihood by letting out mules and carriages. C. Julius Caesar took him into Gaul, and employed him for the remainder of his career in important offices. He rose to be tribunus plebis, then praetor, then pontifex, and lastly consul, B. C. 43. " Mulos qui fricabat consul factus est." Gaining a victory over the Parthians, he celebrated a triumph.

Servius Tullius, the sixth king of Rome, was born of a slave.

201. Servis (as to Tullius), **captivis** (as to Ventidius).

204. Tharsymachi. An emendation of Ritschl (Op. ii. 541), for Thrasymachi of the MSS., for metrical reasons. So the Attic poets interchanged θράσυ, and θάρσος. Cf. crocodilus, corcodilus; tarpezita, trapezita. In translation, use the ordinary form Thrasymachus. It is the name of one of the sophists, who came to Athens about the middle of the fifth century B.C. He was a native of Chalcedon. The scholiast says he hanged himself, but we know nothing further about his "exitus."

Secundus Carrinas was sent by Caligula into exile, because he declaimed in his school against tyrants. The scholiast says, *veneno perit.*

205. Hunc refers probably to Socrates. We should have expected *illum*, but *hunc* may imply greatness and interest in the estimation of the speaker. Mayor, however, says that "*hunc* seems to mean *in our own day*, later still than Carrinas; and *ausae* has little force, unless we suppose that some one is meant, who when banished retired to Athens, and there, as no one would venture to employ him, put an end to his life by taking poison. Nor was Socrates a teacher of rhetoric. Markland supposes that a verse is lost."

206. Ausae, *who* (i. e. Athens) *could bring thyself.*

207 sq. Di .... terram, sc. *dent.* **Sine pondere,** an adjective phrase. See Nägelsbach *Stilistik* 75, 2 (p. 203). The prayer that the earth may rest lightly on the ashes of the dead is very frequent in epitaphs. — Sometimes a sum of money was left in order to secure a constant supply of flowers on a tomb.

211. Patriis in montibus. On Mount Pelion.

Cui (with the subjunctive eliceret) = *talis ut ei.* — Cŭi. Cf. iii. 49. **Tunc,** *then;* in that age of respect for teachers. Mayor.

212. Chiron, the Centaur, taught Achilles music and other accomplishments.

214. This weak disciplinarian, the rhetorician Rufus, was a Gaul, and accordingly his class nicknamed him *the Allobrogian Cicero.*

215. Two grammarians: **Celadus,** hardly known except from this passage, and **Palaemon,** who lived under Tiberius and Claudius, and, though profligate, enjoyed great reputation as a teacher.

217. Autem, *after all.*

218. Custos, the *paedagogus.* (See Lexicons.) Cf. Horat. *Sat.* i. 6, 81 sq.; *A. P.* 161.

Acoenonetus, ἀκοινώνητος, destitute of common feeling, inconsiderate, *selfish.* So Grangaeus, Jahn (in Greek letters), **Weidner.** Hermann Ribbeck, and Mayor read *acoenonoëtus,* after P.

219. Qui dispensat. The *dispensator*, cashier or private secretary of the rich man. — The MSS. and editors vary between *frangit, frangat,* and **franget.**

222. Dummodo non pereat, quod—. *Provided it go not for naught, that —.*

223. Sederet, *would* be willing to *sit.*

224. Obliquo ferro. "The *carding* instrument, consisting of crooked bits of iron fastened in a board." Carding wool prepared it for spinning.

225 sqq. "Boys going to school at night carried lanterns with them. The master had to bear the smell of as many lamps as there were boys, and their class-books were black with the smoke." Horace foresaw that his works would become a text-book (*Epp.* i. 20, 17 sq.).

226. Stabant. In their classes, to recite.

228. The *tribunus plebis* appears to have had a kind of judicial authority under the empire. Cf. xi. 7.

229. Vos, you parents. What follows is ironical. — **Leges,** conditions; demands.

230. That the teacher never be at fault in his accidence or syntax.

231. Omnes is taken with *historias* as well as with *auctores.*

233. Balnea are bathing-rooms or houses, **thermae** large buildings intended for gymnastic exercises and also supplied with hot water and vapor baths. — **Phoebus** was a *balneator* of the day.

234-236. Tiberius used to ask the grammarians such questions as these: "who was the mother of Hecuba?" "what was Achilles' name when he lived among the maidens in Scyros?" "what songs were the Sirens wont to sing?"

235. Anchemolus was a warrior who fought under Turnus. Verg. *Aen.* x. 388-9. — **Acestes.** Verg. *Aen.* i. 195 sqq., v. 73, 35 sq.

236. Phrygibus = Trojanis.

237. Ducat, *mould.*

240. Inquit, he (i. e. any father) says. Often used without a subject expressed. — **Cura;** set. So the best editors. P ω, *curas et.*

241. In the Circensian games the populace sometimes demanded that the *editor ludorum* should give the victorious charioteer an additional reward.

SATIRE VIII.

---oo§o§oo---

ARGUMENT.

1-38. WHAT use are pedigrees, ancestral blood, statues and images, and noble names, if in the face of our great ancestors we live amiss —gambling all night and going to bed at dawn, when they were up and marching? What joy has Fabius of the Allobroges' victor, of the great altar, of his descent from Hercules, if he be covetous, a fool, effeminate, if he bring shame on his rough ancestors, turn poisoner, and disgrace his house? Line your whole house with images, yet still virtue alone is true nobility. Be Paulus, Cossus, Drusus in your morals, and give them place before your images, ay, and your own lictors too. First I claim the goodness of your heart: be holy, just, in word and deed, and then I count you noble. Hail, Gaetulicus or Silanus. From whatsoever stock you come to your rejoicing country, all may cry, "Eurekamen!" as they do who have found Osiris. What man is generous if he be unworthy of his race, illustrious only for his name? Nicknames go by contraries. We call a dwarf Atlas, an Aethiopian Cycnus, a crooked girl Europa, a mangy dog a pard, a tiger, or a lion. See that your great name is not applied to you on the same principle.

39-70. This is for you, Rubellius Blandus, swelling with your descent from Drusus, as if it were a merit of your own that you were born not of a poor weaver, but of the great Iulus' blood. "Low wretches (say you), ye who cannot tell your father's birthplace. I am a son of Cecrops!" Long may you live to enjoy your birth! But in that low rabble you will find a man of eloquence, who shall defend some noble blockhead, or solve the riddles of the law; and some brave soldiers too; while you are all Cecropian, as useless as a Hermes; the only difference is, his head's of marble, yours has life in it. Tell me, O Trojan, who counts animals noble except they're spirited and brave? We praise a horse who has won many races. Wherever he was reared we call him noble who beats the rest, while a mere herd to be put up and sold are the best bred if they but seldom win. There we have no respect for ancestry: they sell for little, and go to draw a cart or grind a mill. So tell me something of your own to engrave upon your bust, besides the honors that we freely give to those to whom you owe all that you have.

199

71-86. Enough for him who, lacking common courtesy (rare in that state of life), is puffed up with his relationship to Nero. But you, my friend, I would not have you valued upon the merits of your family, and you yourself do nothing for future time to praise. 'T is poor to rest upon another's fame; remove the pillar and the roof falls in; robbed of its elm, the vine comes to the ground. Be a good soldier, honest guardian, upright judge, witness inflexible. Count not your life before your character, your life before the causes for which you live; the man that does that deserves to die, though he fare sumptuously and smell of all perfumes.

87-124. When you have got the province that you 've long desired, put reins upon your temper and your covetousness; pity the poor natives; the princes you will see have all the marrow sucked from out their bones. Think of the laws, the trust committed to you, the honors that await the good, the fate of those who were condemned for robbing the Cilicians. Not that such condemnation is worth much, when one takes what another leaves. Go, get an auctioneer to sell your clothes, Chaerippus, and straight say nothing; it were madness to throw away your fare to Rome besides. Those people suffered less when they were beaten first: riches were left them still, shawls and dresses, pictures and statues, and chased silver vessels; then came your governors and carried off more spoils from peace than ever graced a triumph. Now the little that they have they 'll lose it all. You may despise, perhaps, the Rhodians, and Corinth too; but take good care of Spain, of Gaul, Illyricum, the Africans, who send us corn to feed our idleness. Besides, they 've nothing to repay you. Marius has robbed them. Take care you do no great wrong to the brave and poor: take all they have, you will still leave them arms.

125-145. This is no mere opinion of my own; believe, the Sibyl speaks. Be your attendants righteous, no favorite sell your judgments, your wife no harpy, then, though you may trace your birth to Picus and the Titan brood, and claim Prometheus for your ancestor, you are welcome to any pedigree you like, so far as I am concerned. But if ambition, lust, and cruelty carry you headlong, then your ancestors only hold up the torch to expose your shame. The sin is greatest in the greatest sinner. Why boast yourself to me, you who forge wills in temples which your grandsire built before your father's statue, and steal by night in your cowl to a deed of shame?

146-182. Fat consul Lateranus degrades himself as a coachman, driving right past the ashes of his sires by night,— but the moon and stars look on,— and when his consulship is done, he 'll do it in broad day, and meet his aged friend without a blush. He 'll do the menial work of a groom, and when he goes to sacrifice to Jove he 'll swear by Epona and the stable gods. And when he goes to taverns, the greasy host comes out to meet him, and with an air salutes his lordship; while the officious hostess brings the wine. "But we all did the same when we were young." Yes; but we 've left off. Such faults should be cut off with our first beard. Children may be excused; but Lateranus is old enough for the wars. Send him on foreign duty, O Caesar, but seek your legate in the eating-house: you 'll find him there with cut-throats, sailors, thieves, runaway slaves and executioners and drunken priests and undertakers, all pot-fellows together. What would you do, had you a slave such as this? Of course you 'd send him to the slaves' prison and the fields. But you excuse yourselves, ye Trojan-born. Brutus may do what would disgrace a cobbler.

183-210. Bad though this be, yet worse remains behind. His money spent, Damasippus goes upon the stage, and Lentulus acts Laureolus not badly, deserving, as I think, a *real* cross. The people are to blame to sit and see patrician buffooneries. At what price they sell their honor matters not. No tyrant forces them, and yet they gladly sell themselves to the Praetor for his shows. And even if the choice were that or death, which should they choose? Does any one fear death so much that he should act with Thymele and Corinthus? But nobles acting as mimes are not astonishing, when we 've had a harper like Nero for our emperor. After all this, what can there be but gladiatorial shows? This, too, doth shame the town; Gracchus, a noble and a priest, not with helmet or shield, but as a *retiarius*, undisguised and with face uncovered, casts his net, and failing flies the arena round in sight of all the theatre. His tunic and his cap betray the priest of Mars: can we believe it? More shame it is than any wound for him who suffers the degradation of fighting with a priest.

211-230. Were but the people free, who but would choose a Seneca before a Nero? The death of many parricides was his desert. His crime was like Orestes', but it differed in the cause. One, bid by gods, avenged his father's murder; but he slew not his sister or his wife: he poisoned no relations, never acted, never wrote a rubbishy poem on the Trojan War. What is there that Nero did which so deserved punishment at the hands of Verginius, Vindex, and Galba? These are the practices of a high-born prince, who loved to sing in foreign theatres and earn the parsley crown from Greeks! Hang up your dresses and your masks and harp, the trophies of *your* glory, before the statues of your ancestors!

231-268. Catilina and Cethegus were of lofty birth, and yet they would have fired the city, like savages, fit to be punished with the shirt of pitch. But our Consul was awake; a new man and not noble guarded the whole town, and got more fame in peace than all Octavius won at Actium or Philippi. Rome was then free, and called our Cicero his country's Father. His townsman too, Marius, followed the plough for hire, and had the vine-switch broken over his head in the ranks. But he stood single-handed, and withstood the Cimbri and delivered Rome, and when the fight was over he was crowned before his colleague. The Decii were plebeians, yet were their lives offering enough for all the host; they were worth more than all that they saved. A slave's son wore the crown of Romulus, and was our last good king. The Consul's sons would have betrayed the city, a slave betrayed their purpose: he worthy to be wept by matrons, they deserved to die, the first condemned by righteous laws.

269-275. You 'd better be Thersites' son and like Achilles, than like Thersites and Achilles' son. But go as far back as you will, you still come to the asylum, and whosoe'er was founder of your line must have been a shepherd or something worse. — MACLEANE *with modifications.*

1. Stemmata, *pedigrees.* The *imagines* of ancestors in the *atria* of noblemen were painted masks of wax placed upon busts prepared for the purpose. These busts with the portrait-masks were arranged in little shrines (*armaria*), under which inscriptions (*tituli*) proclaimed the names, honors, and exploits of the ancestors. The *imagines* were encircled with wreaths (*stemmata*), running from one to another in such a way as to indicate the genealogical connection of the persons represented. Some scholars suppose that the Romans had family-trees, resembling our own in form, on which were small medallion portraits (*pictos vultus, imagines pictas*), encircled by wreaths running from one to another; and interpret Plin. *H. N.* xxxv. 2, and Sen. *de Ben.* iii. 28, in this manner, rather than in accordance with the explanation given above.

Ponticus was some young noble, to whom Juvenal addresses this satire in the form of an epistle.

2. Pictos vultus majorum. The waxen masks, or the painted faces on the family tree: in either case, *the portraits of one's ancestors.*

3 sq. The only historical **Aemilianus** when this was written was the younger Scipio, P. Cornelius Scipio Aemilianus, who gained the agnomen Africanus. Triumphal statues are probably meant, although paintings may be referred to (Marq. 5, 1, 248). — Dimidios, *broken in half.* — **Umeros minorem,** "short of a head and shoulders."

7. It must be that this verse is an interpolation. What the interpolator meant by *contingere virga* is doubtful. **Virga** has been taken for the *fasces,* for *a broom* to keep the busts clean, for a *wand* with which the busts are pointed out, and for a *branch* of the ancestral tree (like *ramus* (Pers. iii. 28), *linea*). In the latter case, translate **multa contingere virga,** *to reach, through many a branch.*

8. The ancient *imagines* of the masters of the horse are dingy with smoke from the *focus* in the atrium.

9. Coram Lepidis, like ante **Numantinos (11),** under the very eyes of great and noble ancestors. i. e. in the presence of their *imagines.*

Quo, *to what purpose.* Cf. verse 142, Hor. *Epp.* i. 5, 12. *Quo =* quam ad rem. Cf. Cic. *pro Caelio* 52: dixeritne Clodiae *quam ad rem* aurum sumeret; *Ib.* 53: dixit profecto *quo* vellet aurum.

11. Numantinus was an agnomen given to Scipio Africanus the younger after the capture of Numantia, B. C. 133. The plural is generic, as in verse 13, and i. 109. Cf. Cic. *pro P. Sestio* 68: quare imitemur nostros Brutos, Camillos.

12. Quo, sc. *tempore.* — **Duces,** those generals, your great ancestors.

13 sq. Q. Fabius Maximus was surnamed **Allobrogicus** from his
victory over the Allobroges B. C. 121. The **Fabia gens** were said to
be descendants of **Hercules**; hence **natus** in **Hercules lare**, "born
in the household of Hercules." The **ara maxima**, in or near the
Forum Boarium, was consecrated by Evander to Hercules, according
to one tradition; according to another it was built by Hercules himself after slaying Cacus.

15. The **Euganei** were originally the occupiers of all the country
which the Veneti afterwards possessed, but were afterwards driven
farther west and south. The whole region was famous for its
pastures.

16. Effeminate persons smoothed their bodies with pumice-stone.

17. **Squalentis traducit avos,** *disgraces* (exposes to contempt) *his
rugged ancestors.* They are rough, rugged, in comparison with the
fine, soft skin of their degenerate descendant.

18. The busts and statues of those convicted of capital offences
were destroyed by the common executioner. — **Funestat** is properly
"defiles by blood."

21. **Moribus,** *in your morals;* in your character.

22 sq. Hos and illi refer to *moribus.* — **Virgas,** the fasces.

24. **Prima,** in the first place.

25. **Mereris.** The omission of *si* is lively.

26. **Adgnosco procerem,** I recognize the nobleman; the *true* gentleman, *Nature's* nobleman. **Proceres** is generally reckoned among
the *pluralia tantum.*

27, 28. The punctuation is that of **Jahn,** Ribbeck, **Hermann.**

27. **Silanus** was a cognomen in the gens Junia.

28. **Ovanti.** Congratulating itself on the possession of so excellent
a citizen.

29 sq. "The Egyptians worshipped their god Osiris under the
form of a live bull. When the animal grew old, he was drowned,
under the notion that the deity had left his body, to go and inhabit
that of a younger bull. The new tenant was accordingly sought for,
and when recognized, was received with great rejoicing, and a cry of
εὑρήκαμεν, συγχαίρωμεν."

30. **Qui,** sc. *est.*

32. It was fashionable in Rome to keep dwarfs.

33. **Parvam.** A few MSS. have *pravam,* which would be repeated
in *extortam.* — **Extortam,** *twisted out of shape,* distorted, crooked.

34 sq. **Scabie vetusta lēvibus,** "hairless from inveterate mange."

38. **Ne tu,** sc. *sis.* — **Sic,** *in the same way,* on the same principle;

i. e., called a Creticus or a Camerinus in irony and derision. Sic is the conjecture of H. Junius, adopted by the best editors. P *si*, pω *sis*.

40. Blande. So the MSS. Some editors *Plaute*, after Lipsius, hoping to escape a historical difficulty. — Livia, wife of Augustus, had two sons, Tiberius and Drusus, by her first husband Tiberius Claudius Nero. The daughter of Drusus, Livia or Livilla, married her cousin Drusus the son of Tiberius. Their daughter Julia married Rubellius Blandus; from this union Rubellius Plautus was born, who incurred the jealousy of Nero, and was put to death A. D. 62. He was a man of strong character, devoted to the stoic philosophy, and can hardly be the person referred to here. He had children (Tac. 14, 59), and we may suppose that *his son* was named from his grandfather, and is the Rubellius Blandus of this passage. The suspicion was not impossible that Agrippina herself was his mother (cf. Tac. 13, 19); or Juvenal may use the bold expression "te conciperet" of the grandmother of Blandus. (Weidner.)

42. Ut, *so that ;* to bring it about that.

43. Conducta, *for hire.* — Aggere. The *agger* of Servius Tullius.

46. The ἐυγένεια Κέκροπος was proverbial.

47. Ima plebe = *ex ima plebe.*

49. The masculine adjective in the singular used substantively (**nobilis**), itself takes an adjective (**indocti**). Instances are found in Cicero. See Nägelsbach *Stilistik* 25, 6 (pp. 82 sq.). Macleane says neither adjective is used as a substantive, and translates "the nobleman who is unlearned."

Veniet. "There will come one," where we should say "there will be one."

The **plebs togata** is that part of the poorer Roman people which could only be recognized by this national article of dress *as* Roman. It was not respectful for them to appear before their patrons without the toga.

51. Hic, another plebeian. —**Juvenis**, a man of fighting age (from seventeen to forty-five), a *brave soldier.* — The Parthians and Armenians and the **Batavi** were formidable.

52. Custodes aquilas. I. e. the legions left to guard the country.

53. Hermae were statues composed of a head, usually that of Hermes, placed on a quadrangular pillar, the height of which corresponded to the stature of the human body. They were used to mark boundaries, or were set up at the doors of houses, in front of temples, and in various public places. — **Trunco.** I. e. without legs and arms.

56. Teucrorum proles. Cf. i. 100 note.

58. Sic. *It is on this ground that.*—**Facili**—**fervet,** *in honor of whose easy triumph many a hand is warm* (with clapping). Or we may take **facili** of *speed;* cf. Verg. *Aen.* viii. 310 : facilesque oculos fert omnia circum. Manil. i. 647 : **circumfer faciles oculos** (easily turning, hence swift).

59. Rauco, hoarse (with shouting).

60, 61. Notice the rhythm of these fine **verses.**

61. Fuga, speed.

62. Coryphaeus. Some famed racer. Most MSS. *Corythae; P, Coryte.*

63. The race-horse **Hirpinus,** as it appears from an old inscription, won the first prize 114 times, the second 56 times, and the third 36 times. His grandsire, Aquilo, was the first victor 130 times, the second 88 times, and the third 37 times.

64. Ibi = in iis, *in their case;* in the case of horses.

66. Epiredia were freight-wagons which followed **the** *reda* **or** passenger-coach. (This explanation is preferable to that which defines them as "harness.") **Quintilian** (i. 5, 68) remarks **on the word :** cum sit praepositio *graeca,* raeda *gallicum,* neque Graecus tamen neque Gallus utitur conposito, Romani suum ex alieno utroque fecerunt.

67. Nepos is some miller of the day. The other MS. reading *nepotes* is preferred by some editors.

68. Privum. A conjecture of Salmasius, adopted **by the best editors.** Pω *primum.*

1–70. On the sentiment of these **lines, cf.** Chaucer :

> " Look who that is most virtuous alway
> Prive and apart, and most entendeth aye
> To do the gentle dedés that he can,
> And take him for the greatest gentleman.
>   *   *   *   *
>   Men may full often find
> A lorde's son do shame and vilanie.
> And he that wol have prize of his genterie,
> For he was boren of a gentil house,
> And had his elders noble and virtuous,
> And n' ill himselven do no gentil dedes,
> Ne folwe his gentil auncestrie, that dead is,
> He is not gentil, be he duke or erl ;
> For vilains' sinful dedés make a churl."

71. Fama, *report.*

73. Sensus communis, *a sense of what is due to others.* It implies a sympathy with mankind, and a knowledge of men and things, gained by sharing in the common experience of life. More simply, it may be understood as *a sense of equality*, a sense of one's community with others.

75. Sic, *in such a way*, or *on the condition*.

Futurae laudis. Genitive of quality.

79. An arbiter was different from a *judex*, yet not quite the same as our "arbitrator." In a *judicium* the demand made was for a certain fixed sum of money; in an *arbitrium* the amount was not fixed. In a *judicium* the plaintiff gained all that he claimed or nothing; in an *arbitrium* as much was given him as seemed fair. The *judicium* was constituted with a *poena* or *per sponsionem*; there was no *poena* in the case of an *arbitrium*. Lastly, the *arbiter* was possessed of a greater latitude than the *judex*, and was armed with something very closely resembling what we call an equitable jurisdiction. "Hence the more necessary for one filling the office to be an upright man."

81 sq. **Phalaris** with his brazen bull had become proverbial.

83, 84. Pudori, *honor*. These are verses of splendid vigor. — **Vivendi causas.** Cf. Plin. *Epp.* i. 12, 3; plurimas vivendi causas habentem: optimam conscientiam, optimam famam, maximam conscientiam, *etc*. Ejusdem *Epp.* v. 5, 4: qui voluptatibus dediti quasi in diem vivunt vivendi causas cotidie finiunt.

85. Perit (perfect tense; cf. iii. 174, x. 118), *is dead already*.

86. Gaurana = *Lucrina*, as the mons Gaurus was near the Lucrine lake. — **Cosmi . . aëno,** *though he be plunged head over ears in Cosmus's copper*. Cosmus was a noted perfumer; **aenum** is the cauldron in which he prepared his perfumes.

89. Socii refers to Roman subjects beyond the limits of Italy, — the inhabitants of a province.

90. Reges were native princes, like those of India under British rule. — For *medullas ossibus exsugere* we have **ossa** medullis exsuguntur: *the bones sucked dry of the naked marrow*, instead of the *marrow sucked from the empty bones*. On **vacuis** cf. Cic. *pro Marcello* vi. 17: gladium vagina vacuum in urbe non vidimus.

91. Curia. The governors of the senatorial provinces, like those of the imperial, received their instructions from the emperor by *rescripta*. But their appointment was nominally in the senate, whose authority they were supposed to represent. Macleane.

93. Cossutianus Capito was appointed governor of Cilicia A. D. 56, but the next year he was charged with extortion and degraded. (Afterwards, he recovered his senatorial rank through the influence

of Tigellinus, his father-in-law.) **Numitor** is unknown. The name
occurs vii. 74.

94. Piratae Cilicum, "they who robbed the robbers." Cilicia was
a notorious haunt of pirates.

95–97. Sell your old clothes at auction. "Turn all you have into
cash, and hold your tongue (*tace*). Don't think of going to Rome
to obtain redress; you would only be losing your passage-money in
addition to your previous losses." **Chaerippus** represents a delega-
tion sent by the provincials to Rome to complain of the extortion of
the governors.

96. Pansa and **Natta.** Unknown governors.

97. Jam, at once. — **Naulon** = *naulum.*

99. Modo, but recently.

100. Acervos = *acervus.* (Root ak-, *pointed.* Vaniček.)

101. Spartana. The seas off Laconia were among those most
famed for the *murex* fishery. — The island of Cos manufactured light
and transparent cloth or silk, which was sometimes dyed *purple.*

102–104. The great painter Parrhasius of Ephesus flourished at
Athens during the latter part of the Peloponnesian war (about four
centuries B. C.). **Myron,** a great sculptor, the reputed artist of the
Discobolos, **Phidias,** (whose chryselephantine statues, as of Athene
in the Parthenon, and of Zeus at Olympia, are here referred to,) and
Polycleitus (see iii. 217 note) were a little older than Parrhasius.
Mentor was a celebrated Greek artist in silver, about the middle of
the fourth century B. C. — These works of these artists are named as
the *chefs d'œuvre* of antiquity.

103. Vivebat expresses the life-like character of the statues. Cf.
Virgil's "spirantia aera," "vivos de marmore voltus."

104. Multus labor, "many an elaborate work." — Rarae sine Mentore mensae, "few were the tables without a Mentor," i. e. without a
cup of Mentor's chasing : as we say, "a Titian," "a Vandyke."

105. There were three Dolabellas who plundered provinces. Our
reading is a conjecture of Ruperti's, now generally adopted instead
of the MS. readings *Dolabella est adque* (P), *Dolabella atque* (ω).
Notice the hiatus before the principal caesura. To avoid it, Lachmann (followed by Ribbeck and Weidner) reads *Dolabellae, atque
dehinc.* Kiær defends *Dolabella atque.*

M. **Antonius Creticus,** the son of the distinguished orator, and
father of the triumvir, plundered Sicily. His brother, C. Antonius,
was condemned for pillaging the Macedonians.

106. Sacrilegus Verres. Cic. *in Ver.* i. 5, 14 ; neque hoc solum in statuis ornamentisque publicis fecit, sed *etiam delubra omnia, sanc-tissimis religionibus consecrata, depeculatus est;* deum denique nul-lum Siculis, qui ei paullo magis affabre atque antiquo artificio factus videretur, reliquit.

Altis, *deep-laden.*

107. *Triumphs* here for *spoils,* such as graced triumphs. *More spoils of peace* than of war. **109. Capto agello.** Dative.

111, 112. These two verses are found in all the MSS., but are gen-erally suspected by critics. Heinrich would change *unicus* into *unus,* and omit the clause *haec — maxima.*

Aedicula, a niche or recess, for a *shrine.*

113. Unctam, *essenced.*

114. Resinata, with their skin smoothed with resin.

116. Horrida, shaggy, rugged. The emphatic position of this word (which is contrasted with *resinata, lēvia*) supplies the want of an ad-versative particle. — **Axis** = *plaga.*

117. Latus, *coast.*

118. Vacantem, that has leisure *only* for; that gives its time to.

119. Autem, *besides,* moreover.

120. Marius. See i. 47 sqq. note. — **Discinxerit,** has stripped.—As a contrast to Marius, Scipio may be quoted, who said of himself, Cum Africam totam potestati vestrae subjecerim, nihil ex ea quod meum diceretur praeter cognomen retuli (Val. Max. iii. 7, 1). So Horat. (*Carm.* iv. 8, 18) qui domita nomen ab Africa lucratus rediit.

125. Non est sententia, is no mere opinion of my own. — Inferior MSS. and editors omit **est,** connecting **verum** as an adverb with the next line.

127. Comitum. The persons composing the staff and suite of the governor of the province.

128. Acersecomes, ἀκερσικόμης, with unshorn locks; an epithet of Apollo. Here, a long-haired minion.

Conjuge. "The avarice and rapacity of the women, who followed their husbands to their governments, had long been a subject of com-plaint."

129. Conventus, the circuits; used both of the district courts and of the districts themselves.

130. Celaeno. I. e. (like) a Harpy.

131. Licet, *although.* Some MSS. and editors have *tunc licet,* in-stead of *tu licet* (P S *gh* ς). — **Pious,** son of Saturn and father of Faunus, was the earliest mythical king of Latium.

132. Pugnam. For "warriors;" "the whole host of the Titans."

134. Libro, book (of legends).

135. Quod si, *but if.* So Horat. *Epp.* vii. 25. **Praecipitem,** sc. *te.*

139. Pudendis, your shameful deeds.

140 sq. Compare the words of Julius Caesar: in maxuma fortuna minuma licentia est.

142. After quo, to what purpose, there is often an ellipsis. Supply here *juctas.* "What is the use of your boasting of yourself to me, if you're in the habit— etc." — **Signare,** *to set your seal to.*

143. Wills were sometimes executed and kept in the temples.

146. Cf. i. 171 note.

147. There was a T. Sextius Magius Lateranus who was consul A. D. 94.

148. Adstringit multo sufflamine, locks with the frequent drag-chain.

152. Numquam. Jahn and Weidner *nusquam (d f ς).* I follow Pω, with most editors. — Trepidare governing a noun in the acc. is rare and post-classical. Cf. **x.** 21 and Sen. (?) *Herc. Oet.* 1062.

153. Jam, *quite* (in the *English* sense). "Though an old man, and likely to be horrified." Juvenal's dislike for charioteering and horse-racing was (at least relatively) excessive. "It would have been well," as Lewis says, "if the Roman nobility had never amused themselves in a more reprehensible way." The amusement, however, seems to have brought them into low associations. At the present day, it is probably not the most honored and useful members of the English nobility that are found in the " Four-in-hand Club." —**Virga** prior annuet, *will be the first to give him a salute with his whip.* — Maniplos, sc. feni, *bundles of hay.* Old English "bottles of hay," as in Shakspere.

154. Horses in Italy are fed on barley.

155. Interea, meanwhile; so long as he is still consul. — Every year at the Latin holidays the consuls sacrificed to Jupiter Latiaris on the Alban mount. Originally a *white* steer was offered. Some scholars think that *robum* here is simply *robustum.* Cf. Paul. Diac., p. 264.

Robum, *red.* An archaic word, *e re sacra petitum* (Madvig), used here to harmonize with *more Numæ.* It is given by the scholiast, and is now generally adopted. Pω, *torvum.*

157. Epona. From *equus.* In the Italian dialects *p* is often found for *qu,* e. g. pis = quis. — So *sequ-or* is from the same root as ἕπομαι. Among the *facies pictae* over the stalls may have been that of Bubona.

158. Instaurare, to repeat his visits to. The word is used partic-

14 — Juv. S 2

ularly of solemn ceremonies, and there seems to be a certain humor in it here. The solemn rites which he prefers and pays again and again are those of the midnight taverns.

159. Obvius implies "sponte se offerens," "promptus," "paratus."

160. Editors generally mark this verse as of doubtful genuineness. Hermann brackets the first two words in it and the last three in the preceding verse. "The gate of Idumæa" would mean a place through which the traffic of Idumæa passed.

161. *With the officious politeness of a host, he salutes him as "my lord" and "king."*

162. The hostess, with her clothes tucked up to facilitate her movements, bustles in with a bottle of wine (lagona = lagena), for which he will pay a round price.

163. Dicat. So Jahn, Ribbeck, Weidner; *dic*ᵉt P; *dicet* pω.

164. Nempe, *of course.* (And so in verse 180.)

168. Thermae is here generally taken as equivalent to *thermopolium*, a place where hot wine-and-water was sold. But as drinking went on at the baths (Sen. *Ep.* 122; Mart. xii. 70), in or near which there were probably drinking "bars" and *popinae*, it may well be taken in its proper sense. — Inscripta lintea are curtains, or awnings, bearing names or devices to serve the purpose of our sign-boards. They may hang before low eating-houses or stews.

169 sq. He is old enough to protect the empire by arms (bello) against the Parthians and Germans.

170. Nero is used generically, for the emperor of the day.

171. Mitte Ostia, *send (him) to Ostia,* to embark for a foreign war. The name of the town, *Ostia,* is generally of the first decl., fem.; but Charisius says the neut. plural form was often used. So Strabo, v. 2: τὰ δ' Ὤστια ἐστὶν ἐπίνειον τῆς Ῥώμης.

173–178. "The scene is one that Hogarth might have drawn,"—as the commentators have said, one after another.

173 sq. Jacentem, *lying at table.*—**Fugitivis,** sc. *servis.*

176. The priest of Cybele is lying dead-drunk upon his back, with his silent drum (or *tambourine*) beside him. — The tympana, as it appears from old paintings, were struck with the open hand.

·177. Aequa ibi libertas. "It's liberty-hall."

179 sq. On the mood and tense, cf. Hor. *Sat.* i. 1, 63.

180. Lucanos, sc. agros. — **Ergastula** were private prisons attached to most Roman farms, where the slaves were made to work in chains. Sometimes slaves were taken from the *ergastulum,* still chained, to till the fields. In Lucania and Etruria there were great *latifundia*

and pasture-lands, which barbarous slaves were employed to culti-
vate.

182. Cerdoni. Cf. iv. 153 note. — **Volesus Valesius** was the ancestor of the patrician *gens Valeria*, and hence of Valerius Poplicola,
who was associated with Brutus in the first consulship.

185. Damasippus seems to be a typical name, borrowed from Horace (*Sat.* ii. 3), for a man of birth and fortune who had ruined himself.

186. Sipario, *to the curtain,* where we should say, *to the stage.*
The *siparium* answered the purpose of the modern drop-scene; but
it was depressed when the scene began, and raised again when the
play was ended. — The noisy " Ghost " was a mime by Catullus, who
was a noted mime-writer. Cf. xiii. 111; Mart. v. 30.

187 sq. In the mime **Laureolus,** the chief character (here taken
by Lentulus, another dissolute nobleman) was that of an artful
slave who was caught in some knavery and crucified. Lentulus *appears* to be crucified in the mimic scene on the stage, but he deserves
a *real* cross. — **Velox,** because he tried to run away from his punishment.

190. Triscurria (tri- and scurra), *gross buffooneries.* This word is
a ἅπαξ εἰρημένον in the language. The *tri-* is intensive, as in *triparcus,*
trifur, trifurcifer, triportenta, triveneficus, triperditus, " thrice-great
Hermes."

191. Planipedes = *mimi.* The actors of mimes appeared *pedibus
planis* (= *nudis*), unlike those of tragedy, who wore the *cothurnus,*
and those of comedy, who wore the *soccus.*

The **Fabia** gens claimed descent from **Hercules.** Cf. verse 14.

192. The **Mamerci** were a noble family of the *Aemilia gens.* The
whole *gens* traced its descent from Mamercus, a son of Numa.

Alapas. Inferior characters on the stage, — slaves, parasites, buf-
foons, — were slapped on the face and cuffed about by superior personages. Cf. v. 171 note.

Quanti sua funera vendant, *at how great a price they sell the funeral of their honor.* Juvenal says, " their own obsequies," for

> " when honor dies,
> The man is dead."

For *funera* Ribbeck adopts *munera,* a gratuitous conjecture of
Dobree's.

193. Suetonius says **Nero** caused four hundred senators and six
hundred knights to fight in the arena. The number is probably ex-
aggerated.

194. In Juvenal's time the praetor presided over the public games. He sat on his curule chair, raised above the other seats. **Celsi,** *seated on high.* This verse is regarded by Ribbeck and some others as spurious.

196. Quid satius, *which of the two is to be preferred ?* The use of *quid* for *utrum* is not without example in prose. In Juvenal it occurs only here.

Exhorruit = *horret.* Has any one become so terrified at = *is any one so terrified at.* As a present meaning may be conveyed by a perfect, so, on the other hand, a perfect may be represented by a present: thus *ardet* is perfect with reference to *exardescit.*

197. Zelotypus, *the jealous husband* in the play. — **Thymele,** a notorious *mima.* Cf. i. 36. — The **stupidus** is the blockhead who gets knocked about. Cf. v. 171 note. — **Corinthus,** an *actor secundarum,* i. e. of such parts as the *stupidus, morio, parasitus.*

198. Nero appeared on the stage as a harper. — For **mimus** (PΣ) inferior MSS. read *natus.*

199 sqq. Ludus (sc. *gladiatorius*), the school in which they learn the gladiator's art, with a *lanista* for their teacher. (Madvig, *Opusc.* ii. 184.) — **Et illic,** *etc.,* here, too : i. e. in this low art, also, you have — a disgrace to the town — Gracchus fighting in the arena, not even choosing such costume and arms as would serve as a disguise, but as a *retiarius* with uncovered face, and actually wearing the gold-fringed tunic and tall conical cap, with flowing ribbons, which marked him as a priest of Mars. (But see note on 207 sq., *infra.*)

200. The **myrmillones** (mirmillones) were armed with a helmet, short sword, and oblong shield covering the greater part of their body. The Thraces (Threces) also had helmets, swords, and round shields.

201. The **falx** is a short sword or *sica.* — **Supina,** uplifted ; (Heinrich says it is " incurva.")

203 sqq. "*Retiarii* carried only a three-pointed lance, called tridens or *fuscina,* and a net, *rete,* which they endeavored to throw over their adversaries, and then to attack them with the fuscina while they were entangled. The retiarius was dressed in a short *tunic,* and wore no armor on his head. If he missed his aim in throwing the net (" *nequiquam effudit* "), he betook himself to flight (**206**), and endeavored to prepare his net for a second cast, while his adversary followed him round the arena in order to kill him before he could make a second attempt. His adversary was usually a **secutor (210),** or a *mirmillo.*"

205. Spectacula = spectatores.

207 sq. Can we believe our eyes, when we see him fighting in the arena in the dress of the Salii? *Are we to give credence to his tunic, as it stretches all golden from his neck and the twisted strings flutter from his tall cap?* The Salii, who were chosen from the patricians, wore a gold-embroidered tunic with a gold fringe around the border, and a tall conical cap or mitre, fastened under the chin by a gold band of twisted work. Some understand *jactetur spira* of a knot of ribbons floating in the air at the top of the cap.

So commentators generally. A very different (and possibly the correct) explanation of this passage is given by Kiær, who places a semicolon after *harena* (206), and a comma after *credamus*, removes the comma after *tunicae*, and ends verse 208 with a period. His translation, which excludes any reference to the Salii, is this: *We may believe that it is he, when* (in his flight) *the golden cord stretches from the neck of his tunic, and floats out from his long armlet.* "Garrucius dicit **galerum** esse manicam e corio vel aere factam, qua retiarii sinistrum bracchium tegeretur, quaeque supra humerum exstaret. Idem **spiram** docet fuisse funiculum gladiatorium, qui in signis atque tabulis pictis a sinistro humero ad dextram coxam circumcurrens et manicam cum balteo conjungens videri possit."

212. Some of those who joined in Piso's conspiracy against Nero (A. D. 65) had the ultimate aim in view of raising Seneca to the throne. Cf. Tac. *Ann.* xv. 65.

213 sq. Non una, more than one; not one alone. — Parricides were whipped, sewn up in a sack with a dog, a cock, a viper, and an ape, and thrown into the sea, or, where the sea was not at hand, exposed to wild beasts. Nero killed his mother, Agrippina, his wives Octavia and Poppaea, his step-sister Antonia, his step-brother Britannicus, and his aunt Domitia, and is supposed to have had a hand in the death of his father by adoption, Claudius.

215. Agamemnonidae. ·Orestes. There was a verse current at Rome in Nero's days: Νέρων, 'Ορέστης, 'Αλκμαίων, μητροκτόνοι.

216. Ille, that famed man of old (Orestes).

217. Media inter pocula. So Homer, *Odyss.* xi. 409 sqq.:

> 'Αλλά μοι Αἴγισθος τεύξας θάνατόν τε μόρον τε
> ἔκτα σὺν οὐλομένῃ ἀλόχῳ οἰκόνδε καλέσσας,
> δειπνίσσας, ὥς τίς τε κατέκτανε βοῦν ἐπὶ φάτνῃ.

218. *He* did not kill his sister nor his wife.

219. Conjugii = *conjugis*. Orestes married his cousin Hermione, daughter of Menelaus and Helen.

220 sq. Nero went upon the stage first at Naples, where he appeared several times. He wrote an epic poem on the taking of Troy, which he recited publicly in the theatre. He is said to have recited it also as Rome was burning, while he looked out from a tower and admired the beauty of the flames.

221 sqq. Quid is defined by **quod . . . fecit** (223), where *quod* (the MSS. giving *quid*) is a conjecture of Madvig's, now generally adopted. The sense is, Quid ex omnibus ejus factis magis ulcisci debuit? (Madvig *Opusc.* ii. 199 sqq.; Roth *Kl. Schr.* ii. 432.)

"**L. Verginius Rufus** was governor of Upper Germany, when Julius **Vindex**, propraetor of Gaul, rose against Nero, A. D. 68. Vindex having offered **Galba**, governor of Hispania Tarraconensis, the empire, Galba also revolted. Verginius marched against Vindex, protesting that he would acknowledge no one as emperor till he had been proclaimed by the senate. At Vesontio (*Besançon*) the two generals are said to have had a conference, and to have agreed to unite against Nero; but an engagement took place, and Vindex, being defeated, died by his own hand. Verginius afterward aided in the establishment of Galba, and several times refused the empire for himself. His funeral oration was pronounced by Tacitus, who was consul that year (A. D. 97)." "It is rather strange to find Juvenal coupling him with Vindex, as the epitaph composed by himself for his tomb ran thus:

> Hic situs est Rufus, pulso qui Vindice quondam
> Imperium asseruit non sibi sed patriae."

225 sq. Nero went through Greece, A. D. 67, reciting in the theatres and contending for the prizes at the games. He received no less than eighteen hundred crowns, partly in compliment, and partly for his so-called victories; and on his return to Rome he entered the city in triumph, wearing on his head an Olympic crown of wild olive, and bearing in his hand a Pythian crown of laurel, while he had the catalogue of his victories borne before him. The *parsley crown* has special reference to the *musical* contests at the Nemean games, in which a chaplet of parsley was the prize.

228 sq. Nero's father was **Cn. Domitius Ahenobarbus**, for a statue of whom he asked the Senate A. D. 54, the year he came to the throne. — Besides the Greek plays on these subjects, there were Latin tragedies, which were very likely imitations of them. Thus Varius

wrote a **Thyestes,** Nero himself an **Antigone,** and both Ennius and
Accius a **Menalippe.** — The **syrma** (from σύρω) was a robe worn by
the tragic actors, which had a train trailing upon the ground. — Personam, *the mask.* — Menalippe = Melanippe. Euripides wrote a
tragedy with this title.—I read Antigones aut after Hermann. Jahn
and Ribbeck, *Antigonae seu* (P). Many MSS. give *Antigones tu.*

230. The **marble colossus** is probably the colossal statue of one of
Nero's ancestors.

231. Catiline was of the *gens Sergia,* one of the oldest of the
patrician families (cf: Verg. *Aen.* v. 121). **Cethegus,** his chief companion in his conspiracy, was of a still more distinguished family, in
the *gens Cornelia.*

234. The reference is to the Gauls, the inveterate enemies of Rome.
Before the formation of the separate province Gallia Narbonensis,
the Romans gave the inhabitants the name Bracati (Braccati), from
their wearing, like nearly all other nations not Greek or Roman,
braccae, i. e. "breeks" or "breeches." These trowsers were looser
than we wear them now, but not so loose among the European nations
as in the East. There may be an allusion here to the Allobroges, a
Gallic people in this quarter, who had been invited, through their
ambassadors, to join in the conspiracy of Catiline. The **Senones**
were an ancient Gallic tribe on the Seine ; (their name still survives
in *Sens.*) They invaded Italy in the time of the Tarquins, and
settled on the Adriatic (where they have left a record of themselves
in the name of *Senigaglia*) ; and this was the tribe that took and
burned Rome B. C. 390.—Minores, *the descendants.* Weidner understands -que in this verse thus : the sons of the Gauls, *and indeed* the
descendants of the Senones,— that very tribe that took Rome.

235. Tunica molesta, "*with the tunic of torture.*" This was a
tunic covered over with (or made of) paper, pitch, wax, and other
combustibles, which was put upon the victims, who were bound to a
stake, and then lighted.

236. Vigilat consul. Cic. *in Cat.* i. 8 : Intelliges multo me vigilare acrius ad salutem, quam te ad perniciem reipublicae.

Vexilla = troops, bands.

237 sq. Cicero was born B. C. 106 at **Arpinum,** a town of Latium
and a municipium. He was the first of his gens that had curule
honors, and was therefore **novus homo and ignobilis** (*no noble ;* not
"ignoble" in our sense). — **Modo . . eques,** *but the other day only a
municipal knight living at Rome.*

238. Galeatum. Hence, ready for action. Cf. i. 169.

239. Attonitis, "for the bewildered citizens," who knew nothing of the reasons for these things.

In omni monte, *on every hill* (of Rome), i. e. throughout the whole city. **Monte** (S) is now adopted by the best editors.. Other readings are *gente* (pω) and *ponte* (" legitur et ponte " S). In P the first two letters are erased or illegible.

240. The **toga** represents *peace,* and civil functions.

241 sq. *From Leucas* means from the battle of Actium, which place was about thirty miles north of the island of Leucas or Leucadia. *From the plains of Thessaly* refers to the battle of Philippi, — inaccurately, as Philippi is in *Macedonia adjecta,* a district originally Thracian. — The original name of Augustus was C. Octavius ; but he dropped this at his great uncle's death, and then became C. Julius Cæsar Octavianus, to which the title of Augustus was added B. C. 27. — In 241 with Ribbeck I adopt Hermann's conjecture, viz. The MSS. give *in* (P S f g h), and *non* (pω). *Non* is certainly inadmissible. The true reading may be *quantum Leucate* (Kiær, p. 87).

243 sq. Set — dixit. But Rome called Cicero "Parent," Rome called him "Father of his Country," *when she was free.* It was an *enslaved* Rome that gave that title to Augustus.

245. Arpinas alius. C. Marius.

247. The vine switch was the centurion's baton of office, and was also used for military floggings.—" Broke with his head " = had the switch broken over his head.

248. The **dolabra** was a hatchet on one side, but had a pick on the other. Ancient writers speak of breaking through ice, felling trees, breaking through and undermining walls, and performing various other operations, with *dolabrae.*

249. In B. C. 101 Marius and Q. Lutatius Catulus defeated the **Cimbri** on a plain called Campi Raudii, near Vercellae in Gallia Cisalpina. — **Rerum,** *of the State.*

252. Majora cadavera. The Cimbri were remarkable for their size.

253. Nobilis, nobly born.

254-258. "The **Decii** were a plebeian family, but a very old one; for at the secession of the plebs, B. C. 494, M. Decius was one of the deputies sent by them to treat with the senate." P. Decius Mus, father and son, devoted themselves to death in battle, thereby securing the victory to the Romans : the first in the war against the Latins (Liv. viii. 9), the second in that against the Gauls (Liv. x. 28). The formula of devotion, after calling on the gods, finished with these words : Pro re publica Quiritium, exercitu, legionibus, auxiliis populi Romani Quiritium legiones auxiliaque hostium mecum *diis Ma-nibus Tellurique* devoveo (Liv. viii. 9). — Quae **servantur.** In this concise expression, *quae* suggests everything that was great in Rome, her wealth, her power, her splendor, her dominion.

259. Ancilla natus. I. e. Servius Tullius. — The trabea was a white robe, with stripes of purple, supposed to have been worn by the kings. — The diadema was a band or fillet.

260. Meruit, *earned* by his merits; *won.*

261-268. Juvenal refers to the participation of the sons of Brutus, the first consul, in the conspiracy for restoring Tarquinius Superbus. They were the very men from whom *some great exploit in behalf of liberty only partially established* (dubia, still *doubtful)* might have been expected, *such as Mucius* (who thrust his right hand into the fire) *in unison with Cocles* (who kept the bridge) *might admire, and the virgin* Cloelia, *who swam across the Tiber* and escaped from the camp of Porsena.

261. Laxabant, were on the point of loosening; were ready to loosen.

265. Imperii fines. After the surrender of the city to Porsena, the Romans lost their territory on the right bank of the river.

Tiberim. Accusative of the space over which the action extends. More simply, we might have had *Tiberim tranatavit.*

266 sq. He that revealed the crime was a slave; and he deserved to be mourned by the matrons, even as was the consul Brutus himself.

268. *The first axe of the laws* signifies the first execution under the laws of a free state. The constitution of Massachusetts indicates the difference between arbitrary and republican government, in the happy phrase, "to the end that it may be a government *of laws, and not of men.*"

269 sqq. Thersites, the deformed and odious braggart and slanderer in Homer (*Il.* ii. 212 sqq.). — **Aeacidae,** Achilles. — **Vulcania arma.** Cf. Hom. *Il.* xviii. 369 sqq.

272. Et tamen, *and after all.* — **Ut longe,** *however far back.*—**Revolvere nomen** = revolvendis voluminibus quaerere nomen.

273. Asylo. Cf. Liv. i. 8; Dionys. Hal. ii. 215.

275. Even Romulus and Remus had been brought up as shepherds.

* This satire abounds in sharp contrasts, as those between Nero and Seneca, Cicero and Catiline, Marius and Catulus, the Decii and the patricians, the sons of Brutus and the slave; so also the picture of a worthy noble is followed by examples of the opposite,—noble-born coachmen, actors, gladiators. (Weidner.)

SATIRE X.

———o-o:o:o:oo———

ARGUMENT.

1-11. IN all the world, but few can tell good from its opposite. When are our fears or hopes guided by reason? What wish when gained is not repented of? The gods, too kind, ruin whole houses at their own desire. In peace and war we pray for what must hurt us: the gift of eloquence or sinewy arms are fatal both alike.

12-27. But more are choked with money, that theirs shall excel all other men's fortunes. For this in tyrannous times by Nero's bidding Longinus, Seneca, and Lateranus were shut up in their houses: but guards are seldom set to watch a garret. The empty traveller sings in the robber's presence; carry a little silver cup or two and you shall start at every reed that moves. But wealth is our first prayer; and yet no poison lurks in earthen mugs, 't is in the jewelled cup and Setian wine you have to fear it.

28-53. Did not the sages well then, one who laughed and one who wept whene'er he went abroad? Any can laugh, but where the other got his store of tears we well may wonder. Democritus could laugh forever, yet those towns had no abuses like our own. Suppose he had seen the Praetor going to the games in his tall chariot with Jove's tunic on, with folds of purple toga, and a great crown, too big for any neck, borne by a slave placed in the same chariot with him, of course to lower his pride; an eagle on his ivory staff, on one side trumpeters, on the other friends and citizens in white, friends whom his dole makes such. Why, even there he laughed at every turn, showing that men of mind are found even in dullest times. He mocked the cares, the joys, sometimes the very tears of men, bade Fortune hang herself, and pointed at her.

54-113. So all our prayers are idle or they're mischievous. Some by the envy which is linked with power, some by long rolls of honors are undone; their statues fall, triumphal chariots are hacked to pieces. The flames are crackling, see Sejanus burns, and from that face, second to only one, are pots and pans and kettles made. Rejoice! Sejanus through the streets is dragged, and all are happy. "Look at his lips, his face: I never loved the man; but who accused him, how has the offence been proved?" "A wordy long epistle came from Capreae." "No more, I ask no more. But what of the

218

rabble?" "They follow fortune and they hate the fallen. Had but the Tuscan prospered and taken the old man off his guard, that self-same hour they had hailed him emperor. We 've grown indifferent since our votes were sold, and they who once gave all the honors now mind nothing but their belly and the games." "I hear that many are to share his fate." " Of course ; the fire is large." " I met Brutidius looking rather pale ; Ajax will be for punishing us all for not sup-porting him : let 's run and tread upon the corpse, and let the slaves be witness." This was what people whispered of Sejanus. Would you be bowed to as he was, and have his power, and be the guardian of a tyrant, living on a lonely rock, surrounded by astrologers? Of course you like promotion, and why not? But what is rank, if mis-ery be its measure? Which would you rather take, Sejanus's toga or the rags of a country Aedile? He then, you must allow, knew not what he should ask : for he who prayed for too much power did only build himself a tower to fall the farther from. What ruined Crassus, Caesar, and Pompeius? The rank they sought by every art, and gods too prone to listen to their prayers, Few kings and tyrants die a natural death.

114–132. Boys pray Minerva for Demosthenes's or Cicero's elo-quence, and yet 't was this that killed them. 'T was genius that lost its head and hands. Small pleaders never dyed the rostra with their blood. Had he writ all as he wrote poetry, then Cicero might have mocked Antonius's swords. I 'd rather be the author of his poems than of his famous speech. A cruel death was his, too, who held the reins of the full theatre before admiring Athens, whom with bad omens born his father sent to school from the forge.

133–167. The spoils of war some count the height of human hap-piness ; for this do all great captains rouse themselves. The thirst for fame is greater than for virtue ; for take away her honors who would love her? The glory of a few then, thirsting for epitaphs to be inscribed upon their tomb till the fig splits it, has wrecked their country : tombs themselves must perish. Put Hannibal in the scales ; how many pounds in that great general, whom Africa could not hold? He wins Hispania, leaps across the Pyrenees, and splits the Alps with vinegar. Now he 's in Italy ; that 's not enough ; he counts it nothing till he plants his flag in the streets of Rome. A glorious picture that, the one-eyed captain on his elephant! What was the issue then? O glory! he himself is beaten, sent into exile, and there sits at the king's door till he be pleased to wake. The soul that shook the world, a ring laid low. Go, fool, and scale the Alps, that boys may learn to wonder and declaim! 168–173. For Pella's boy one world was not enough : its narrow limits were to him as Gyarus or Seriphus : yet when he came to Babylon a coffin satisfied him. Death reveals how small we little men are. 173–187. The credulous believe that Xerxes cut through Athos, and all the lies of Greek historians : he bridged the sea and drank up rivers, flogged the winds, and chained the earth-shaker — how merciful not to have branded him! Sure any of the gods would have been glad to be his slave! But how did he get back from Salamis? Why, with one ship, through seas choked with the corpses of his men. This was the penalty his glory found.

188-245. "Give me long life, O Jove, and many years!" So unabashed and eagerly you pray. But age is full of ills : an ugly face,
tough skin, cheeks flabby, wrinkles like a monkey. In youth there's
some variety, old men are all alike ; with trembling voice and limbs,
bald head and running nose, and toothless gums, a burden to themselves and all about them. His taste is gone of meat and drink ; the
finest music gives him no enjoyment. What matter where he sits at
the theatre? He cannot hear the very horns and trumpets. His
slave must bawl when visitors are announced or when he tells him
what's o'clock. The blood runs cold and scanty in his veins, and it
requires a fever to keep him warm. A troop of all diseases dances
around him; so numerous I could sooner reckon Hippia's lovers,
Themison's victims, how many villas my old barber has. One has
the rheumatism, one the lumbago, one sciatica : this one is blind,
that one is fed by others; he would grin once at the sight of dinner,
now gapes like a young swallow for his food. But worst of all is
dotage that forgets its servants, friends, and children : makes a will
and gives its money to a harlot. But though he keeps his senses, he
must see his friends all dying round him. This is the penalty of
age, to pass its days in mourning for the dead. **246-257.** Nestor of
course was happy, who lived to be as old almost as the crows. But
see him mourning by Antilochus's pyre, asking what crime he had
done that he should live so long. See Peleus weeping for Achilles,
Laërtes for his wandering son. **258-288.** Had Priam died before
the war of Troy, his sons had carried him to burial with solemn
rites and mourning women, his daughters at their head. What did
he get by living? He saw all Asia fall by fire and sword, then put
his armor on and ran to the altar like an old ox to perish. His
death, however, was a man's : his wife survived him and she died a
dog. But passing by Pontus's king and Croesus and the lesson
Solon gave him, look at Marius, exiled, imprisoned, swamped, and
begging bread where he was late a victor. Who had been happier
had he breathed his last when he came down from his triumphal
chariot? Pompeius had a fever sent him, but the prayers of many
towns prevailed, and so his fortune saved him to lose an army and
his head. This Lentulus was spared, Cethegus too died whole, and
Catilina fell no mangled carcass.

289-329. Mothers will pray for beauty for their children. Why
should they not? Lucretia bids us ask not for form like hers : Vir-
ginia would have changed for the hunchback girl. Seldom do
chastity and beauty go together : though your child be trained with
all simplicity, though nature guard him with a modest mind and
blushing face, great risks attend him. "But if he's chaste, his
beauty will not hurt him." Nay, did Hippolytus's virtue profit him,
or did Bellerophon's?

329-345. How would you counsel Silius, when Messalina had resolved to marry him? The best and handsomest, a noble youth, is
hurried to his death by the Empress's eyes. The veil is on her head,
the portion settled, and the auspices declared. Is it a private business? No, she must marry as becomes her state. Now make your
choice, marry *or* die before the evening falls; marry *and* die when
the Prince hears of it. You'll have a few days' reprieve; he'll be

the last to learn his own disgrace: so do her bidding. Either way, thy fair neck suffers for it.

346–366. Must we then ask for nothing? Leave the gods themselves to settle what is good for us. They give us what is best, not pleasantest. We ask in the heat of passion for wife or children, and know not what they 'll prove. But if you must pray, let it be for health, a healthy body and a healthy mind; for a stout heart that fears not death, but counts the end of life a gift of nature; able to bear its toils, patient, content, preferring the labors of Hercules to lust and appetite and luxury. This you may give yourself; a tranquil life lies in the path of virtue. Fortune, thou hast no power, if we have Prudence at our side: 'tis we, 'tis we, make thee a goddess, and set thee up in heaven. MACLEANE, *with modifications.*

1 sq. Usque Auroram et Gangen. The use of the adverb *usque* as a preposition is rare, even in the poets. It is generally followed by *ad*, except before terminal accusatives of the names of towns (as Cic. *in Pis.* 51: a Brundisio *usque Romam* agmen perpetuum).

3. Illis multum diversa. A euphemism for *vera mala.*

4. Nebula, *mist.* — Ratione, intelligently, with right understanding.

5. Quid tam dextro pede concipis, *what purpose do you conceive so auspiciously.* The expression *dextro pede* implies a happy approach, — a felicitous coming up to, or starting out for, some object. Porters in Rome used to call out to guests about to enter the house, *dextro pede !* — The reading of inferior MSS. *concupis* is a clerical error; and Ribbeck's conjecture *conripis* is uncalled for.

5, 6. Ut — peracti, that you do not repent after you have made your attempt and accomplished your wish. Conatus of course genitive.

7. Evertere. The perfect here resembles a gnomic aorist; but it could not be replaced by *evertĕre solent.* The English, *have overthrown*, very well represents it. In the Greek gnomic aorist the *historical* element is always a part of the meaning; it is said that something happened in the past, and it is left for the mind to take it as an example of what often or customarily happens. Sometimes our idiom compels us to sink the historical statement in translation, and use our present of a general truth; but in such cases we lose the *vividness* and the pictorial character of the original.

Domos, families.

Optantibus. Ribbeck read *operantibus*, with cod. Bernensis 61.

8. What is the force of **faciles ?**

Toga = in pace.

9. Torrens. Cf. iii. 74 : Isaeo torrentior ; x. 127-8.

10. Sua, his native, his inborn (eloquence).

Viribus ille confisus. *Ille* would seem to indicate some one well known. The scholiast says the reference is to Milo of Crotona, the athlete, wedged in the trunk of the tree which he strove to rend, and devoured by wolves. Macleane refers *ille* to the soldier, as opposed to the orator. Heinrich and Macleane read *admirandusque* (**11**), after a few inferior MSS.

11. Periit. The last syllable is lengthened here in the arsis, before the caesura. The fact that *i* in the termination of the perf. 3 sing. was *originally* long (Lachmann, Fleckeisen, Ritschl, Corssen), explains its frequent occurrence as long in the oldest poets, and, after it had become short, made it easier for the poets of the Augustan age to lengthen it, when metrical considerations urged them. But Juvenal is very ready to lengthen a short syllable in this situation, and needed not the aid of any historical consideration.

13. Before **exuperans** (exsuperans) supply *tanto*, to correspond with *quanto* (14). Cf. xiii. 31.

14. Ballaena (balaena). "In Juvenal's time, whales probably came as far south as Great Britain more commonly than they do now."

15. Temporibus diris, " in the reign of terror."

16 sq. Longinum **clausit** = *Longini domum* clausit. Cf. *Juno regina* dedicata est, for *fanum Junonis; Nägelsbach Stilistik* ₴ 16. **C. Cassius Longinus,** a distinguished jurist, was consul and praetor, and a man of wealth. Nero in jealousy, banished him. — The philosopher **Seneca,** the tutor of Nero, was enormously wealthy. The conspiracy of Piso gave the emperor a pretext for putting him to death. He was dining at his villa, four miles from Rome, when the tribune came with the fatal mandate. Tacitus says (*Ann.* **xv.** 60): illo propinqua vespera tribunus venit et villam globis militum sepsit. — The patriotic **Plautius Lateranus,** consul designatus, also suffered death for complicity in the conspiracy of Piso.

18. Cohors, sc. praetoria. — Varro (*L. L.* v. 33, 45) shows how *cenaculum* came to mean a garret or chamber in the attic : ubi cenabant cenaculum vocitabant; posteaquam in superiore parte cenitare coeperunt, superioris domus universa cenacula dicta.

19. Puri, plain ; without any figures or chasing.

21. Ad lunam, *in the moonlight.* Cf. Verg. *Aen.* iv. 513. More strictly, it is *before* the moon, *in the presence of the moon,* and is thus vivid and poetical. — **Trepidabis umbras.** Cf. viii. 152, note.

25. Foro. The bankers' offices were in and about the forum.

27. Setinum. The favorite vintage in Juvenal's time. Cf. v. 34; xiii. 213.

Ardebit, shall glow; shall give its color in the cup. I prefer this to Mayor's explanation, which refers the word to the wine's *burning* the palate.

28. Jamne. The enclitic *-ne* is used here, where we should expect *nonne,* an affirmative answer being called for. So in Greek we find ἄρα for ἄρ' οὐ. — **Jam** = quod cum ita sit. — **Laudas.** Do you not *think it well,* — approve the fact.

29, 30. The laughing philosopher was Democritus of Abdera; the weeper, Heracleitus. — **Contrarius auctor,** the opposite authority; the teacher of the opposite view.

31. Rigidi censura cachinni, *the censure of a hard sardonic laugh.* The genitive is specific. Laughter is the kind of censure which Democritus employs.

34. Urbibus illis. Abdera, Ephesus, and the cities of those days.

35. The **tribunal** was a raised platform (βῆμα, French *tribune*) in the basilica, on which the praetor and the **judices** sat when they held their courts of law.

36 sqq. The Ludi Circenses were preceded by a grand procession in which the praetor rode in a triumphal chariot with all the insignia of a triumph. — The **tunica Jovis** (called also *tunica palmata*) was worn only on triumphal occasions. Together with the *toga picta* (38, 39), it was kept in the temple of Jupiter Capitolinus. — **Pictae sarrana aulaea togae,** *the purple hangings* (i. e. cumbrous folds) *of the embroidered toga.* **Pictae,** sc. *acu.* **Sarrana,** *Tyrian,* Sarra (Sara) being a name in one of the Greek epics which was ascribed to Homer, and in the early Latin writers (Ennius, Plautus), for Tyre.

39–42. One of the slaves owned by the state rides in the same chariot as the triumpher, to keep down his pride; this slave holds a heavy golden crown set with jewels. The victor himself wore a crown of laurel. — The praetor is here called **consul,** from the original association of the two names, and because, before the reign of Augustus, it was the consul that presided at the Circensian games.

43. Da nunc = *add now.* — **Volucrem,** the eagle. — **Sceptro.** Abl. of point of origin or departure. Juvenal omits the preposition (*e*), as in iii. 271.

44 sq. Praecedentia longi agminis officia = praecedentes longo

agmine officiosos, the clients marching before him in long array.
Officia, abstract for concrete, as often *consilium, conjugium, remi-gium, servitium,* and other words. Weidner takes *officia* for the *officials;* but **officium** is often used of attendance on the great. Cf.
iii. 239. — **Niveos.** White was the color worn on festive occasions.
Men wishing to make a good appearance at such times sent their
togas to the *fullo* to have an extra whitening.

Ad frena, *by his bridle;* walking by his horses' heads.

46. Defossa, *buried deep.*

47. Invenit. Sc. Democritus. — **Omnis.** Accusative plural.

50. Vervecum in patria, "in the native country of mutton-heads"
(blockheads). The people of Abdera were proverbial for dulness.
Mart. x. 25: Abderitanae pectora plebis habes.

53. Medium unguem. The middle finger, *digitus infamis, the
finger of scorn.*

54. Ergo, *so then.* — **Aut vel,** *or even.* — **Aut** vel is a conjecture of
Doederlein's, adopted by Hermann, Jahn, and Weidner. The MSS.
(one excepted, which gives *vel* alone) read simply *aut,* thus leaving
an hiatus. Among the conjectural readings proposed are *aut et* and
haec aut. Lachmann proposed ergo, supervacua aut ne perniciosa
petantur, placing an interrogation mark at the end of verse 55; Ribbeck follows Lachmann, placing, however, a colon at the end of line
54, and no mark of punctuation after ergo. But considering the fre-
quency with which Juvenal uses a short vowel in the arsis before
the caesura, and even admits an *hiatus* there, Kiær may be right in
reading with the MSS. simply *aut perniciosa.*

55. "For which we deem it right to cover the knees of the gods
with the waxen tablets of our vows." The custom alluded to is that
of placing in the lap of the statues of the deities supplicated waxen
tablets containing vows written out. Madvig proposes the emendation of reading *incerate* in the imperative, which Jahn adopts; this
change requires a period or colon after *petuntur.*

56. Subjecta, *exposed.*

57. Mergit, sc. *eos* (the same persons as *quosdam*).

57, 58. Honorum pagina, the list of their honors, inscribed on a
bronze tablet set up before the busts.

58–64. Their statues are pulled down and dragged along by ropes;
the triumphal chariots and horses of bronze or marble are broken
up; the brazen statues are melted down.

62. Ingens, as Lewis says, seems to have a double reference to the
greatness of Sejanus himself, and the size of his colossal statue.

63. Sejanus, favorite of Tiberius, and practically left to wield the supreme power in Rome, as "the second man in the world," while that tyrant was living in debauchery at Capreae, at last excited the emperor's suspicion, and fell suddenly from the height of greatness. Tiberius sent a dispatch to the senate, expressing (with his usual vagueness and indirection) his apprehensions. The senate at once decreed the death of Sejanus, and he was executed the same day. His body was dragged about the streets, and finally thrown into the Tiber.

65 sq. Ornament the house, and offer sacrifice, as for a festive occasion. — **Cretatum.** "Either = *candidum,* or else in allusion to the habit of chalking over any dark spots when an ox white all over could not be found." The scholiast cites here from " **Lucretius** " (regarded universally as misplaced for *Lucilius*), *Cretatumque bovem duci ad Capitolia magna.* — **Unco,** the hook by which the bodies of condemned criminals were dragged to the Tiber or the Scalae Gemoniae.

67–88. A conversation between two citizens, returning from the execution ; one, (who is always the questioner,) curious, anxious, time-serving ; the other, (who may be regarded as expressing the views of the poet himself,) dignified, calm, judicious.

70. Indicium is the evidence of an accomplice turned informer.— **Probavit,** sc. Tiberius.

72. Bene habet, it's all right ; that's enough.

73. Remi is used by the Roman poets where we should expect *Romuli,* when metrical considerations demand. — Other readings are *tremens* (ω), *fremens* (ς).

74. Nortia (perhaps = Nevortia, "Ατροπος, cf. Bergk, Philol. 16, 443), an Etruscan deity of *Fortune* or Destiny. Into the wall of her temple at Volsinii a nail was driven every year ; there was a similar custom in the temple of the Capitoline Jupiter at Rome.

Tusco, i. e. *Sejano.* Sejanus was an Etrurian by descent, and born at Volsinii.

75. Oppressa foret secura, had been caught off its guard.

77. Ex quo (sc. *tempore*) **suffragia** nulli vendimus. With bitter sarcasm, Juvenal speaks of the people's loss of the right of suffrage as the loss of the right of *selling their votes.* Tiberius, two years after he became emperor, put an end to the little influence in public affairs which Augustus had left with the people, by transferring the elections from the Comitia to the senate. *Neque populus ademptum jus questus est nisi inani rumore.* (Tac. *Ann.* i. 15.)

15 — Juv.

78. Effudit, sc. *turba Remi.* — **Curas,** (public) cares.

79. Imperium, fasces. Dictatorships, consulships, praetorships.— Legiones. Perhaps the command of armies; or the military tribune-ships, two-thirds of which were assigned in the *comitia.*

81. Panem, i. e. the public distribution of bread. Cf. **vii.** 174. Macleane takes it as simply "bread," the want of *all*, whether they received the public dole or not.

82. Magna est fornacula. It can hold many statues besides those of Sejanus.

83. Brutidius Niger was a distinguished orator and rhetorician in the time of Tiberius. He was probably a partisan of Sejanus, and trembled lest he should share his fate. — The **altar of Mars** was in the Campus Martius.

84 sq. "I very much fear lest the baffled Ajax will wreak his vengeance upon him, for his feeble defence." Lewis explains the reference of **victus Ajax** to Tiberius as follows. "The poet has in his mind the legend of Ajax conquered by Ulysses, and the mad rage which seized on him after his defeat, when he butchered the sheep, thinking they were his enemies. So the speaker is repre-sented as fearing that a similar butchering frenzy will seize Tiberius, whom he compares to Ajax, and, as Ajax was conquered, he affixes the epithet *victus* to him, without seeming to notice that it does not fit Tiberius. 'I am afraid that we are going to have a repetition of the story of conquered Ajax, — an undiscriminating massacre.'" In like manner Macleane comments on **male defensus**: "Under the character of Ajax, enraged with the leaders of the army for not tak-ing his part against **Ulysses** [Sejanus], the man means Tiberius, who in his letter to the senate expressed great alarm, and begged them to send one of the consuls with a guard to conduct him, a poor solitary old man, to their presence. These apprehensions, whether real or pretended, the senate might well fear would be visited on them, and they hastened to remove the cause of them, and everybody con-nected with him. This is what Niger had to fear."

Madvig (*Opusc.* i. 44) proposes a very different explanation. The controversy between Ajax and Ulysses, he says, for the arms of Achilles, was a frequent subject for *declamationes* (cf. vii. 115), and had been taken by the rhetorician Brutidius, who espoused the cause of Ajax. The speaker says, jokingly, he fears Ajax is going to exact the penalty of the death of the declaimer, for his frigid de-fense of his cause. Mayor and Anthon follow Madvig.

87. The testimony of slaves against their masters could be received

only in cases of high treason, when they could be examined by torture. (Cod. x. 11, 6.) Tiberius evaded the rule by ordering that the
slaves should be purchased by the *actor publicus.* (Tac. *Ann.* ii. 30.)

87. In jus. Augustus made the senate a high court of justice, and
gave it the right of taking cognizance of crimes against the state and
the person of the emperors.

88. Cervice obstricta. With a rope about his neck : the common
way in which a resisting culprit was taken before a magistrate.

90. Salutari. To have your morning levees thronged.

91, 92. Illi, illum. Like τῷ μέν, τὸν δέ.

Summas curules, sc. sellas, the highest curule offices, — consulships, censorships, praetorships, curule aedileships.

Tutor, *guardian.* Sejanus was virtually regent at Rome, and for
a time had Tiberius completely under his control.

94. Grege Chaldaeo. Chaldaea was looked upon as the head-
quarters of astrology, magic, and sorcery ; as may be gathered from
the book of Daniel. Tiberius was slavishly devoted to the astrologers in his latter years : "superstition and vice are often comrades."

94 sq. Vis . . . domestica. Variously taken as meaning, Do you
wish for yourself promotion (as *primipilus centurio, praefectus co-
horti, eques egregius,* and *praefectus praetorio*): Do you wish the
power of promoting others to these offices: and Do you wish for
javelins, cohorts, a brilliant train of equestrian attendants, and a
domestic camp, — i. e. do you wish to be attended by a guard, as Sejanus was. We may translate, with Weidner, At least you wish to
be centurion, tribunus militum, praefectus alae, with *equites illustres*
in your staff, and to have a body-guard at your house? — Under the
republic, **equites egregii** were such knights as were illustrious for
birth, wealth, or fame. Under Augustus they were men of fortune,
not necessarily of the equestrian order, to whom he gave the privilege of wearing the *latus clavus.*

96. Et, *even.*

97 sq. But what glory or prosperity is worth the condition that
our sufferings must be proportioned to our success?

99. Hujus. I. e. of Sejanus.

100. Fidenae and Gabii, and so **(102) Ulubrae** (cf. Hor. *Epp.* i. 11,
30), are mentioned as small, unimportant towns.— **Potestas,** abstract
for concrete. Cf. the Italian podestà.

101. Minora, too small ; below the standard measure.

102. Vacuis. Cf. Sat. iii. 102.

103. Quid optandum foret depends upon *Sejanum ignorasse.*

106. Unde, *so that from it.* — **Altior,** from a greater height.

107. Et . . . ruinae, "*and dreadful the headlong descent of the ruin once set in motion.*" Macleane would translate *impulsae,* " beaten by the storm," or " struck by the bolt or lightning." **Praeceps** is used substantively. There is no instance of an adjective agreeing with it earlier than Juvenal.

108. Crassos, Pompeios. Used generically. — Illum, C. Julius Caesar. The names are those of the so-called first triumvirate.

109. Domitos deduxit flagra **Quirites,** *tamed the Romans and brought them under his lash.*

110. Locus is the subject of *evertit* understood, in reply to the question.

111. Exaudita, heard too well. (Macleane.)

112. Who married the daughter of Ceres ?

113. Sicca, i. e. *bloodless.*

115 sq. The **Quinquatria,** a feast of Minerva, received its name from being originally celebrated on the 19th March, five days after the Ides. It was afterwards extended to the 23d, so as to occupy five days. These were holidays in the schools; on the first of them scholars paid the master the entrance fee, or *minerval.* — Uno . . . Minervam, *pays his court to frugal Science with a single as,* i. e. is in the lowest or alphabet class, where the school-fee is the smallest. Minervam = *litteras.* — **Parcam,** P and the best editors : pω *partam.*

117. A little homeborn slave, *capsarius,* carries the boy's *capsa* or box of books and paper and pens.

118. Perit. Perfect tense ; a contracted form not used by writers of the golden age. Kiær makes it present, the final syllable regarded as long *in arsi quarti pedis* by the aid of the caesura (hephthemimeris).

120. Ingenio. Best taken as dative, and abstract for concrete; *genius* for *man of genius.* Otherwise, it would be ablative of cause.

121. Causidicus is always an inferior term, as compared with *orator* and *patronus.*

122. A line of Cicero's which was much ridiculed on account of the jingle *fortunatam natam.* Cf. Quintil. ix. 4. A contrary instance, where the repetition is, as Lewis says, a great beauty, is in the well-known verse of Terence, *Eun.* ii. 3, 6 : taedet quotidianarum harum formarum.

123. Founded on Cicero's own words, *Phil.* ii. 46 : contempsi Catilinae gladios, non pertimescam tuos. — Contemnere **potuit,** *he really could have scorned.*

126. Volveris a prima quae proxima. A periphrase for *the second.* This second Philippic cost Cicero his life.

Volveris, *art unrolled.* An allusion to the form of Roman books. **Illum.** Demosthenes.

128. Theatri. In the time of Demosthenes, the assemblies of the people were frequently held in the theatre of Dionysos.

129 sqq. Juvenal abuses a poet's license. "The father of Demosthenes was a man of means, — the proprietor of a sword manufactory, it is true; but not 'a blear-eyed, smutty-faced blacksmith,' as he is here represented as being." The father died when Demosthenes was seven years old.

133. Truncis, "trunk-formed." Trophies were made of arms taken from the enemy and piled up on the trunk of a tree or a wooden frame.

135. Curtum temone jugum, a war-chariot shorn of its pole.

136. Captivos = captivus. — **Arcu.** I. e. a triumphal arch.

137. Humanis majora = μείζω ἢ κατ' ἄνθρωπον, superhuman.

138. Induperator. Cf. Sat. iv. 29, note.

148. Non capit, οὐ χωρεῖ, does not contain, is not large enough for.

150. Rursus, again, in another direction. Repeat *admota*, or supply *pertinens.*

152 sq. There is nothing harsh in the sequence of the present on the perfect. The obstacles which nature *has placed* in his way, *are* confronting him.

153. Aceto. Cf. Liv. xxi. 37; Plin. *H. N.* xxiii. 21, 71.

155. Cf. Lucan. ii. 657: nil actum credens dum quid superesset agendum. — **Portas,** sc. *Romae.*

158. Luscum. Hannibal got ophthalmia and lost one of his eyes in the marshes south of the Po, B. C. 217. Cf. **Liv.** xxii. 2.

162. Bithyno tyranno. Prusias, to whom Hannibal betook himself upon leaving Antiochus, king of Syria, whither he had first fled.

Vigilare, *to wake up.*

163. Res humanas miscuit, threw the whole world into confusion. *Miscere* = συγκυκᾶν.

166. The Romans sending a demand for the surrender of Hannibal, which Prusias was not able to resist, the great Carthaginian took poison, which he carried about with him in his signet-ring (anulus). In **Cannarum vindex** there may be an allusion to the bushels of rings of Roman knights picked up after the battle.

167. Declamatio, the theme for a declamation or school-exercise.

168. Alexander was born at Pella.

171. Babylon is said to have been built of brick cemented with asphalt.

U

172. Fatetur, betrays, reveals. Cf. Juv. ii. 17.

172–3. Cf. Shakspere, Henry iv. :

> "When that this body did contain a spirit,
> A kingdom for it was too small a bound;
> But now, two paces of the vilest earth
> Is room enough."

174. Juvenal now takes Xerxes as his example. Traces of the ship-canal cut to avoid the dangerous promontory of Mount Athos are still visible, although Juvenal treats the story as an invention.— The final syllable of **Athos,** though short, stands for a long syllable by the aid of the caesural pause.

175 sq. Constratum . . . **mare.** This refers to the bridge of boats over the Hellespont. Cf. Lucret. iii. 1029 sqq. — Ribbeck has *contractum*, the reading of P *a prima manu*. Some MSS. have *cum stratum*, which Kiær would adopt.

176. The punctuation is Kiær's. Editors generally put a semicolon after *mare*, and no mark after *credimus*.

177. Herodotus speaks of several rivers as having been drunk dry by the enormous host of Xerxes.

178. Prandente, *at his lunch.* — **Sostratus.** An unknown poet, who, it seems, sang of the exploits of Xerxes. — **Madidis alis,** *in his drunken flights* (Lewis). *Madidis* has been explained in three ways: (1) *steeped in wine;* (2) *drooping;* (i. e. his song was feeble); and (3), *moist with perspiration*, in which case *alis* would be *armpits*, and the reference to the labor and heat of recitation.

179. Qualis, *in what plight.*

180 sq. Xerxes's custom of flogging whatever winds opposed him, making him a harder master than their king Aeolus (cf. Verg. *Aen.* i. 52 sqq.), may be a playful invention of Juvenal's.

182. Aeschylus (*Pers.* v. 745 sqq.) and Herodotus (vii. 35) say that Xerxes chained the Hellespont for breaking his bridge.

183 sq. *This is quite merciful, to be sure, that he did not think him deserving also of being branded.* So the MSS. As Herodotus says he had heard a report that Xerxes sent persons to brand the sea, editors have fancied it necessary to alter the text. So Jahn, at the suggestion of Weber, reads *mitius id sane, quid? non et stigmate dignum Crediderit?* Hermann and Weidner follow Jahn; Ribbeck, Mayor, and Macleane follow the MSS.

185 sq. Juvenal's story of the manner in which Xerxes escaped from Salamis differs from other accounts, but is good for his purpose.

189. Recto vultu. I. e. in health; "with the erect look of health." This seems the best antithesis to *pallidus*. Heinrich takes the words to mean *unabashed*, impavidus, understanding *pallidus* as "pale with anxiety."

192. Dissimilem sui, unlike its (former) self. Escott compares with this expression the Greek δυνατώτεροι ἑαυτῶν γιγνόμενοι.

194. Thabraca (Tabraca) was a town in Numidia, surrounded with jungles which abounded in monkeys.

199. Lêve. I. e. bald. — **Madidi,** *drivelling.* — **Infantia,** (second) infancy.

200. Misero, sc. *ei.* The so-called dative of the agent. — **Gingiva inermi.** *A gum unarmed* is a *toothless* gum.

201. Usque adeo gravis, *so utterly burdensome is he.* — **Sibi.** Juvenal lengthens the last vowel here in the arsis of the last foot. Cf. xv. 98 (*mihi*).

202. Even a persistent fortune-hunter cannot stomach him.

204. Partis, organ, *sense.*

210. Cantare is used of instrumental as well as of vocal music.

211. Seleucus must have been some famous singer or musician.

212. The costume of the citharoedi was the *palla* (here called *lacerna*) and the *syrma.* — **Aurata,** *gold-embroidered.*

214. Horns and trumpets were sounded at the beginning and end of games and plays. Cf. Serv. *ad Verg.* v. 113.

216. Nuntiet horas. There were public water-clocks (*clepsydrae*), as well as sun-dials, at Rome. The wealthy had clocks or dials sometimes at their own houses. A slave watches the timekeeper (public or private), and reports the hours to his master.

221. Themison, the name of a celebrated physician before Juvenal's time, is here put for any medical practitioner. Dryden's translation of this line,

"Or how *last fall* he raised the weekly bills,"

(i. e. the bills of mortality), is noticeable for its use of a term which has been alleged to be an Americanism.

228. The connection of the perfect and present here is perfectly natural; because he has lost his eyes, he is envious of the one-eyed. Cf. Verg. *Aen.* vi. 747 sq.

Luscis, *one-eyed men.*

238. Phialen. An impure woman. — **Artificis oris,** *of an artful mouth.*

239. Quod steterat, *which had been stationed.* — **Carcere,** *the cell.*

240. Ut, *even if*.

242. Plenae sororibus, *full of one's sisters' ashes*.

246. Rex Pylius. Nestor.

247. A cornice secundae, *next after the crow* (in longevity). See note on Sat. xiv. 251.

249. Jam dextra computat annos. I. e. has begun his second century. Men counted up to one hundred on the left hand, then up to a thousand on the right, then over a thousand on the left again.

252. Nimio stamine, the too-long thread of his life. — Acris, brave, spirited.

253. Ardentem. I. e. on the funeral pile. — **Ab omni** quisquis **adest socius** = ab omni socio quisquis adest.

256. Haec eadem Peleus, sc. *queritur*.

257. Alius. I. e. Laertes. Alius as in i. 10. — **Fas, a** natural right. — Ithacum. I. e. Ulysses. — Natantem. Afloat; at sea. Cf. Propert. iii. 12, 32. The translation "swimming from the wreck" is less suitable.

259. Assaracus was Priam's great-uncle.

261. Primos edere planctus. Cassandra is the leader of the dirge. Cf. Il. xxiv. 723 sqq.

265. Dies, when meaning a space of time, and not a literal day, is feminine. Longa dies here has been well translated *length of days*.

265 sqq. Cf. Verg. *Aen*. ii. 506–558, and Cic. *Tusc. Disp*. i. 35, 85, together with the lines there cited from the Andromache of Ennius:

> Haec omnia vidi inflammari,
> Priamo vi vitam evitari,
> Jovis aram sanguine turpari.

267. Curtius (iii. 3, 19) defines **tiara,** " regium capitis insigne, quod caerulea fascia albo distincta circumibat."

270. *Ab aratro*, as *fastiditus* ("scorned") attributes feeling and mental action to the plough.

271 sq. Torva canino latravit rictu, barked savagely with the jaws of a dog. On Hecuba's metamorphosis into a dog, cf. Eurip. *Hec*. 1265; Ov. *Met*. xiii. 565 sqq.

272–277. Notice the *stabiles spondei*, skilfully introduced " *ut res tardior atque gravior ad aures veniat*."

272. On the tenses here Simcox remarks, "[the Latin implies,] his wife, who had survived him, lived to bark. We observe this distinction of tenses in telling a *new* story, but not in alluding, as here, to an *old* one."

273. Regem Ponti. I. e. Mithridates VI., not undeservedly called

by modern historians the Great, who at last, on the successful insur-
rection of his son Pharnaces, took poison, and when it proved in-
effectual (cf. xiv. 252, note), compelled one of his Gaulish mercenaries
to despatch him with his sword.

274. What is the story of the visit of Solon to Croesus? (See Herodotus i. 30–32.)

275. Spatia ultima, the closing scenes. Literally, *the last heats.*
The competitors in the chariot-races in the circus had to run seven
times round the *spina*, and each course round was called a *spatium.*

276–282. Juvenal goes on to speak of C. Marius, to whose conquest
of the Cimbri and Teutones (Teutonico, verse **282**), and triumph,
we have had allusion in viii. 245 sqq. At this triumph Marius was
fifty-five. In B. C. 88, when he was in his sixty-ninth year, he was
obliged to fly from Rome to escape from Sulla, and in his flight tried
to hide himself in a marsh near Minturnae on the Liris. He was
caught, and kept in custody for some time, but was allowed to escape
by sea, and went to Carthage, as Velleius says (ii. 19), *inopemque vitam
in tugurio ruinarum Carthaginiensium toleravit.* Plutarch (*Marius* 37–40) has also the story of Marius sitting on the ruins of Carthage, which may be founded on some commonplace in the declam-
atory exercises of the imperial period. The following year, his
party having gained temporary success, he returned to Rome, where
he made a fearful example of his enemies, but died in January B. C.
86, in his seventh consulship. (Macleane and Long.)

278. Hinc. I. e. from length of life.

281. Observe the hiatus after pompa. — Macleane's "his full soul"
is perhaps the best rendering that can be given of animam opimam.
"It seems to involve a reference to the *spolia opima*, and is particularly suited to a conqueror."

282. Vellet = ἔμελλεν. *When he was on the point of* getting down.

283–286. Provida. Foreseeing what was coming upon him. —
Cicero enlarges on the same thought in regard to Pompey, in *Tusc.
Disp.* i. 35, 86; which passage, as well as the one on Priam immediately preceding, must have been in Juvenal's mind. — His fever
ought to have been prayed for, to remove him from impending
calamities; but many cities prayed that he might recover, and their
prayers prevailed (vicerunt. — Victo (**286**), sc. *ei.* Dative of disadvantage.

287 sq. Lentulus and Cethegus, fellow-conspirators with Catiline,
were strangled in prison by the common executioner. Catiline fell
on the field of battle.

289. Majore, *louder.*

291. Usque ad delicias votorum, *even to the luxury of vows;* even to delighting herself in fancying details of loveliness and vowing offerings for each charm. Various translations of this phrase have been proposed, as *even to a foolish fondness in her vows, even to fastidiousness in her prayers, even till she dallies with her prayers, even to caprice in her vows, even to enticements* (of the gods) *in her vows,* etc., etc. — The subject of *inquit* is not *mater,* but a supposed objector representing the common opinions, *some one.*

294. Rutila is any one with a hump on her back.

295. Suam, sc. *faciem.*

298 sq. Horrida, sternly virtuous; of old-fashioned strictness. For such morals the Sabines were famed.

300 sq. Modesto sanguine ferventem, *glowing with modest blood;* i. e. blushing.

304. Esse viro, to be a man (in the full sense of that great word).

325. Hippolytus resisted the advances of Phaedra, who was the daughter of Minos, king of Crete, and so is called **Cressa (327).** — **Grave propositum,** *his stern resolve.* — **Bellerophon** would not yield to the solicitations of **Stheneboea (327).** Anteia is the name generally given, instead of **Stheneboea.**

326. Haec. I. e. Phaedra.

Repulsa (pω Kiær, *when refused.* Heinrich, Jahn, and Ribbeck, read *repulso,* after P Sç. M. Haupt would read *hac* for *haec,* (*hac ... repulsa.*) Kiær would omit the pronoun altogether, making *Stheneboea* the subject of *erubuit.* If repulso is read, it must be taken, as Heinrich says, as "an ablative absolute of the participle, = *quum accidisset repulsa.* Cf. Gronov. ad Liv. i. 41. Perizon. ad Sanct. p. 574 ed. Scheid."

327 sq. Se concussere. "Aroused themselves to vengeance" is the stock translation here. Comparing Verg. *Aen.* vii. 338 and Ov. *Met.* iii. 726 and iv. 473, we find a better interpretation, *were excited to madness.* So Heinrich, Macleane, Weidner.

329 sqq. Elige . . . destinat. "Choose what advice should be given to him whom Caesar's wife resolves to marry." **C. Silius** (optimus . . . patriciae) was a handsome youth whom the Empress **Messalina** fell in love with and married publicly during the absence from Rome of her husband Claudius. The latter remained ignorant of the whole affair till it was revealed to him by his freedman Narcissus, whereupon Silius and Messalina, with many others, were put to death.

334. Tyrius. I. e. covered with purple spreads. — **Genialis,** sc. *lectus* or *torus.* — **In hortis,** sc. Luculli. Cf. Tac. *Ann.* xi. 37.

335. A dowry will be given after the old custom ; a dowry amounting to a million sesterces. This seems to have been the usual dowry among the upper classes, like £10,000 with the English. Cf. Lips. ad Tac. *Ann.* ii. 86 ; Sen. *Consol. ad Helv.* 12.— For et Kiær suggests the emendation *ex,* to accord with Juvenal's frequent practice, in a sentence of four members, to connect the first two by a conjunction, and add the second two without a copula. In this instance the change to asyndeton would neatly concur with the change in tense.

336. The signatores were witnesses to the marriage-contract. — The auspices attended at weddings, though the practice of taking *auspicia* had been given up. Val. Max. ii. 1, 1.

345. " Decapitation and strangling were the common way of executing criminals, **except the lowest and slaves,** who were crucified."

347. Permittes, *you will leave it.* Cf. Hor. *Carm.* i. 9, 9 : permitte divis cetera.

354. Ut tamen et poscas aliquid, *if, however, you must e'en ask for something.* **Et** is used for emphasis, as the Greeks sometimes καί. — Another translation is possible : That, however, you may e'en ask for something, and make your little offering to the gods, pray *etc.* With the ancients, prayer was inseparable from offering. — **Sacellis** "means the chapel in every man's house, in which were images of the Lares, to whom the offering of a pig was common (Hor. *Carm.* iii. 23, 4)."

355. Divina, *dear to the gods.* — Tomacula (τέμνω), cut pieces of flesh, to be burnt on the altar. Conington (on Pers. ii. 30) remarks that the details in this line are mentioned contemptuously, and compares xiii. 117 sq.

358. Inter munera naturae. " And counts it *nature's privilege* to die." (Dryden.) Weidner, very differently, translating *spatium vitae extremum* " the farthest bounds of life," considers the especially kind gift of nature to be length of days.

362. Pluma. Beds of down.

365. **Habes.** So most MSS. and recent editors; but P has *abest, and the line is quoted with *abest* by Lactantius. Hermann and Macleane read *abest.* I have modified Macleane's Argument (p. 221) to bring out the true meaning. — **Numen,** as often, is *divine power.* — **Prudentia** is *moral* prudence ; involving forethought.

363–366: "Man is his own star, and the soul that can   ·
      Render an honest and a perfect man
      Commands all light, all influence, all fate." — *John Fletcher.*

SATIRE XI.

———◦◦◦◦◦———

ARGUMENT.

1-20. IF Atticus lives well, he's reckoned generous; if Rutilus, a madman. All men laugh to see a pauper epicure, and so all talk of Rutilus. He's young and stout enough for the wars, and yet, he is impelled (the prince consenting) to train for the arena. There's many a man who lives but for his palate, for whom his creditor looks out at the entrance of the market. The poorest live the best, just on the verge of bankruptcy. Meanwhile they search the elements for dainties, regardless of the price, or in their hearts preferring what is dearest. For men so reckless it is not hard to get the money. They'll sell their dishes or their mother's image, to season for four hundred sesterces a glutton's crockery. 'T is thus they come to gladiator's fare.

21-55. That, then, which riches make respectable is wanton luxury in the poor. The man of learning who knows not the difference between a cash chest and a little purse, I do well to despise. That rule came down from heaven, "KNOW THYSELF." Remember it when you think of marrying or entering the Senate (Thersites did not seek Achilles' armor in which Ulysses made a doubtful figure); or if you aim at pleading some great cause, think who you are, whether a mighty speaker or mere mouther. In great things or in small, a man should know his own measure. Buy not a mullet if your purse will go no further than a gudgeon. What can you come to, if your appetite grows larger as your purse grows emptier; when all you have is buried in your belly? The ring goes last, and Pollio with bare finger begs. Wantonness fears not early death, but age much worse than death. The steps are these. Money is borrowed first, and spent at Rome; but when the usurer begins to trouble them, then off they go to Baiae and the oysters. To run away from the forum is no worse than from Subura to migrate to Esquiliae: they only care that they must lose the games: they never think of blushing: Modesty is laughed at as she flies the town, and few men care to stay her.

56-129. To-day, my friend, you'll see whether I practise the fine things I preach, or praise plain fare but call for rich. You'll find in me Evander as the host, you shall be Hercules or Aeneas. Now listen to your dinner. A young kid from my farm, and wild herbs gathered by my gardener's wife; fresh eggs warm in the nest, and hens that laid them; grapes fresh as when plucked; the finest pears and apples, the crude juice dried from out them. Such was the dinner of our senators when first they grew luxurious. The herbs he gathered in his little garden, such as a ditcher now turns up his nose at, Curius would boil with his own hand. The flitch hung up to dry in former times they kept for holidays, and lard for birthdays for their blood relations, and part of the victim's meat. The great man who had thrice been consul, dictator too, went to such feasts stalking along with spade upon his shoulder. In the strict Censor's days no one would ask what sort of turtles might be found in the sea, to ornament the rich man's couch: they were content with a rude ass's head. Their food and house and furniture were plain alike. Unskilled in art, the cups they got for plunder the soldiers broke to ornament their harness or their helmets. The only silver that they had adorned their arms. Their homely fare was served in earthen-ware. If you're inclined to envy, you might envy those good times. The gods were nearer unto men; they warned the city of the Gauls' approach, such care for Rome had Jupiter when made of clay. The tables then were made of home-grown wood. But now the richest viands have no flavor except on a round table with a carved ivory stem; a silver one to rich men is rude as an iron ring upon the finger.

129–182. I'll have no guest, then, who despises poverty. I have not an ounce of ivory in all my house; the very handles of my knives are bone; and yet they do not spoil the meat, or cut the worse for that. And I've no carver taught by first-rate artist, who teaches them to cut up all fine dishes. My man's a novice too, and cannot filch except in a small way, a chop or so. I've only a rough boy in woollen clothes to offer you my vulgar herbs, no eastern bought for a vast price from dealers. Whatever you may ask for ask in Latin. They all are dressed alike, their hair cropped straight, combed out to-day in honor of my guest; boys from the farm, modest as those should be who wear the purple. One shall bring you wine grown on his native hills. And for our sports, we'll read what Homer wrote and his peer Maro. It matters not what voice recites such verses.

183–208. But come, put care away and take a rest. We'll have no word of debts or jealous thoughts; before my door you must put off all this, home and its troubles, slaves and their breakages, and, worse than all, the ingratitude of friends. The great Idaean games are going on. The praetor, victim of his horses, sits as a conqueror in triumph; all Rome (the multitude must pardon me) has poured into the Circus, and by that shout I know that Green has won the day. For had it not, you might have seen the city all in mourning as on that day of Cannae. Let boys go look at games, boys who can shout and bet and sit by girls they love. Let my shrunk skin drink in the sun, and put the toga off. To-day, an hour ere noon, you may go to bathe: you must not do so every day of the six, for even such a life as that would pall. Pleasures are sweeter for unfrequent use. — MACLEANE, *with modifications.*

1–3. Atticus is used here for any rich man, and **Rutilus** for one who has beggared himself. T. Pomponius Atticus, the friend of Cicero, was very wealthy, and his name may have become proverbial. Apicius was a noted *gourmand*. **Pauper** Apicius, *a poor Apicius.*—**Eximie** = *prae aliis.*

4. Convictus = *convivium.* **Omnis convictus**, every dinner-table. — "Around the **thermae**, or public baths, there were promenades and spaces, called *scholae*, where people were in the habit of sitting, walking about, and gossiping." — **Statio**, in post-Augustan use, is any place of public resort.

5. De Rutilo, sc. *loquuntur.* — **Juvenalis** implies *validus ;* **juveni-**lis is allied to *lĕvis* and *temerarius.*

6. Galeae, sc. *ferendae.* — **Ardent.** So Jahn, Ribbeck, Hermann, on the conjecture of C. Barth and others. Most MSS. ardens; two give *ardenti* and one *ardentis.* Weidner *ardet*, after Guietus.

7. The **tribunus plebis** appears to have had some kind of judicial authority, a *cognitio extraordinaria*, under the empire. The tribune here is the emperor himself. — **Prohibente** = *intercedente, interfering to stop it.*

8. To sign the bond and take the oath, such as a tyrant imposes, of the trainer of gladiators. — **Verba scribere** suggests *verba praeire.* Upon entering the service, the gladiators swore *uri, vinciri, verberari, ferroque necari*, and to suffer whatever else the trainer commanded, — truly *regia verba*, from the mouth of the trainer who imposes them as the oath. — Many commentators understand *scribere* here simply of writing out the rules etc., in order to learn them by heart.

12. Egregius. An unusual comparative form, from the adverb *egregie.* — **Egregius meliusque,** sc. *ceteris.* Or, as Heinrich says, the sense is : quo quisque horum miserior est et citius casurus, eo melius cenat.

13. Casurus. I. e. about to become bankrupt. — **Perlucente ruina.** A metaphor from the daylight shining through the cracks in a ruined house.

14. Interea. I. e. before the final crash. — **Gustus,** *dainties;* not necessarily the *relishes* eaten at the *promulsis*, or preliminary course, to whet the appetite. (Hor. *Sat.* ii. 8, 7 sqq.) They were sought *elementa per omnia*, from water, air, and earth, fish, fowl, and vegetables.

15. Animo, *their fancy.*

17. Perituram arcessere summam, "to fetch the money which they are bent on throwing away."

18. *By pawning their plate, or the broken statue of a mother.* — Imagine, a silver statuette or bust.

19. **Nummis.** Sesterces (*not* sestertia). — **Condire gulosum fictile,** *to season a savory dish on earthen-ware;* i. e. to compound some rich and luxurious viand, which he has to serve up in earthen-ware, as all his silver is pawned.

20. **Sic,** i. e. by such extravagance. — **Ad miscellanea ludi,** to the hodge-podge served in the gladiatorial school.

21. **Ergo,** *as I said;* (going back to verse 1.) — **Nam,** in every other case in Juvenal, is found at the beginning of the sentence; similar inversions of *nam* are found in Catullus, Virgil, and Horace.

22. **Ventidius** is put here for any man of wealth. — Kiær puts a semicolon after **nomen,** and finds the subject of *sumit* and *trahit* (23) implied in *quis haec eadem paret* (21).

25 sq. **Hic tamen idem ignoret** = *si tamen idem ignoret.*

26. **Ferrata arca.** Cf. i. 90, note.

31. **Se transducebat,** made but a sorry figure; exposed himself to ridicule.

34. Two windbags are mentioned. On Matho, cf. i. 32; vii. 129.

38. **Crumina** (crumena). So the best editors, except Jahn, who has *culina,* after two French MSS. and a doubtful reading in P.

41. **Argentum** grave is heavy plate; massive articles of solid silver.

42. **Exire a domino** is allied to the juristic expression on inscriptions and in the digests, exire de nomine familiae, as said e. g. of a sepulchral monument, *peto non fundus de familia exeat,* or *ut fundus de nomine vestro numquam exeat,* etc. On *exire* with *a* cf. Cic. *Verr.* ii. 60: ad istum non modo illos nummos, qui per simulationem ab isto exierant, revertisse, etc. (Weidner.)

43. **Anulus.** The badge of equestrian or senatorial rank.

44. **Acerbum,** *untimely;* from its meaning, *unripe.*

45. **Luxuriae.** The so-called "dative of the agent." — Kiær would place lines 42 and 43 after lines 44 and 45; and I agree with him.

47. **Dominis.** I. e. the money-lenders.

49. **Qui vertere solum,** *they who have made off;* literally, they who have shifted their quarters.

50. **Cedere foro,** "to abscond from 'change," or to become bankrupt.

Deterius, *more disgraceful;* more discreditable.

51. **Ferventi,** *bustling, noisy;* the Esquiline was quiet. Some translate **ferventi** here *hot;* the Esquiline was cool and healthy.

53. Anno uno. The ablative of duration of time is very rare in the golden age, but more frequent afterwards.

54. Sanguinis non gutta, no flush of shame, no blush from a sense of honor. — **Haeret,** *remains.* — **Morantur,** *seek to detain.*

55. Et fugientem. So Jahn, Hermann, Ribbeck, Weidner, after gs *Priscian.* Other readings are *effugientem* (Pω), *fugientem* (s).

57. Persicus is some unknown friend of the poet's. — **Vita vel moribus et re,** *in my life, that is my character and actions.* Vel, *or if you please to say,* offers a choice of expressions. Jahn and Ribbeck give *nec* (adgs), but *vel* (pω. In P the word is erased) is better.

58. Si. So Jahn, Ribbeck, Weidner, after S and one MS. Pω, *sed,* and so Hermann.

59. Puero = servo. — Dictare for *imperare* belongs to the later Latin.

60 sqq. Habebis Euandrum. You shall have in me a host as simple and frugal as Evander. — **Tyrinthius.** Cf. Verg. *Aen.* viii. 362 sq. — **Minor . . . . caelum.** The reference is to Aeneas, the son of a goddess, though inferior to Hercules. Cf. Verg. *Aen.* viii. 102 sqq.

63. Aeneas, according to one legend, was drowned in the Numicius; Hercules was burned on Mount Oeta.

64. Nullis ornata macellis, *furnished by no markets.*

65. It would appear from this that Juvenal had an estate near Tibur.

69. Asparagi. Cf. v. 82. The term includes several herbs besides the one we know by that name.

70. Torto calentia foeno. The eggs were wrapped up warm in the hay in which they were laid.

72. Parte anni. About half a year, as (according to verse 193) the dinner is given in April. The ablative resembles *anno uno* (53).

73 sq. The **Syrian** pear, a kind of bergamot, is placed by Pliny next to the Crustumian, which he calls best of all. The pears from **Signia** (in Latium) were of a reddish color, and thought particularly wholesome (Cels. ii. 24). The apples of Picenum were celebrated; cf. Hor. *Sat.* ii. 3, 272; ii. 4, 70.

75 sq. Siccatum . . . . succi, *now that they have put away their autumn (crudeness), dried out by the frost, and the perils of their unripe juice.*

77. Jam luxuriosa, when it had grown to be luxurious; even a luxurious (dinner).

78. M. Curius Dentatus, the conqueror of Pyrrhus, often served the Roman poets as a pattern of the good old times.

80. The **fossor** here is a fettered slave from the'**ergastulum** (see viii. 180, note), set to work in the fields.

81. **Vulva.** The *matrix* of a pregnant sow was regarded as a great luxury.

82. **Rara pendentia crate,** *hanging from the wide-barred frame* among the rafters.

85. All but the legs and entrails of a victim were eaten.

88. **Solito maturius,** *earlier than his wont.*

89. **Domito a monte,** from the hill where he had been digging. *Domare* is used of subduing the earth by ploughing, digging, etc.

90–91. **Autem,** *moreover.*—The proper names represent censors of the old time. — **Postremo.** So P, and Jahn, Hermann, Ribbeck, Weidner. The MSS. other than P, *rigidique.*

92. The allusion is to C. Claudius Nero and M. Livius Salinator, colleagues in the censorship B. C. 204. For the story, see Liv. xxix. 37 and Val. Max. ii. 9, 6. — Kiær would place a period at the end of this verse, and a comma at the end of verse 89.

95. **Fulcrum,** *couch-foot.*

96 sq. **Nudo . . . aselli,** *on small couches with bare sides a front of bronze displayed the rude head of a little donkey crowned with a garland.*

98. **Ad quod lascivi ludebant ruris alumni,** *by which* (i. e. near which) *the sportive sons of the country* (i. e. the farmers, the rustics) *made merry.* Though the furniture was rude and the fare simple, the rural guests amused themselves and were happy. — Kiær has exploded the old notion that the allusion here is to boys' " poking fun " at the head of the donkey.

101. **In parte.** I. e. in his share.

103. **Ut,** etc. He broke them up *in order to* make trappings for his horse, and an embossed helmet for himself.

104 sq. **Ferae,** i. e. the she-wolf. — The **twin** Quirini are Romulus and Remus. Compare the name *Castores* applied to Castor and Pollux. — **Sub rupe.** Like Virgil's *in antro* (Aen. viii. 630).

106 sq. **Venientis dei.** Mars coming to visit the twins. — **Pendentis.** Hanging in the air, (not yet having alighted.)

108. **Tusco.** I. e. of earthen-ware, which Etruria produced in great quantity.

111 sq. **Vox.** Livy (v. 32) and Cicero (*de Divin.* i. 45; ii. 32) tell the story of one who heard a voice louder than that of man in the dead of night, near the temple of Vesta, ordering him to report to the magistrates that the Gauls were coming (about B. C. 390). — **Audita,** sc. *est.*

16 — Juv.   V

114. His. I. e. hac voce et hujusmodi signis.

116. The earthen-ware images of the gods came from Etruria. — **Violatus,** *wronged;* as if it were an insult to gild him. Cf. iii. 20.

121. Dama, the gazelle.

122. Orbes. Round tables, of costly material, supported by a single foot. Cf. i. 137.

123. The ivory table-leg is carved in the form of a leopard rampant.

124. Porta. Either *gate,* because the traffic of Aethiopia passed through Syene, a frontier town, or *pass,* because the valley of the Nile is greatly narrowed below Syene.

125. Obscurior, darker, " of duskier hue."

127. The elephant changes its tusks only once in its life; and *not* then, as Juvenal says, because they have grown " too large and burdensome for his head."

131. Adeo nulla, etc. " I have actually not an ounce of ivory."

132. Nec, *not even.* — Tessellae, dice, of six sides. — Calculus. A counter used in a game resembling draughts.

136. Structor. Cf. v. 120, note.

137. Pergula, (carving-) school. — **Aput quem,** *at whose house.*

138. Sumine. The breast of a sow, before she had been suckled, was a great delicacy with the Romans. — " The *boar* was commonly the chief dish (caput cenae) of a large dinner, and served whole."

139. Sythicae volucres. I. e. pheasants, *Phasianae aves.*

140 sq. Oryx. An African *wild-goat,* with one horn. (Plin. *H. N.* viii. 53.) — **Lautissima ulmea cena,** " *a most dainty supper made of elm.*" Wooden models were used in the carving-schools to practise upon, the parts being slightly fastened together, so that they could be separated with a blunt knife. The clatter the pupils made with them, says Juvenal, resounded over the whole Subura, — in which quarter of the city we must place Trypherus's school.

142–144. Afrae avis. The guinea-fowl. — **Noster,** sc. *puer.* " My young attendant, a mere novice, has not the chance of making off with the remains of costly delicacies. He knows nothing of the dainties served up at great houses and the ways of the servants there. At most, his peccadilloes consist in clearing off some scraps of steaks or chops." — **Rudis omni tempore,** " untutored all his days." — **Et,** *and* (*only*).

146. A frigore tutus. Warmly, but coarsely clothed; not rustling in silks, like a dainty page in a great house.

148. Magno, sc. pretio. — **Latine.** He does not know Greek.

155. Quos ardens purpura vestit. Those who wear the toga prae-texta, — (boys born of free parents.)

180 sq. Cantare = recitare. A reader (ἀναγνώστης) was employed at refined entertainments. — **Dubiam palmam.** The comparative merits of Homer and Virgil were much discussed at Rome.

182. Such poetry commends itself, even if poorly read.

193. At the festival of the Magna Mater, the Idæan Mother, which was held in April, there were *ludi circenses* as well as *ludi scaenici*. The praetor gave the signal for the beginning of the chariot-races with a kind of banner.

194. Colunt, sc. cives. — **Similis triumpho.** The praetor went to these games in procession and presided in state, as at the Ludi Circenses (x. 36, note).

195. Praeda caballorum. The *caballi* are the horses, now worn out, that have won the race. The praetor is a prey to them, or their victim, because he had to provide from his own means the sum needed for the prizes in addition to the sum furnished by the state. — **Pace,** *by the leave.*

198. **Viridis panni.** Cf. vii. 114, note.

200. Livy (xxii. 43, 46) says that at the battle of Cannae a wind arose, blowing the dust in the face of the Romans and blinding them.

202. **Cultae,** *well-dressed.*

204. At the games spectators were obliged to wear the toga, the dress-coat of the Romans.

205. You may go to the bath at 11 o'clock. The usual hour was from 2 to 3. — **Salva fronte,** without shame. *Frons* as the seat of modesty.

SATIRE XIII.

ARGUMENT.

1-22. BAD acts displease the doers. Conscience convicts them, though the praetor's urn be false. All your friends feel with you; you are not so poor that you should sink with such a loss; besides, the case is common, one out of fortune's heap. Put off excessive grief; the sorrow of a man should not blaze up too high, the pain should not be greater than the wound. A trifle, a mere scrap of ill you scarce can bear, and all your entrails burn because a friend will not give up a deposit: and you a man of sixty! Has not experience taught you? Wisdom is great, mistress of fortune: those we count happy, too, whom life has taught to bear the yoke of life.

23-33. No day so holy but it puts forth thieves and liars. The good are rare, not more in number than gates of Thebes or mouths of Nile. We live in the ninth age, an age so bad no metal is so base that it should give it name. And yet we call upon the faith of gods and men, as loudly as the clients of Faesidius when he pleads!

33-70. Say, art thou in thy second childhood, that thou knowest not the charms of other people's money, or how they laugh at thy simplicity in expecting that any man should not forswear himself or should think that fanes and altars have their gods? The natives in the golden age thought so, before the skies were filled so full of gods and hell so full of victims. *Then* was dishonesty a prodigy. 'Twas a great crime if youth rose not to age, yea children to their seniors by four years. But *now*, if friends should not deny a trust but pay it back entire, it is more wonderful than all the prodigies that ever were; an honest man is a *lusus naturae*.

71-85. Complain that you've been impiously cheated of ten sestertia! What if I tell of one who's lost two hundred, and another more than he can cram into his chest? 'Tis easy to despise the witness of the gods, if human there be none. See with what voice and face the man denies it. He swears by all the gods and goddesses, their bows, spears. tridents, all the armory of heaven: yea, he will offer to boil his son and eat him pickled, if he be a father.

86-119. Some say 'chance governs all things, nature rules the world,' and so they fearless go to any altar. Others believe in gods and punishments, but argue thus: " Let them do with my body what they will, and strike me blind, so that I keep my gains. We may bear all for that. Let even a Ladas not hesitate, if he be poor, to pray for the rich man's gout, unless he be insane. The racer's barren crown, what does he get by that? The gods may punish, but they punish slow: my turn will not be yet; besides, it may be they will pardon me; the fault is venial. It's all a chance, one gains a cross by his crimes and one a crown." 'T is thus they quiet conscience, put a bold face upon it, go to the altar of their own accord, abuse or beat you for mistrusting them, and get believed for their audacity. And so they act their farce, while you cry out with voice like Stentor or like Mars, "Jove, hearest thou in silence? Why do we bring thee sacrifice and incense? As far as I can see, your images are no better than the statues of Vagellius."

120–161. Now take such comfort as you may from one unread in all philosophy. Patients in danger may consult great doctors, do you submit to an humbler. If you can prove there never was a crime so bad in all the world, I hold my peace, mourn as you will; I know the loss of money is greater grief than loss of kindred; in *its* case mourning is not feigned, the tears are real. But if it's everywhere the same that men deny their hand and seal, are you, fine gentleman, to be excepted? How do you make yourself the chick of a fine bird and us the produce of an humble nest? It's but a small thing after all if you compare it with the greater crimes, the hired assassin, the incendiary, the sacrilegious robber who plunders temples, or the petty thief who scrapes the gold from statues; the poisoner, the parricide. How small a part is this of all the crimes the praefect listens to from morn till night! His court alone will teach you what men are. Spend a few days there, and talk about *your* misery if you dare.

162–173. None wonder at swelled throats in the Alps, or blue eyes and curly hair in Germany, because the people are all the same. So no one in the land of the pygmies laughs at their battles with the cranes, though they are only a foot high.

174–192. "But must not perjury and fraud be punished?" Suppose him carried off and put to death, your loss is still the same, and all you get is odium and a drop of blood shed from a headless corpse. "Oh! but revenge is pleasanter than life." This is fool's language, who flare up for nothing. Chrysippus, Thales, would not say so, nor Socrates, who would not share his cup of poison with his enemy. Philosophy corrects our faults of nature and of practice: she first taught us right from wrong, for only little minds care for revenge, as you may see from women's love of it.

192–235. But why think they escape, whom conscience whips? Their punishment is worse than any down in hell, who night and day carry their witness with them. The Spartan once tempted the oracle and got his answer, which the event established, for he and all his house, though old, have perished. Such was the penalty of even a bad desire. For he who thinks to do an evil deed incurs the guilt, as if he'd done the deed. What if the man has carried out his purpose? Ceaseless anxiety haunts him at meals, parched mouth, contracted brow; bad dreams, through which the altars he has sworn by pass, and your tall ghost, most terrible of all, that drives him to confession. 'T is these who tremble at the storm and think each bolt a messenger of wrath. If one storm passes, then they fear the next, and tremble at the calm that goes before it. Every disease they count a stone or dart from heaven. They dare not sacrifice in sickness; what can the guilty hope for? What victim is not worthier to live than they? **236–249.** The wicked commonly are changeable; they are firm enough while tney're engaged in crime; when it is done, they learn the difference between right and wrong. Yet nature will go back to its old ways. Who ever puts a limit to his guilt? Who ever got back modesty once lost? Who is contented with a single crime? He will be caught some day and pay for it by death or banishment. You shall be happy in the sufferings of him you hate, and shall confess at last the gods are neither deaf nor blind. MACLEANE, *with modifications.*

1. Exemplo malo. Ablative of quality, used predicatively: quodcumque ita committitur ut malo sit exemplo. Cf. Näg. *Stil.* § 9, 1.

3. Absolvo was the legal word for acquittal. Three tablets were given each judex, on one of which was written A (= absolvo), on another C (= condemno), and on a third N. L. (= non liquet, "not proven").— Racine expresses the same sentiment as Juvenal:

> "De ses remords secrets triste et lente victime,
> Jamais un criminel ne s'absout de son crime."

4. In criminal trials a **praetor** usually presided. Urna is either the urn into which the names of the *judices*, who were to be impannelled, were placed, or that into which the *judices* threw their votes. Either could be called the praetor's urn, inasmuch as he drew the lots in the first place and counted the votes in the second; and in the performance of either of these duties he might betray his trust.

5. Juvenal writes this satire to a friend of his, whom he calls Calvinus, who is in a state of great excitement about a fraud practised upon him by a man to whom he had given in trust a sum of money, and who had denied the trust on oath.

6. Sed, *and besides.*

13. Quamvis levium, *"be they as light as they will."*

17. There was a **C. Fonteius Capito** who was consul A. D. 59 with C. Vipsanius Apronianus. There was another consul **Fonteius Capito** A. D. 67; and as he is named *first* of the two consuls of his year, and it was the custom to use the name of the first of the consuls in designating dates, many scholars think that he is the one here referred to. This supposition brings the date of this satire as far down as A. D. 127.

20. Sapientia, *philosophy*.

22. Jactare jugum. The opposite of Horace's *ferre jugum*.

25. Puxide = pyxide. Here for *poison;* the container for the thing contained.

27. Bæotian Thebes had seven gates, the Nile seven mouths.

28. I read **nona**, with most of the MSS., as do Hermann, Mayor, and Macleane. P has *nunc*, which Jahn, Ribbeck, and Weidner adopt. The division of the ages of the world into the golden, silver, bronze, and iron is well known. Juvenal says we have got down in the descending scale as far as the ninth age, for which nature herself has found no name nor any metal base enough to designate it. *Ninth* may be simply a humorous taking of a low number, or may involve an allusion to the Etruscan notion of ten ages, in which the last but one indicates the lowest degradation before the restoration of primitive innocence in the tenth.

31. Clamore, sc. *tanto*.

32 sq. Faesidius is an advocate, whose *clientes*, bribed by the *sportula*, come into court and applaud him loudly. Vocalis sportula is bold metonymy for the partakers of the dole: Heinrich translates, *die brüllenden Couverts;* Weidner, *die brüllende Tisch.*

33. Senior. This comparative has a diminutive force, and is used familiarly or kindly.

37. Rubenti. Red with the blood of victims.

40. Fugiens, as an exile. When Saturn was deposed by Jupiter, he went to Italy and engaged in tilling the earth.

41. Privatus adhuc, "not yet a public character."

43. Puer Iliacus. Ganymede. — Formonsa (formosa) **Herculis** uxor. Hebe.

44 sq. Et is awkward after nec, but it serves to connect *Herculis uxor* and *Vulcanus* closely together, making one picture of the two well-contrasted personages. "He comes in reeking from his work. She is at her task on Olympus, and hands him a cup to refresh him, which he first drains and then wipes off the **sweat**" and soot "from his black arms."

Liparaea nigra taberna, *sooty from his forge on Lipara.*

46. Sibi, *by himself.* Literally, for himself.

47. Talis ut = *tanta, quanta.*

48. Atlanta. Cf. Verg. *Aen.* iv. 482.

49. Profundi. I. e. the sea. Some refer it to Hades, to which they think the epithet *triste* is more appropriate. But the Romans, as Macleane says, had a great dread of the sea.

50. Pluto carried off his wife Proserpina from Sicily.

51. Reference is made to Ixion, Sisyphus, and Tityos.

54. Quo. So P, Jahn, Hermann, Ribbeck. Other readings, *hoc* (ς) Macleane, and *quod* (pω).

55. "Thou shalt rise up before the hoary head and honor the face of an old man."

57. Greater wealth is implied by larger stores of food. The *wild strawberries* and *acorns* indicate the simplicity of the times.

59. The order of the words in this verse is noticeable, — the first, third, and fifth go together, and the second, fourth, and sixth. *So fully was the first down held equal with sacred old age.*

62. Tuscis libellis. I. e. the books of the Etrurian soothsayers, in which, among other things connected with religion, various wonderful portents were set down.

63. Coronata, *garlanded* for sacrifice. — **Lustrari** = *procurari.*

64–70. Livy (xli. 26) speaks of a *two-headed boy* as a prodigy auguring evil. — **Miranti.** The plough is personified. (Jahn, Hermann, and Ribbeck read *mirandis*, with P.) — Theophrastus, Pliny, and Livy (xlii. 2), mention the digging up of sea-fish in the land. — **Fetae,** *with foal.* (Liv. xxxvii. 3; Spallanzi *Mem. sopra i Muli*, Modena, 1768, p. 8.) — **Uva,** *a cluster.* (Liv. xxi. 46; xxiv. 10; xxvii. 23. Plin. *N. H.* xi. 18, 55; Tac. *Ann.* xii. 64.) — **Amnis.** I. e. the Tiber. — **Miris** = prodigiosis, *unnatural.* Cf. Hor. *Epod.* xvi. 31.

73. Arcana. Given as a trust in secret: deposited, with the gods only as witnesses.

78. Tarpeia. I. e. of Jupiter Capitolinus.

79. Cirraei vatis. I. e. Apollo. Cirrha is near Delphi. Cf. vii. 64.

80. Venatricis puellae. Diana.

83. There is no need of inserting et at the end of the preceding verse, with Heinrich and Hermann. After two or more clauses connected by conjunctions, a third or last may be added without a conjunction, when, as here, it sums up everything in the genus to which the things spoken of in the preceding clauses belong, and thus comprehends them also.

84 sq. He says he will boil his son and eat his poor head, first dipping it in Egyptian vinegar (which was very strong), if he is not speaking the truth.

89. *Tangere aliquid* = to swear on something. Cf. Liv. xxi. 1: *tactis sacris* jure jurando adactum se.

91. Et, *and yet.* — Secum, *sc.* cogitat.

94. Quos abnego, *which I deny having received.*

95. Vomicae, *abscesses.* — Dimidium **crus**, *a broken leg* (cf. viii. 4; xv. 5, 57). According to Lewis, *a withered leg* (reduced to half its natural size).

96. Sunt **tanti**, *are worth bearing for their sake*, i. e. for the sake of the moneys (94); are not too great a price to pay. Cf. Cic. *in Cat.* i. 9; ii. 7. Madvig (*Opusc.* ii. 187–194) has given a masterly exposition of the various significations of the phrase *est tanti.*

Locupletem. I. e. *cum divitiis conjunctam.*

97–99. **Ladas** was the name of two celebrated victors in foot-races at the Olympic games, which were held on the plain of Olympia, near Pisa in Elis. The prize was a wreath of olive; the olive-branch of victory is called *hungry* because it bore no fruit, and was a mere worthless symbol. Anticyra, in Phocis, was the chief place whence *hellebore* was procured, the supposed remedy for insanity. **Archigenes** was a well-known physician. The last *e* is long, as in the Greek name. Juvenal introduces Greek proper names rather frequently. On Ladas's speed there is an epigram in the Anthology (N. 312):

Λάδας τὸ στάδιον εἴθ' ἦλατο εἴτε διέπτη,
δαιμόνιον τὸ τάχος οὐδὲ φράσαι δυνατόν.

99. **Praestat**, *brings in.*

100. "And after all, though the wrath of the gods be great, assuredly it is slow."—**Ut**, *grant that.*—100 sqq. "Because sentence against an evil work is not executed speedily, therefore the heart of the sons of men is fully set in them to do evil." For **tamen** certe we should have in good prose simply *tamen* or *certe*, or *at . . . certe.*

102. Sed, *besides.*

107. **Confirmat.** So Jahn and Ribbeck, with Sꜱ. Macleane and Kiær *confirmant* (Pω). Hermann *confirmans*, without MS. authority. Kiær makes *culpae* the subject of *confirmant.*

108. Trahere, *sc. te.* — **Vexare**, *to hustle.*

109. Superest, with the dative, "belongs in abundance to." Or as others, from a popular misuse of this word to which Gellius (i. 22) and Suetonius (*Aug.* 56) allude, we may translate it, "appears as the advocate of."

110 sq. "'T is as good as a play." He is acting just such a farce as the runaway slave in witty Catullus (or Catulus, a celebrated mime writer in the reigns of Caligula, Claudius, and Nero).

112 sq. Stentor was a Greek herald (Hom. *Il.* v. 785 sq.) whose shout was as loud as that of fifty other men together. Ares (**Gradivus**), when wounded by Diomed, roared as loudly as ten thousand men (Hom. *Il.* v. 859 sq.).

116 sqq. Carbone. I. e. altar-fire.—Charta soluta, *from the opened paper* (i. e. *wrapper*).—There is a slight tone of sarcastic depreciation in Juvenal's reference to the sacrifice here, as in x. 354 sq.

119. Vagellius. Some unknown man, of whom the scholiast says, "stultissimus accepit statuam." The same name occurs xvi. 23.

120. Ferre, *to offer.*

121. Et qui, *even one who.* Ribbeck, *is qui.*

122. The Cynics wore no tunic under their pallium.

123. Suspicit (looks from under at, looks up to), *admires.*—Epicurus, according to Pliny (*H. N.* xix. 4), was the first to plant a garden at Athens. In this garden he taught.

124. Dubii, *in a critical state.*—Notice the absence of the preposition a from **medicis.** Cf. i. 13, note.

125. Philippus may be, as most of the commentators say, some obscure practitioner; but the name is that of the celebrated physician of Alexander the Great, who certainly belonged to the *medici majores.* The emphasis is on discipulo, *even to a raw apprentice.*

129. Claudenda est janua, as in the case of a death in the house; for the loss of money is something still more dreadful!

132 sq. "He is not content to tear only the top of his tunic instead of rending it from top to bottom, and to torment his eyes with forced tears (crocodile's tears)."

135. Cuncta fora, all the courts. There were several *fora* at Rome at this time; but the three in which the most legal business was done were the Forum Romanum, Forum Julium, and Forum Augusti.

136 sqq. If, when the bond has been read over ten times on the opposite side, they whom their own handwriting and seal convict, declare their note of hand to be void and the tablets worthless.—Diversa parte, i. e. by the advocates of the other party (the creditors). So Madvig. Others, on both sides; both parties pass the document back and forth, and the debtor pretends to examine the document honestly, to see if it is genuine. Macleane, "in various places, i. e. in all the fora," connecting the words with the main assertion *dicunt,* etc.—Ligni, the waxed tablets of thin deal on which they wrote.

138, 139. The seal used by the man who denies his bond is carved on the choicest of sardonyxes, kept in an ivory purse. Pliny (*H. N.*

xxxvii. 6) says that the sardonyx was the principal gem employed for seals.

140. Ten' = *te-ne.* — **O delicias,** *my sweet sir.*

141. Gallinae filius albae = *feliciter natus,* white being the lucky color. So the French proverb, *le fils de la poule blanche.*

144. Si flectas, *if you'll turn.* The subjunctive suggests a prior clause like this : *as you'll see.*

147, 149. Vetus is used of what has **been** in existence for a long time ; **antiquus** of what existed in old time.

148. Adorandae robiginis. I. e. of venerable antiquity.

150–152. Exstat, *there starts up.* — **Qui radat.** Subjunctive of the purpose. — **Bratteolam** = bracteolam.

153. I have adopted Mayor's emendation, **solitumst** (solitum est), which makes sense of a passage which commentators have considered as hopeless. *It is a common custom to melt down a whole statue of the Thunderer* (i. e. Jove). The common reading is *solitus,* with either no pause after *dubitet,* or nothing but a comma.

154. Mercatorem, *the purchaser.*

155 sq. " The man who should be launched into the sea in a bull's hide," is a parricide. **Cf. viii. 213 sq.,** note.

157. Haec quota pars, *how small a part is this ?* Cf. iii. 61, note. — **Custos urbis** = *praefectus urbi,* an officer who at this time held almost the whole criminal jurisdiction of the city (Tac. *Ann.* vi. 10– 11). C. Rutilius Gallicus was praefectus urbi in the reign of Domi- tian, and his name may be used for that of the praefect at the later day when this satire was written.

161. Veneris. Future perfect.

162. Tumidum guttur. The goître.

164 sq. Cf. Tac. *Germ.* 4 ; Hor. *Epod.* xvi. 7. — **Flavam . . . cirro,** *at his hair, of yellow hue, and making twisted horns with its moist- ened locks.* Cf. Tac. *Germ.* 38. So Kiær. Commentators generally have supplied *Germanum* for *torquentem.*

167 sqq. Ad, *to meet.* Cf. Hand *Turs.* i. 84. — **Thracum volucres** are the cranes, of which *Threiciae, Strymoniae,* are constant epithets " In the East," says Macleane, " the *sudden* (subitas) appearance of *clouds* of birds, no one can tell where from, when any prey is to be got, is very surprising. The *cry* of the crane is such that the flock may be heard very high up in the air after it has passed out of sight." — The fabulous people of the *pygmies* lived in India, or at the sources of the Nile. On their battles with the cranes, cf. Hom. *Il.* iii. 3–7.— **Sed illic,** etc. However frequently such sights occur, and however numerous the spectators, nobody laughs, because *all* the pygmy warriors are small enough to be carried off by a crane. — Pede uno. The pygmies were a Greek πυγμή in height, or thirteen and a half inches.

175. Graviore catena. Modal ablative (of description).

178. Sospes. Cf. Hor. *Carm.* i. 36, 4: Hesperia *sospes* ab ultima.

179. Invidiosa, *full of odium.* You will be detested for taking so cruel revenge.

181. What verb is to be supplied, of which indocti is the subject?

183. Adeo, *in fact.*

185. Dulci. Hymettus was and is famed for its honey. — **Senex.** Socrates.

194. Surdo verbere, *with the noiseless lash.* Cf. Pers. vi. 28. So *caeca* for *invisible*, as caeca saxa.

195. Animo, (tamquam) tortore, flagellum quatiente.

197. The scholiast says that **Caedicius** was a courtier and most cruel satellite of Nero. Take *gravis* with *Caedicius*.

198. Cf. Ausonius:

Turpe quid ausurus te sine teste time.

And Sen. *Ep.* xliii.: Si honesta sunt quae facis, omnes sciant; si turpia, quid refert neminem scire cum tu scias? O te miserum, si contemnis hunc testem!

199-208. The story is told in Herodotus (vi. 86). A person named Glaucus bore the highest reputation for honesty in all Sparta. A man of Miletus came to him and said that, in consequence of his reputation for just dealing, he wished to deposit half his fortune with him. Glaucus accepted the deposit, and promised to restore the money to any one who should produce certain tokens and claim it. This the man's sons afterwards did, but Glaucus professed to have forgotten all about the matter, and required four months to refresh his memory. When he consulted the oracle at Delphi as to whether he might not keep the money and swear he had never received it, an answer was returned denouncing dreadful punishment on the breaker of oaths; and Glaucus, begging pardon of the god, paid the money. The priestess warned him that he who tempts God is as bad as he who does the wickedness which it is in his mind to do. Terrific punishment came; and the whole house of Glaucus became extinct. (Macleane.)

200 sq. Quondam, *one day;* (at some future time). — **Dubitaret retinere,** *he hesitated about keeping back.*

205 sq. Probavit extinctus. We should say, "his death, with that of all his relations, proved."

207. "And his relatives, although derived from a remote *common stock*" (or collateral line).

211. Nec mensae tempore. Post-classical for *ne mensae quidem tempore.*

212. Ut morbo, as from disease; i. e. as from fever.

213. Difficili crescente cibo, when his food, hard to swallow, seems to swell between his teeth. — **Setina.** Herel's conjecture, adopted by Jahn, Hermann, Ribbeck. The MSS. *sed vina.*

215. Melius, sc. *vinum.*

218. Jam, *at last.*

221. Tua sacra imago, *thy awful apparition.*

226. Vindicet. So Ribbeck and Weidner, after ς *Serv. Aen.* iv. 209; vi. 179. The ordinary reading is *judicet* (Pω).

228. Hoc dilata sereno, put off by this short lull. The ominous character of the first lull, says Macleane, is well known by all those who have witnessed a tropical storm.

234. Nocentibus aegris, *the sick if they be guilty.* (Macleane.) Weidner remarks that *nocens,* as compared with *noxius,* denotes an *habitual* quality.

235. The life of any animal that could be offered in sacrifice were worth more than his.

236. Malorum. Masculine; (*of the wicked.*)

237. Superest constantia. "They have resolution enough and to spare."

244 sq. In laqueum. I. e. to be strangled. Cf. Sall. *Cat.* 55: laqueo gulam fregere. — The body was dragged out of the prison with the uncus. — Other interpretations are, of *in laqueum,* "into the snare" (i. e. of temptation, or "he will be caught in his guilt"), and of *uncum,* "the hook or ring in the prison wall to which the culprit's chains are attached."

246. Places of exile are here referred to, as Gyaros, Seriphos.

248. Nominis, *person,* man.

249. Tiresias, the Theban prophet, was *blind.*

⁂ Macleane remarks upon the subject of this satire: "There never was a time when conscience did not exist in the mind of man, however completely the habit of guilt may have seared it in some, and given a color of innocence to wickedness in the judgment of whole communities. The picture Juvenal draws is taken from ex-

W

perience, the experience of those who were no Christians, and had no knowledge to deter them but that which was suggested from within. If we are surprised to read in Juvenal language or sentiments which, if delivered from a Christian pulpit, would be appropriate and searching, it is because we are apt to forget that human nature, with its desires, its corruptions, and its self-deceptions, has always been the same in the main, and that God has never been without his witness against guilt in the heart of man. This satire represents the common moral sense of mankind. The law of Christianity *confirms* the unwritten law of which conscience has always been the guardian and the exponent, and of which such writings as Juvenal's, especially this poem, are the clearest evidence."

SATIRE XIV.

———o◦⊃❂⊂◦o———

ARGUMENT.

1–30. THERE'S many a wrong act, Fuscinus, which is taught both by precept and example. The old man games, his boy too shakes the dice. What hope is there of him who learns in youth to season fig-peckers and mushrooms? Give him a thousand teachers, he will never cease to be a gourmand. Does Rutilus train his son to gentleness, holding that servants and masters are one flesh, or cruelty, when all he loves is the sweet sound of the lash, the monster of his trembling household, happiest when a wretched slave is tortured for a trifle? What does he teach his boy who loves the grating of the chain, the brand, the workhouse?

31–43. It is but nature; home examples come with great authority, and so corrupt more speedily than any. One or two of better sort may spurn them, but others follow in their elders' footsteps and the old track of crime long put before them. So keep from wrong, if for no other reason, yet for this, that those who are born of us will imitate our faults, for all are teachable in vice; a Catiline you'll find in every town, a Cato or a Brutus nowhere.

44–85. Let nothing evil come near the young. Great reverence is due to boys. If you are meditating wickedness, think not the child too young to see it. Whatever wrong you do, he'll grow up like you not in face alone, and stature, but in morals, and follow in your footsteps: and after this you'll punish him and disinherit him forsooth! When guests are coming, you will sweep your house and scold and rave for fear a speck of dirt offend the company, and yet you take no care that your son should see his home all spotless. You give your country a great boon if you shall make him a good citizen. It matters much how you shall train him up. The bird when fledged will seek the food his mother brought him in the nest.

86–95. Cetronius took to building everywhere grand marble houses, and so broke his fortune: but he left his son no small inheritance, which he wasted in his turn in building finer houses than his father. **96–106.** The father shows respect to the Jews' worship, the son becomes a Jew and goes all lengths with the law of Moses.

107–134. But though the young are prone to imitate all other vices, to avarice they're actually forced against their will. It looks too

255

much like a virtue, to attract them of itself. They 're cheated with
the show of gravity it wears, the praise it wins for carefulness and
skill in getting. These are the craftsmen to make fortunes grow!
Yes, anyhow, the forge and anvil working on forever. The father,
too, thinks only misers happy, and bids his boys go on that road
with those philosophers. All vices have their rudiments, in these
he trains them first and afterwards they learn the insatiable desire
for money. He pinches his slaves' bellies and his own : saves up the
fragments and puts them under seal for next day's supper, a meal
the beggars would not share.

135-151. What worth is money got at such a price? What madness is it to live a pauper's life in order to die rich ! As money grows,
the love of it grows too. He wants it least who has it not. So you
go adding house to house and field to field, and if your neighbor will
not sell, you send your beasts to eat his crops. 'T is thus that many
properties change owners.

152-172. But what will people say? "And what care I for that?
I do not value at a beanshell all the world's praise, if I am to be
poor to earn it." Then you are to escape the pains and cares of life
and live for many a year, because you 've land as much as Rome
possessed when Tatius reigned! And after that two jugera was
counted ample for old soldiers broken in the wars, and they were
well content. For us 't is not enough for pleasure-ground.

173-255. Hence come more murders than from any cause, for he
who would be rich would be so quickly. And who that hastens to
be rich cares aught for laws? The old Sabellian spake thus to his
sons : " Be happy with your cottages and mountains : let the plough
get us bread ; so shall we please the country gods, whose help and
favor got us corn for acorns. That man commits no crimes who
wears rough boots and clothes himself in hides. Outlandish purples
lead to every crime." Now all is changed : the father wakes his
son at midnight. "Up, get out your tablets, write, read, study law,
petition for a centurionship : let the commander see you rough and
hairy. Go fight, and in your sixtieth year you 'll get the eagle. Or
if your courage fails turn merchant : don't be particular, stinking
hides will do. Money smells sweet wherever it may come from.
The poet's words be ever on your lips, well worthy of the gods and
Jove himself, — 'whence you get no one asks, but get you must.'"
This is what nurses teach, the boys and girls learn this before their
alphabet. When I hear fathers urging thus their sons, I answer,
What need of all this haste? I warrant you the pupil will outstrip
his teacher. Make yourself easy, he 'll surpass his father, as Ajax
Telamon, Achilles Peleus. He 's young, when he begins to shave
he 'll swear and lie for a mere trifle. Woe to his wife if she is rich !
He knows a shorter way to wealth than ranging sea and land. Crime
is no trouble. "I never taught him this," you 'll say some day.
But you 're the cause of all his wickedness. Who trains his son to
avarice gives him the reins, and if he tries to check him he refuses,
and spurns his driver and the goal. He thinks it not enough to err
as far as you will let him. Tell him the man's a fool who helps his
friend, teach him to rob and cheat, by every crime get money, which
you love as ever patriot loved his country, and then you 'll see the

spark yourself have lighted blown to a flame and carry **all before it**:
you'll not escape yourself, the lion you have reared **will tear his**
keeper. Your horoscope is told, you say: but he'll not **wait, he'll**
weary of your obstinate old age. Buy yourself antidotes, **such as**
kings and fathers should take before their meals.

256-302. No play is half so good as to look on and see **what risk**
they run to increase their store. Can the petaurista or the rope-dancer
amuse us more than he who lives **at sea,** a wretched trafficker in
perfumed bags **or raisin wine from Crete?** The dancer does it for a
livelihood, you **but for countless** gold **and houses. The sea** is full of
ships; more **men** there than ashore; **wherever** gain may call them
there they **go.** A fine return for **all your** toil, to come with full
purse back and **boast** you've seen **the monsters** of the deep. Madness may vary, **but** that man is **mad** who fills his ship and risks his
life for silver cut in little heads **and letters.** The clouds are lower-
ing; "'t is nothing," cries the master, "**mere summer** thunder," and
that night perhaps his ship is lost **and he himself must** swim for
life; and he who thought **the gold of** Tagus and Pactolus little,
must beg in rags, carrying **with** him the picture of **his wreck.**

303-331. What danger gets, anxiety must guard. Licinus posts
his regiment of slaves with buckets all the night, in terror for his
plate and marble **and all his finery.** The Cynic's tub burns not;
break it, and he will make **another or** patch up the old one. So
Alexander, when he saw the man who made that tub his home, then
learnt how happier far **was he who wanted nothing,** than he who
coveted a world and **went through every toil to get it.** All gods are
there where Prudence is; 't is we who **make Fortune a** goddess. If
any ask me what is the measure of a private fortune, I tell them just
as much as nature wants, or Epicurus for his little garden, or Socrates
before him. Nature and Philosophy always speak alike. But if I
seem too hard upon you, mix a little **from our** habits with the old.
Make up a knight's fortune: if that be not enough, then two, or even
three. If that does not suffice, then will not Croesus's treasures or
Persia's kingdom **or** Narcissus's wealth.—MACLEANE, *with modifications.*

------

1. **Fuscinus.** Some friend of Juvenal, unknown to us.

2. **Nitidis rebus.** "The minds of the children, in their first innocence, are the '*bright things.*'"

5. **Bullatus.** Cf. v. 164, note. —**Fritillus** is a *dice-box.* —**Arma,** i.
e. the dice. Cf. Verg. *Aen.* i. 177: Cerealiaque arma expediunt.

7. **Radere tubera terrae,** *to peel truffles.*

9. **Ficellas** (= ficedulas). So Mayor, after Lachmann. The MSS.
ficedulas, which alone will be found in the Lexicons. The *beccafico*
was the only bird of which epicures allowed the whole to be eaten.

10. **Monstrante,** *showing the way.*

12. **Barbatos.** Beards were much affected by those who set up for
philosophers.

15. Modicis erroribus aequos, *indulgent to small transgressions.* Cf. Hor. *Sat.* i. 3, 118, 140.

16 sq. Nostra is taken with **materia.** On the sentiment cf. Macrob. I. xi. 6 : tibi autem unde in servos tantum et tam inane fastidium, quasi non ex eisdem tibi et constent et alantur elementis eundemque spiritum ab eodem principio carpant?

18. Rutilus. Some father. Hardly the same person as in xi. 2.

19. Nullam Sirena. I. e. *no Siren's song.*

20. *The Antiphates and the Polyphemus of his trembling household.* **Antiphates,** the grewsome king of the Laestrygones, ate up one of the three men whom Ulysses sent out as explorers, and sunk all his ships but one. (*Odys.* x. 80–132.) The story of the cyclops **Polyphemus** (*Odys.* ix. 182–542; *Aen.* iii. 618 sqq.) is well known.

22. Duo propter lintea, *for the loss of a couple of towels.*

24. Inscripta ergastula, *the branded slaves in the workhouse.* (Cf. viii. 180, note.) In **ergastula** we have a bold metonymy, — the container for the thing contained. **Inscriptus** is not found elsewhere in Juvenal in the sense of *branded,* but is so used by Pliny, Martial, and Gellius. The common word is *inustus* or *compunctus.*

33. Cum subeant. Subjunctive as giving the reason. Pg, *subeunt.*

35. The **Titan** is Prometheus, (a son of the Titan Iapetus,) the fabled creator of the human race.

38 sq. Hujus .... **est,** *for there is at least one reason that commands this* (i. e. to keep clear from grievous sins).

43. The *uncle of Brutus* was Cato Uticensis.

45. A (ah) is the interjection. It is a conjecture of Cramer's, adopted by the best editors. The MSS. have *hinc, hanc, ac* (P).

46. The *parasite that makes a night of it* is "the contemptible guest who for a dinner sits up all night drinking or gaming, or both, and singing low songs."

49. Notice the hiatus before the caesura in the third arsis.

52 sq. Qui .... **peccet,** one to follow in your steps and exaggerate all your faults.

55. Tabulas. I. e. *your will.*

56. Unde tibi frontem, etc. On the ellipsis, cf. Hor. *Sat.* ii. 7, 16 : unde mihi lapidem? ... unde sagittas?

57 sq. Vacuum .... **quaerat.** You are mad, and want cupping. The cupping-glass is called *windy,* perhaps from the pressure of the external air. In the Middle Ages the adjective *ventosa* itself became a noun signifying a cupping-glass, and hence the Italian *ventosa* and French *ventouse*.

59. Tuorum, sc. *famulorum*.

62. **Leve**, *plain*. — **Aspera**, *embossed*.

67. Saw-dust was thrown before sweeping, like our **tea-leaves**.

68 sqq. An *argumentum ex contrario*. — Omni sine labe, for *sine ulla labe*, is post-classical.

71. Utilis **agris**. The art of agriculture was held in very high esteem, and its importance for the national welfare recognized.

75. **Devia** = deserta.

77. **Crucibus**. The crosses bearing bodies of malefactors. ·

80 sqq. In point of fact, vultures build their nests in rocks, and eagles (*famulae Jovis et generosae aves*) are scarcely more delicate in the choice of their food than vultures. Juvenal follows popular tradition, often against the facts of natural history; thus he speaks of beavers as mutilating themselves (xii. 34), ants as laying up stores for winter (vi. 361), cranes as having talons (xiii. 169), elephants as shedding their tusks when they have grown too heavy (xi. 126), the ibis as eating snakes (xv. 3), and tigers and boars as never fighting among each other (**xv.** 160 sqq.).

83. **Levavit**. So Priscian, Ribbeck, Weidner. Hermann reads *levabit* (ω), Jahn and Mayor, *levarit*, P *levaret*.

86. **Aedificator**, *passionately fond of building*. The verbal substantive in *-or* implies a continued and constantly repeated activity in the actor. Cf. Nägelsbach *Stil.* § 54.

90. There was an ancient and celebrated temple of Fortuna at Praeneste, and one of **Hercules** at Tibur, whence the town is often called *Herculeum*.

91. **Posides** was a freedman and favorite of Claudius. Pliny mentions the *aquae Posidianae*, a splendid bathing-house on the shore at Baiae. — **Capitolia**. Pluralis majestatis.

94. Turbavit, *squandered*.

96–106. With Juvenal's account of the Jews, cf. Tac. *Hist.* v. 4, 5.

96. **Metuere** and metus are the words used for *religious* fear.

103. **Non monstrare**, sc. *solent* or *consueverunt*. Juvenal says that the Jews will not show any one the way except he be of their faith, nor tell the tired traveller, if he be uncircumcised, where he may quench his thirst.

110. **Habitu**, *in bearing*. — **Vultuque et veste severum**, *severe both in countenance and attire*.

114. The two dragons referred to are the one that watched the

Hesperides, as they watched the golden apples, and the one that guarded the golden fleece of Colchis in Pontus.

115 sq. Adquirendi artificem, "*an adept in the art of getting rich.*"

117. Crescunt quocumque modo. Hor. *Epp.* i. 1, 65 : rem facias, rem; si possis, recte, si non, quocumque modo rem.

119. Et pater ergo, *and so the father too.*

120 sq. Madvig would read (with inferior MSS.) *mirantur, putant.*

126. Modio iniquo. Cf. *Dig.* xix. 1, 32 : *iniquis ponderibus.* Slaves had a certain allowance of corn, olives, dates, figs, vinegar, and wine, either by the month or the day.

127. Neque enim sustinet umquam, for indeed he can never bear.

129 sq. Medio Septembri. In the very season when the heat was excessive and the air pestilential.

131. Lacertus. A coarse sea-fish, eaten in summer dried or salted. Translate, *salt-fish.*

132. Signatam, *sealed up,* so that the slaves could not eat it.—**Siluro,** *sheat-fish.* Cf. iv. 33.

133. Fila, *shreds,* slices. Weidner translates it, *blades.* — Sectivi porri. Cf. iii. 293, note.

134. Aliquis de ponte, *any beggar from the bridge.* Cf. iv. 116, note; v. 8, note.

135. Sed quo, sc. *habes* or *possides.* Cf. viii. 9, note.

140. The subject of **optat** is *qui non habet.*

142 sq. Major et melior. Sc. than your own.

144. Densa qui canet oliva, *which is hoary with the thickly-planted olive.* The hoary, gray, silvery, *dusky* hue of their foliage, makes olive-trees a very striking and peculiar feature in a landscape.

147. Hujus, refers to dominus (**145**).

152. Quam . . . famae, "*what a foul blast will rumor blow!*" — P (alone) has *foede,* and so Jahn and Ribbeck; but even in P, as Hermann says, it may be that *foede* stands for *foedae.*

155. Secantem, while reaping *merely.*

156. Scilicet, of course; *no doubt.* Sarcastic.

160. Tatius is the legendary Sabine king under whom and Romulus the Romans and Sabines formed one united kingdom.

162. The **Molossi** were a people of **Epirus.** Pyrrhus is called *rex Molossus* xii. 108.

165 sq. Ingratae curta fides patriae, a scant discharge of her promise on the part of their thankless country.

169. The slave played with his *three young masters;* the title do-

minus being given to *a master's son* as well as to a master. Cf. Plaut.
Capt. Prol. 18.

178. **Properantis.** Cf. Prov. xxviii. 22: He that *hasteth to be rich*
hath an evil eye.

180 sq. The people mentioned were all of that Sabellian stock
which was proverbial for severity and simplicity in its way of living.

187. **Inversis.** I. e. *with the hair inside.* — **Peregrina purpura.**
Phoenician, Laconian, and African purples were most esteemed.

188. **Quaecumque est** indicates at once disdain for, and ignorance
of, the foreign innovation.

191. **Accipe,** "*here, take!*"

192. **Rubras leges.** The titles and beginnings of laws were written
in red, with ink made of *minium*, vermilion, or *rubrica*, red ochre.
Hence *rubrica* came to mean the civil law ; hence too our word *rubric.*

193. **Vitem,** *the vine-switch* of the centurion (viii. 247, note), used
here for a centurion's commission. — **Libello,** a *petition.*

195. **Laelius** is put for the commander of the troops to whom the petition would be referred. Let him see what a stalwart fellow you are ;
(for it was thought well that centurions should be big and burly.)

197. **Locupletem aquilam.** " The *primipilus centurio* had charge
of the *eagle* of the legion, and was above all the centurions in rank
and *pay.* Lipsius says they rose from the lowest grade to the highest
by rotation, except in cases of extraordinary merit. The ten cohorts
of the legion consisted of thirty *manipuli*, and in each *manipulus*
there were two centurions."

199. **Solvunt,** *relax.* — **Solvunt ventrem.** "A common result,"
says Lewis, "of the first sound of cannon in modern actions."

201. **Pluris dimidio.** For more than half as much again as it cost
you.

202. Trades of an offensive kind, such as tanning, had to be carried
on *Tiberim ultra*, i. e. in the Trastevere.

206. **Poeta,** *as its author.*

208. **Vetulae assae,** *old dry-nurses.*

212. **Praesto,** *I warrant.* — **Meliorem,** sc. fore.

215 sq. **Nondum** . . . nequitiae, "the evils of matured vice have
not yet filled the marrow of their bones."

217. **Cultri,** *of the razor.*

218 sq. There are three possible translations of vendet perjuria
summa exigua: " he will sell his perjuries for a trifling sum ;" "he
will perjure himself most heavily for a trifle ;" or "he will perjure
himself in any way you like, little or great."—**Et,** *even ;* and that too.

219. Tangens pedem. Like devotees.

220 sq. Elatam, *borne out to burial.* — **Limina subit.** The bride, on entering her new home, was lifted across the threshold.

224. Magni sceleris, *in the case of* a great crime. Cf. Cic. *Tusc.* iv. 6, 14 : *praesentis* autem *mali* sapientis affectio nulla est.

227-231. Pueros producit avaros, *schools his sons in avarice.* — Conduplicare, sc. *praecepit.* — Commentators generally confess themselves unable to extract any sense from verse 229. Kiær meets the difficulty by considering verses 227, 228, and 229–231 (curriculo) as containing two parallel statements; *nam . . . amorem* is the first protasis, *et . . . avaros* the first apodosis; *et . . . conduplicare* is the second protasis, *dat . . . curriculo* the second apodosis. With this interpretation et in verse **228** must be taken as equivalent to *etiam.*

231. Quem must be regarded as a careless expression, in a carelessly written satire, **referring to** *juvenis,* or some such word suggested by *curriculo* or by the whole phrase *dat . . . curriculo.*

238. Quarum amor, sc. *tantus est.* Before the correlative adjectives *qualis* and *quantus,* Juvenal almost always omits *talis* and *tantus.*

240. Menœceus, son of Creon, gave his life for his country when the seven came against Thebes.

241. Quorum is used as if *Thebani* had preceded, and not *Thebas.*

243. Tubicen. To give the signal for battle.

244. Ergo, *so then* (as I was saying).

247. Leo alumnus, *the lion you have reared.* — **Tollet,** *will make way with,* will destroy.

249. Colus. The distaff of the Fates.

251. Cervina. Hesiod (according to Pliny, *H. N.* vii. 48) attributes to the raven nine lives of man, to the stag four lives of a raven, and to the crow three lives of a stag. To man he gives ninety-six years.

252. Archigenes was a celebrated physician of this period, a Greek, born in Syria. — **Mithridates VI.,** king of Pontus, was in the habit of taking antidotes, and had so fortified his constitution by their means, that when he wished to poison himself he could not, and was obliged to get a soldier to kill him.

257. Praetoris. Cf. viii. 194, note. The praetor presided at the *ludi scenici* in the time of the emperors. He is called *lautus* on account of the magnificence of the games.

258. Discrimine. Ablative of price. — **Constent,** *cost.*

260 sq. The **temple of Castor** was in the Forum Romanum, and near it the bankers had their places of business. They kept the cash-chests of their customers in this temple, where there were sentries. The temple of **Mars Ultor**, in the Forum Augusti, had been used (it would seem) as a place of deposit of this kind, but it had been robbed, or possibly damaged by fire (Weidner), and Mars had lost his helmet *also*, as well as other treasures.

262 sq. The festival of Flora was celebrated at Rome from the 28th April till the 3d May, every year. The Cerealia were held in the middle of April. On the festival of **Cybele**, also in April, the Megalesian games (cf. xi. 193) were celebrated. At each of these festivals there were dramatic representations. — Aulaea. I. e. *the plays*.

265. Petauro. A flying-machine, or stage from which persons took flying leaps.

266. **Rectum funem,** *the tight-rope*.

267. **Corycus** was the name of a city and promontory in Cilicia. There was a promontory of the same name in Crete.

271. Passum, *raisin-wine*. See Lexicon, s. v. *pando*. — **Lagonas** = lagenas. They are called "*compatriots of Jove*" from the tradition of the education, and even of the birth and burial, of Jupiter in Crete. When the people of Crete asked aid of America in their attempt to throw off the Mohammedan yoke, they began their appeal with the words, "We, the descendants of Minos and of Jupiter."

273 sq. Illa mercede = illius rei mercede. — **Illa reste,** i. e. *recto fune* (266).

274 sq. Tu . . . temerarius. The rope-dancer hazards his life to avoid starvation; you hazard yours for superfluities.

280. **Herculeo gurgite.** In the Atlantic. "Posidonius and Epicurus pretended that when the sun sank in the Atlantic, it hissed like red-hot iron plunged into water. According to the popular belief, the Sacrum Promontorium, on the Atlantic coast of Hispania, now *Cape St. Vincent*, was the place where the sun plunged with his chariot into the sea."

283. **Juvenes marinos.** Tritons, Nereids, and the like.

284 sq. **Non unus furor,** not one *kind only of* madness. — **Ille.** I. e. Orestes. — **Sororis.** I. e. Electra, who throws her arms around her brother to prevent him from leaping from his couch in his terror at the apparition of the Furies. The scene is from the Orestes of Euripides. — Igni. I. e. the torches.

286. **Hic.** I. e. Ajax. The scene is from the Aias of Sophocles.

287. **Ithacum.** I. e. Ulysses. — **Parcat . . . lacernis.** Though he may not tear his clothing, like some other lunatics.

288. **Curatoris.** In accordance with the provisions of the Twelve

Tables, a curator or *guardian* was appointed by the praetor in the cases of persons of unsound mind. Cf. Hor. *Epp.* i. 1, 102, 103.

289. Ad summum latus, to the topmost edge: i. e. *to the very top of the bulwarks.* — **Tabula distinguitur unda,** *is separated from the water by a* single *plank :*

> "digitis a morte remotus
> quattuor aut septem, si sit latissima taeda." —*Sat.* xii. 58 sq.

291. Silver cut up into small coins, having on them the "image and superscription" of the emperor.

292. Solvite funem, *loose the cable.* Cf. Verg. *Aen.* iii. 266 sq.

294. Fascia nigra, this black streak or *black belt* of clouds.

298, Modo, *but now.*

300. Sufficient, sc. *ei,* the antecedent of *cujus* (298).

301 sq. Shipwrecked men had paintings made of the scene of their misfortune, and carried them around with them to gain sympathy and alms. — **Picta se tempestate tuetur,** *maintains himself by a painting of the storm.*

305. Amis = *hāmis.* — "In the days of the empire there were seven cohorts of night police, whose business it was to ensure to the citizens protection from fire. The wealthy, however, who kept an immense number of slaves (cf. iii. 141), did not trust to this common protection, but had their own private watchman (here *cohortem servorum*). Nero ordered all who could afford it to keep *custodes et subsidia reprimendis ignibus in propatulo* (Tac. *Ann.* vi. 43). They were furnished with *hamae* — buckets filled with water — and with *siphones,* and other instruments for checking conflagrations."

306. Attonitus, "wild with fear."

307 sq. Electro. Cf. v. 38. — **Signis.** Cf. viii. 110. — **Phrygia.** Synnada, in Phrygia, was famed for its marble. — **Ebore.** Cf. xi. 123 sqq. — **Testudine.** Cf. xi. 94 sq. It was common to inlay furniture with tortoise-shell. Or *lata testudo* may refer to the vaulted and highly ornamented roof of the palace.

308 sqq. Dolia. The "tub" of Diogenes was made of clay. If any one broke it, he could make another next day, nay more, he could patch the old one with lead. — **Commissa,** *soldered.*

311 sqq. The story of Alexander's visit to Diogenes, and how the Cynic told him not to stand between him and the sun, when asked if there was anything that could be done for him, is told by Plutarch (*Alex.* 14).

319. Hortis. Cf. xiii. 123, note.

320. The extreme frugality of Socrates's mode of life was appealed to by himself in proof of his disinterestedness (*Apol.* xviii.), and is attested by Xenophon and Aristophanes.

322. Cludere = claudere. "Do I seem to confine you by too rigid examples?"

323. Nostris, *our* (*modern*).

324. On the *fourteen rows* and *the law of Otho*, cf. iii. 154, note.

325. If this makes you knit your brow and pout your lip.

326. Duodecies sestertium was the census senatorius.

327. Gremium. The fold of the toga (*sinus*), in which the purse was commonly carried. Cf. vii. 215. — Ultra, i. e. for more.

329. Narcissus was the chief favorite of Claudius Caesar. He made a fortune of about four million of our money. It was he, and not Claudius, who ordered the death of Messalina. The subject of paruit is Claudius. Cf. Plin. *Epp.* viii. 6: imaginare Caesarem liberti precibus vel potius imperio . . obtemperantem.

X

SATIRE XV.

———○○⦂●⦂○○———

ARGUMENT.

1-32. ALL know, **Volusius**, the monsters Egypt worships, here 't is the crocodile, the ibis there; the long-tailed ape at Thebes where Memnon strikes his lyre; cats, river-fish, and dogs (but not Diana). Onions and leeks no tooth may harm. O holy people, whose gods grow in their gardens! A sheep or goat they may not eat, but human flesh they may. When once Ulysses told such marvellous tales to Alcinous and his guests, some more sober than the rest no doubt were wroth, and would have thrown him into the sea, with his tales about Laestrygones and Cyclopes. His Scylla and his clashing rocks and bladders full of storms and comrades turned to swine, were not so hard to swallow. He had no witness to support him; but my story, a crime not known in all the tragedies, was acted publicly the other day.

33-71. Two neighboring peoples, Ombites and Tentyrites, have long fallen out with deadly hatred, only for this, that each maintain there are no other gods but those they worship. It was a holiday at Ombi, a fit occasion for the enemy, who were resolved to spoil their seven days' sport (for these barbarians vie with the infamous Canopus in good living): and they expected easy victory when they were drenched with wine. On one side there was dancing, flowers, perfumes (such as they were); on the other, hatred and an empty belly. First, they cry out words of abuse, with hot courage; this is the trump of battle. Then they charge with mutual shout: their weapons are their fists; scarce any cheeks were left without a wound, or any nose unbroken. Faces contused you 'd see throughout the host, cheeks burst and bones all starting through the skin, fists reeking with the blood of eyes knocked out. But this is child's play: what use is such a crowd of combatants if none are killed? So they grow fiercer and throw stones, not such as Turnus, Ajax, or Tydides threw, but such as men can wield in these degenerate days, when all are bad and puny, so that heaven laughs at men and hates them.

72-92. But to return. One party reinforced get bold and ply the sword and bow; and Tentyra flies, as they pursue. One slips and falls in his haste; they take him prisoner and cut him up and eat him raw. How lucky they profaned not the holy element! But they who ate had never a more happy meal. Don't think it was the first taste only that was sweet; the last man when the carcase was

266

all gone, scraped up the blood on the ground and licked it from his fingers.

93-131. Vascones, they tell us, lengthened life by food like this: but that was fortune's spite and war's extremity, a long blockade and famine. Such cases we should pity, when, after all their food is gone to the last blade of grass, men eat each other, as they would themselves: these gods and men may pardon, as the ghosts would do of those they've eaten. Zeno may teach us all things must not be done even for life; but how should they be Stoics, and that in old Metellus's time? Now all the world have got our learning and the Grecian too. Gaul teaches Britain how to plead, and Thule talks of hiring soon a rhetorician. But yet that noble people and Saguntum had some excuse for what they did. But Egypt was more savage than the Tauric altar; for there (if we're to trust the story) the goddess only sacrificed the men, and nothing more. What led these people to their crime, what accident, blockade, or famine? Suppose the Nile had left the country dry, what greater insult could they show the god? The Cimbri, Britones, and Scythians were never yet so savage as this useless cowardly herd, who swarm upon the river in their painted boats. No punishment is hard enough for those whose passion is as bad as famine.

131-174. Nature has given soft hearts to men, as tears will prove. She bids us weep for friends in sorrow, for the poor wretch on trial for his life, or boy, that brings his fraudulent guardian to justice, with weeping face and streaming hair. She bids us weep when a young maiden dies or little babe. What good man and true but counts all human miseries his own? 'T is this distinguishes us men from beasts; for this we've minds to take in things divine and exercise all arts; and sense from heaven, which they have not who look down to the earth. They've breath but we have soul, so that sympathy bids us seek mutual help, join in communities, and quit the woods our fathers lived in, build houses, join our habitations for mutual safety, stand by each other and protect the fallen, fight side by side at one signal, share the same walls and towers. But now the snakes are more harmonious than we are; the wild beast preys not on his kind: but as for man 't is not enough to have forged the fatal sword, though the first smiths knew only to make tools. But now we see whole peoples not content with killing in their passion, but they must eat each other. What would Pythagoras say, where would he run to, if he saw these monstrous doings, he who abstained from all kinds of meat and ate not every kind of vegetable ?—MACLEANE, *with modifications.*

---

1. Of **Volusius Bithynicus**, to whom this carelessly written letter is addressed, we know nothing.

3. The ibis does not eat snakes, although Herodotus (ii. 75, 76) and Cicero (*N. D.* i. 36) speak of it as destroying flying serpents.

4. **Nitet aurea,** *glitters in gold.* So **jacet obruta** (6), *lies in ruin.*

5. "Memnon's statue that at sunrise played" was *mutilated* (di-
midio). It was afterwards restored, perhaps by Septimius Severus.

7. Aeluros, *cats* (αἴλουρος). An emendation of Brodaeus, now generally adopted. P has *acruleos*, the other MSS. *caeruleos.*

9. Cepe = *cuepe.*

10. Haec = *talia.*

17. Abicit = *abjicit.*

19 sq. Concurrentia saxa Cyaneis. Either *the rocks that dash
against each other in the Cyanean sea* (i. e. the Symplegades), or
* *the rocks that clash with the Cyanean waves* (dative), or *the rocks that
dash against the Cyanean isles.* I prefer the first interpretation. Cf.
Soph. *Antig.* 966 : Κυανέων πελαγέων. Juvenal confounds the Symplegades, at the entrance of the Thracian Bosporos from the Euxine,
with rocks in the Sicilian sea which Circe advised Ulysses to avoid.

20. When Ulysses was leaving the island of Aeolus, the king gave
him a leathern bag containing all the winds. His companions let
them out of the bag, causing a tempest. (*Odys.* x. 19, 46.)

22. Et = *etiam.*

26. Canebat, chantait, = *recitabat.*

27. Junco. So P, Jahn, Hermann, Ribbeck, Mayor, Weidner.
There was a consul of the name of Juncus under Hadrian, A. D. 127
(Dissertazioni della pontificia Acad. Rom. di Archeologia vi. 231.)
From ignorance of this fact, other MSS. and editors altered the read-
ing to *Junio.*

28. Super, *above,* i. e. to the south of; up the country.

30. A Pyrra. As we say, *since the flood.* — **Syrmata.** For *tragoe-
dias.* Cf. viii. 229.

33. Finitimos. The term is used laxly.

39. Alterius populi. The people celebrating the festival were the
Ombites.

40. Inimicorum. The Tentyrites.

45. Quantum ipsi notavi. These words imply that their author
had visited Egypt. Most lives of Juvenal, following the pseudo-
Suetonius, relate that he was sent to Egypt, when eighty years of
age, as prefect of a cohort stationed at Syene, and that this, under
the appearance of an honorary appointment, was in reality meant as a
species of exile. The story is incredible in itself, and apparently derived from the present passage. (Mayor.)

46. Canopus, though in Egypt, was a cosmopolitan city, a centre
of Greek and oriental culture and luxury; and its manners were no
type of those of Egypt in general.

48. Inde, *on one side,* i. e. among the Ombites. — **51. Hinc,** *on the other side,* i. e. with the Tentyrites.

52. Haec tuba rixae, *this was the trumpet of the fray.* Cf. i. 169.

53–56. Dein . . . . integer. The two clauses connected by a conjunction (et) represent the action; the two added without any conjunction represent the effect of the action.

64. Domestica seditioni **tela,** *the familiar weapons of sedition.* Cf. Verg. *Aen.* i. 148–150.

65 sq. Hunc = *talem.* — **Qualis,** accusative plural. — Turnus et Ajax, sc. torquebant. — On the proper names, cf. Verg. *Aen.* xii. 896 sqq.; Hom. *Il.* vii. 268 sqq.; v. 302 sqq.

69. Genus hoc, *this race of ours.*

73. Aucti. Plural, appositive to the noun of multitude **pars.** — Pars altera, i. e. the Ombites.

76. There were groves of palm in the neighborhood of Tentyra.

77. Hinc = *ex hac parte,* on the side of the Tentyrites.

86. Te perhaps does not refer to Volusius, but is a bold address to fire itself.

88. Sustinuit, *had the heart to.*

90. Prima gula = qui primus gustavit hanc carnem.

93. The Vascones were a people of Spain on the upper Ebro. They had a town Calagurris (now *Calahorra*), of the man-eating of the inhabitants of which, when oppressed by siege A. U. C. 682, we read in Valerius Maximus vii. 6: qui quo perseverantius interempti Sertorii cineribus, obsidionem Cn. Pompei frustrantes, fidem praestarent, quia nullum jam aliud in urbe eorum supererat animal, uxores suas natosque ad usum nefariae dapis verterunt: quoque diutius armata juventus viscera sua visceribus suis aleret, infelices cadaverum reliquias sallire non dubitavit.

95. Ultima, sc. discrimina.

97. Miserabile debet esse, *ought to excite our compassion.*

102 sq. Esse, from *edo.* — **Et sua.** Cf. Ov. *Met.* viii. 877 sq.:

> ipse suos artus lacero divellere morsu
> coepit et infelix minuendo corpus alebat.

109. Q. Metellus Pius conducted the Sertorian war together with Cn. Pompeius.

110. Graias nostrasque **Athenas,** *the Grecian Athens and our own,* i. e. *the Grecian culture and our own.* — Athens is the worthiest metonym for intellectual and ethical culture, — the city *unde humanitas, doctrina, religio, fruges, jura, leges ortae atque in omnes terras*

distributae putantur (Cic. *pro Flac.* 62); the παίδευσις τῆς Ἑλλάδος
(Thuc. ii. 41), the κοινὸν παιδευτήριον πάντων ἀνθρώπων (Diodor.).

114. For the siege of Saguntum (Saguntus, Zagynthos, Ζάκυνθος), see
Liv. xxi. 7–15. Augustin (*Civ. Dei* iii. 20) says that it is believed
that some of the besieged citizens ate the corpses of their friends.

115. Tale quid excusat, *had excuse for any such conduct.* — The
Maeotic altar is the altar of the Tauric goddess, called by the Greeks
Artemis, on which all strangers who came to the country were sacri-
ficed. Cf. Eurip. *Iph. in Taur.*

117. Ut jam, *supposing only.*

119. Quis modo casus, *what mischance even.* On *modo* in the sense
of *even, at all,* cf. Cic. *Tusc.* v. 66 : quis est omnium, qui modo cum
Musis habeat aliquod commercium?

120. Hos, the Ombites. — **Vallo,** *their ramparts.*

122 sq. Anne .... Nilo? *could they, if the land of Memphis were
dried up, do anything worse to spite the Nile because he would not
rise?* Cf. Ov. *Met.* iv. 547 : invidiam fecere deae. Others (as Mayor,
Weidner), translate aliam invidiam facerent Nilo, *bring any greater
infamy* (or *odium*) *upon the Nile.* . Drought would cause famine.

124. By Britones Juvenal seems to mean the Britons, whose
human sacrifices were well known. As Juvenal in all other places
calls them *Britanni,* some suppose that the reference here is to some
German tribe.

133. Quae dedit, *in that she has given.*

134 sq. *She bids us, then, weep for the squalid plight of a friend
when he pleads his cause and is accused;* or as we should say, *who is
accused and pleads his cause.* Some inferior MSS. give *casum lugentis* instead of *causam dicentis.* Kiær would emend by reading **squa-
lorem atque** insteat of *squaloremque.*

137. Incerta is explained by some as meaning hard to be distinguished from a girl's, by others hard to be recognized (i. e. so that
it is not easy to tell *who* he is).

140. Minor igne rogi, *too young for the fire of the funeral-pile.*
Children who died before they had a tooth were buried, not burned.

140 sq. Face arcana. On the fifth day of the Eleusinian mysteries
the initiated carried torches to the temple of Demeter (Ceres), led by
a priest. Of every neophyte the hierophant demanded moral purity.
— Qualem esse, sc. *hominem.*

142. Ulla aliena sibi credit mala. Every one will remember the
noble verse of Terence (*Heaut.* i. 1, 29):

homo sum, humani nihil a me alienum puto.

143. Macleane takes **venerabile** as having an active meaning, *reverential,* or *capable of reverence,* which suits the context better than the passive sense. Forcellini cites two examples of the active use of this verbal from Valerius Maximus.

147. Prona **et terram spectantia,** sc. *animalia.* Cf. Ov. *Met.* i. 84–86:

> pronaque cum spectent animalia cetera terram,
> os homini sublime dedit, caelumque tueri
> jussit et erectos ad sidera tollere voltus.

Dryden adds a magnificent epithet in his translation of Ovid:

> "Man looks aloft, and with erected eyes
> Surveys *his own hereditary skies.*"

149. "Animus est quo sapimus, **anima** qua vivimus."

151. In populum, *into* one *people.*

157. Defendier. Notice this archaic form of the present infinitive passive.

160. Cognatis maculis, *kindred spots,* i. e. animals of the same species; the leopard recognizes the leopard and spares him.

166. Produxisse, *to have beaten out,* i. e. to have forged. "Producere" like "extendere" (168). — **Cum,** *although.*

67. Coquere, *to forge.*

68. Extendere = *excudere.*

170 sq. Sed crediderint = *sed qui crediderint,* the *qui* being suggested by *quorum* (169). Subjunctive, **because** *qui* = *tales ut ii.* Kiær makes *crediderint* a "dubitative" **subjunctive,** "quos credidisse probabile est."

174. The story that Pythagoras abstained from beans is probably a fable; but Juvenal follows the common tradition.

SATIRE XVI.

———··⊙⋅⊙⊙··———

ARGUMENT.

1-6. O GALLIUS, who can tell the advantages of lucky service? Give me a crack regiment, and I'll enlist and think my stars have favored me. Of course a fortunate hour avails one more than if he had a letter of recommendation to Mars from his wife Venus or his mother Juno.

7-34. First, the advantages that all soldiers enjoy. The greatest is that no civilian dares to strike you, nay more, if you strike him, he holds his tongue, and dares not show his grievance to the praetor. If he would have revenge he has his judge, a stout centurion in the camp, for soldiers may not go beyond for trial. Most just, no doubt, is the centurion's judgment, and if I've right upon my side he'll give me satisfaction. But all the camp will see that my revenge shall prove a greater trouble than the wrong. And he's a bold man who would dare offend so many boots and hobnails. And who would come so far to give his evidence? Let's dry our tears, nor trouble friends who will not fail to excuse themselves. The man who dares to witness to the assault is worthy of the good olden times: a lying witness may be easier got against a townsman than a true against a soldier's fortunes and his honor.

35-50. And if a scoundrel neighbor moves my landmark, or debtor will not give me back my own, then I must wait and go through all the law's delays; but soldiers are allowed their own time for suing and no drag stops their suit.

51-60. The soldier too may make a will while yet his father lives, for all he gets in service is his own. The old man therefore courts his lucky soldier who by fair favor is rewarded as his gallant deeds deserve. For 'tis the general's interest that the brave should also be the lucky and pride themselves upon their trappings and collars.— MACLEANE, *with modifications.*

———··⊶⊷··———

1. .It is idle to ask who is the **Gallius** (or Gallus, *Galli* P, *Galle* ω) to whom this unfinished satire is addressed.

2 sqq. Si . . . sidere, " if a fortunate corps is being entered, may

its gate receive me, a timorous recruit, under a favorable star."
Priscian quotes verse 2 twice, with *quod si* instead of the *nam si* of
the MSS.

6. Samia. Cf. Verg. *Aen.* i. 16.

8. Ne. . . . audeat follows illud erit (commodum), because "*subest
notio impediendi vel prohibendi*" (Hand. *Turs.* iv. 42).

9. Immo, *nay more.*

11. Offam, *swelling.*

12. Medico nil promittente, of which the doctor gives no hope.

13 sq. " He who would have redress for these injuries has assigned
to him for judge a Bardaic shoe, and big legs at big benches."   The
Bardaici or Vardiaci (called also Vardaei) were an Illyrian tribe.
The *Bardaicus calceus* represents here a centurion.   " Judicem dare
was properly said of the praetor urbanus, who could appoint, if he
pleased, a judex privatus to hear a private case at the instance of the
plaintiff. "   Here the praetor sends the plaintiff to a military court.

14. Grandes *dantur* magna ad subsellia *complenda* surae.   Cf. Nägelsbach *Stil.* § 122, 2.

15. More Camilli is not to be taken strictly, but represents generally the ancient military usages of Rome.

18. Cognitio, *the jurisdiction.* — Derit = *deerit.*

19. Justae querelae. Genitive of quality.

20. Each cohort was divided into six centuries or three maniples.

23. Corde, *understanding.* — Who Vagellius was we know not.

26. Tam Pylades, i. e. so devoted a friend. — Molem aggeris ultra,
beyond the mole of the rampart, i. e. within the rampart of the camp.
Agger is the rampart of Servius Tullius, which overlooked the praetorian camp.   A friend must be ready to give his life, as was Pylades,
or he must live so remote from the city as to have no cause to dread
the wrath of the praetorians, to be willing to give testimony in your
behalf against a soldier.

31. I will deem him such a man as the noblest worthies of the good
old times.   The Romans wore their hair long and their beards uncut
until 300 B. C., when barbers were introduced from Sicily.

33. Paganum, *a civilian.*   Properly, a rustic, a countryman.

34. Fortunam, the interests.—Pudorem, *honor;* good name.

36. Sacramentorum, *of military life.* Literally, of the soldier's oath.

38 sq. Medio, *intervening;* which separates our estates. — At the
Terminalia, every February, the owners of adjacent property made
offerings of cakes of meal and honey, etc., to the god Terminus.
Sometimes a lamb, or a sucking pig, was slaughtered. — Patulo,
        18—Juv.

broad. — Any one whose landmark was removed had an *actio termini moti* against the person who did it.

40. Pergit, etc., *persists in* not restoring money deposited with him. In this case the aggrieved party had an *actio depositi.*

41. Repeated from xiii. 137.

42 sq. *I shall have to wait for the year in which the suits of a whole people begin* (literally, which begins the suits, *etc.*). "These suits would be brought before the centumviral court. Suits could be begun only in the half year from the 1st of March to the 1st of September (Mommsen, *Histor.-Philolog. Gesellsch. Breslau,* 1857, i. 2, 1). If the suit was not brought to an end within a magistrate's year, *praescriptio,* or limitation ensued. To avoid this, it was necessary to await the beginning of a new magistrate's term of office, in order to obtain at least the longest possible time for the action. (Keller, *Litis Contestation,* 135 sq.) "

43. Tunc quoque == si litibus inchoatis petitori praetor formulam dedit, i. e. causam recepit.·

45. Sternuntur. I. e. with cushions.

45 sq. The court is broken up on some pretext or other, just as Caedicius is taking off his cloak to plead, or Fuscus is preparing himself for a long speech.

47. Lenta . . harena, *and we contend only with the retarding sand of the forum.* Instead of a contest *jure et disceptatione fori,* we have only the trouble of going away. (Weidner.) Others translate, "and the forum is but a slow arena for our combat."

49. Agendi, *of going to law.*

51 sqq. "According to Roman law, all the property amassed by a son during his father's lifetime belonged to the latter (was in his *potestas*), and could be disposed of by him only. The early emperors, with a view to making military service popular, allowed an exception to this law in the case of the earnings of soldiers. The *castrense peculium* was the private property of the soldier and at his disposal."

53. In corpore census, incorporated in the private fortune; a part of the property which was under the father's control.

54. Omne regimen, *unlimited control.* — The name Coranus may be borrowed from Hor. Sat. ii. 5, 55 sqq.

56 sq. Hunc —— labori, *such an one deserved favor advances, and returns its due rewards to his honorable service.* — **Favor** is a conjecture of Ruperti's, now generally adopted. The MSS. give *labor.*

60. The satire breaks off abruptly, and was evidently left unfinished.

THE FIFTH SATIRE OF PERSIUS.

———o○◦○◦oo———

THIS satire is addressed by **Aulus Persius Flaccus**, — the young
Etruscan nobleman, whose pure morals, attractive character, and untimely death excite an even greater interest than the few works he
left behind him, — to his friend and teacher, the philosopher, grammarian, and rhetorician **Lucius Annaeus Cornutus**. Persius went to
this distinguished master at the age of sixteen (A. D. 50 or 51) to be
instructed in the Stoic philosophy, and afterwards, it appears, received him into his house, leaving him at his death (A. D. 62) his
library and a large sum of money, of which the former only was
accepted by Cornutus.

  "In style no less than in matter" the fifth is generally regarded as
"*facile princeps* amongst the Satires of Persius." I give the Argument in the words of **Pretor.**

ARGUMENT.

  1-4. 'O that I had a hundred tongues!' says Persius.
  5-18. 'Why so?' (asks Cornutus): 'they are not needed by the
Satirist.'
  19-51. 'True enough: but I require them to enable me to sing your
praises worthily, that I may leave a fitting record of my gratitude to
you (21-29), of your kindness to me (30-40), and of our mutual
friendship (41-51).
  52-61. Men's lives are varied, but most men feel when life is ending that they lack something.
  62-72. You supply that want by bidding them seek philosophy
betimes;
  73-90. which alone can give a liberty far surpassing that of the
slave set free by the magistrate, or of the self-styled 'independent'
man;
  91-104. for no magistrate can impart to you a knowledge of the

real duties of life, and no man may do just what he pleases, but only
that for which nature has fitted him.

105–114. If philosophy has taught you to distinguish between
virtue and vice, and to free your soul from the dominion of the
passions, you are really and truly free;

115–123. but, if you are not entirely in the right, you *must* be altogether in the wrong.

124–131. You are thinking only of *bodily* slavery, and forget that
you may be the *slave of your passions:*

132–141. as of Avarice;

142–153. of Luxury;

154–160. (from one or other of which you are seldom altogether free;)

161–174. of Love;

175–179. of Ambition;

180–188. of Superstition.

189–191. Tell all this to a captain in the army, and he 'll laugh at
us for our pains.'

1, 2. Vatibus hic mos est, *this is a way bards have.* Examples
are familiar and abundant; cf. Hom. *Il.* ii. 488 sqq.; Verg. *Aen.* vi.
625; *Georg.* ii. 43; Ov. *Met.* viii. 532. Valerius Flaccus (vi. 36)
thinks a thousand mouths too few.—In carmina, *for the purposes of
song* (Conington).

3. Ponatur, *is set on the stage.* Others, *is taken in hand.*

4. Parthi may be either subjective or objective genitive; the
wounds may be those he inflicts, drawing his scimitar from (near) his
groin, or those from which he suffers, as he drags the dart that shot
him from his groin. The last interpretation is much to be preferred.

5 sq. Quantas ... **niti,** *what lumps of solid poetry are you cramming, so big that you require to strain a hundred throats?*

7. Nebulas Helicone legunto, *gather fogs on Helicon* (Macleane).

8,9. *If there be any who are going to set Progne's or Thyestes's pot
a boiling, to be the standing supper of poor stupid Glycon* (Conington). — Glycon was a tragic actor of those days, who could not understand a joke. "He was probably *too* tragic, and seemed as if he had
really 'supped full of horrors,' in spite of the frequent repetition of
the process."

10–13. *But you are not squeezing wind with a pair of panting
bellows, while the ore is smelting in the furnace, nor with pent-up
murmur croaking hoarsely to yourself some solemn nonsense, nor
straining and puffing your cheeks till they give way with a* "plop."
— Stloppo. A word occurring nowhere else, perhaps coined by Persius. The scholiast says, "*stloppo* dixit μεταφορικῶς, a ludentibus

pueris, qui buccas inflatas subito aperiunt, et totum simul flatum cum sonitu fundunt." **Stloppo** here represents the explosion of the poetic bombast which in the two preceding lines has been represented as gathering. Some MSS. read *scloppo*, and so Jahn (1868).

14. **Verba togae,** the language of every-day life at Rome, especially the simple and easy, but refined, *language of good society.* — Junctura callidus acri, "with dexterous nicety in your combinations." Cf. Hor. *A. P.* 47 sq.: dixeris egregie, notum si *callida* verbum reddiderit *junctura* novum; *A. P.* 242 sq.: tantum series juncturaque pollet, **tantum** *de medio sumptis* (cf. "verba togae") accedit honoris.

15. **Ore teres modico,** *with diction well-turned and smooth.* — **Pallentis radere mores,** *to rasp unwholesome morals.* **Pallentis,** pale from vice and its consequent diseases.

16. **Et ingenuo culpam defigere ludo,** *and carry off vice on your lance, in sport that's fit for gentlemen.*

17. **Mycenis.** Dative. " *Leave Mycenae its feasts.*"

18. **Capite et pedibus.** These were reserved to convince Thyestes of the real character of the food he had been eating.

Plebeia prandia. The full opposition is between banquets of an unnatural sort in the heroic ages at Mycenae, known in these days only as stage-horrors, with no lesson for life, "raw head and bloody bones," as Dryden renders it, and every-day meals (*prandia,* not *cenae*) of the simplest kind, in common society at Rome, which show ordinary men as they are. (Conington.) **Mensa** is contrasted with **prandia** (cf. Sen. *Ep.* 83, 6: *sine mensa prandium*) as *banquet* with *meal, Tafel* with *Tisch.* (Gildersleeve.)

Noris. The subjunctive used imperatively. *Novi* has no imperative of its own. And Persius does not hesitate to connect imperatives and imperative subjunctives; cf. Sat. iii. 73: disce nec invideas.

19. **Bullatis nugis,** " *air-blown trifles,*" "frothy nothings."

22. **Excutienda,** *to be sifted thoroughly.* (Conington and Pretor.) The metaphor is from shaking out the folds of a robe, to see if anything was concealed in them.

24. **Ostendisse.** Once for all. (Gildersleeve.)

Pulsa, *strike it,* knock against it; (to judge of its solidity by the ring.)

25. **Pictae tectoria linguae,** the stucco of a painted tongue, for " *painted tongue-stucco.*" (Conington, "the mere plaster of a varnished tongue.")

26. **Hic** = *in hac re.* Others read *his,* which would mean *ad haec.*

Deposcere. Notice the determination that lies in *deposcere.* (Gildersleeve.)

27. **Sinuoso in pectore,** "in the very recesses of my breast."

28. **Voce pura.** Opposed to *pictae linguae.*

29. **Fibra,** "*heart-strings.*"

30. "*When first the purple resigned its dreaded guardianship over me.*" — **Pavido.** I. e. trembling under those who watched over me.— **Purpura.** I. e. the *toga praetexta,* with its purple border, which was worn by boys, but laid aside when they took the *toga virilis.* On the praetexta as a symbol of sanctity, cf. Quint. *Decl.* 340 : sacrum praetextarum, quo sacerdotes velantur, quo magistratus, quo infirmitatem pueritiae sacram facimus ac venerabilem.

31. On the day when the *toga virilis* was assumed, the boy dedicated to the gods his bulla, his playthings, and his long locks.

Persius calls the Lares succincti, *girt up,* in allusion to the *cinctus Gabinus,* in which they were always represented ; the free movement of the body which this style of dress allowed befitted them as deities ever ready to act and help.

32 sq. **Cum blandi comites,** *when companions were enticing.* — **Totaque . . . Subura,** and my new *toga virilis* allowed me to go freely in every part of the town. — The Subura was the most thronged and the busiest part of Rome. Cf. Juv. iii. 5 ; xi. 51. — **Jam candidus.** No longer with the purple border, but *now all white,—toga pura,* the toga virilis. — **Umbo,** the gathering of the folds of the toga over the breast ; here put for the whole toga.

34. **Iter,** *the way* of life.— **Vitae nescius error,** ramblings, through ignorance of life.

35. **Deducit.** Certainly the right reading, although Jahn (1868) adopts *diducit.* Gildersleeve cites Schlüter's neat distinction : *homines in compita ubi viae diducuntur, deduci dicuntur.*— **Trepidas,** *bewildered.*—**Ramosa in compita,** to the fork where the roads branch off. Persius alludes to the old image of the two diverging paths, which represent the alternative offered to youth of virtue or vice, at the end of the unconscious life of infancy and childhood.

36. **Me tibi supposui.** "I threw myself as a son into your arms." (Gildersleeve.) "I put myself under your teaching." (Macleane.)

37 sq. **Fallere . . .** *sollers, your ruler, skilful to surprise, straightens my moral twists to which it is applied.*—**Intortos mores,** "my warped nature."

39. **Premitur,** *is moulded.* Or, *is broken in ;* cf. Verg. *Aen.* vi. 80. — **Vincique laborat,** *and struggles to be subdued.*

40. **Artificem,** *artistic,* finished. —**Ducit,** *takes on ;* "like saxa . . ducere formam (Ov. *Met.* i. 402)."

42. Primas noctes, *the early hours of the night.* — **Epulis.** Either "*for* feasts," or "*from* the banquet, (for study)."

43. Requiem, sc. *unam.*

45. Non with the imperative subjunctive, instead of the regular *ne*, is found also in Pers. *Sat.* i. 5. It is frequent in Juvenal.

46. Cf. Hor. *Carm.* ii. 17, 21 sq.: utrumque nostrum incredibili modo consentit astrum.—**Duci,** *are guided.* So Conington translates, although he says in his commentary, "*duci*, apparently = cepisse originem."

48. Nata fidelibus hora, *the birth-hour ordained for faithful friends.*

49. In, *between.* "**Dividit in Geminos,** like *dividere nummos in viros.*"

50. Gravem. The influence of Saturn was regarded in astrology as *malignant.* — **Nostro Jove,** *our own Jupiter,* Jupiter who to us is propitious.

51. Nescio quod astrum, *some star there is.* **Nescio quod** is a livelier substitute for *aliquod.* Conington most unaccountably prefers the reading **nescio quid.** We want the *adjective* pronoun here, not the substantive. — **Me tibi temperat,** *blends me with thee.*

52. Rerum usus, *the practice of life.* — **Discolor,** *of various hue;* "wears the most different colors."

53. Velle suum, *his own desire.* Persius is very fond of the use of the infinitive as a regular substantive. Conington cites i. 9: *nostrum istud vivere triste;* i. 27: *scire tuum;* i. 122: *ridere meum;* iii. 17: *pappare minutum;* iii. 18: *mammae lallare;* vi. 38: *sapere nostrum.*

54. Recenti, i. e. *eastern.* Conington compares Verg. *Georg.* i. 288: *sole novo* terras inrorat Eous.

55. Rugosum piper. "The shrivelling, being the effect of the sun, distinguishes it from the Italian pepper." — **Pallentis cumini.** Effect for **cause**; *pale* because *producing paleness.* Cf. Hor. *Epp.* i. 19, 18: *exsangue cuminum.* Cumin was a favorite condiment.

56. Inriguo turgescere somno, "to bloat himself with balmy sleep." Some take *inriguus* as implying that the man has well drunken; one commentator is vulgar enough to make it "sweaty."

57. Campo. The sports and athletic exercises of the Campus Martius. — **Decoquit,** *runs through with.*

59. Veteris ramalia fagi, "like the boughs of an old beech-tree." "Mr. Paley has suggested to me," says Pretor, "that φηγός and *fagus* are probably identical, and represent the edible acorn tree (*quercus*

aescula) rather than the beech as the latter word is ordinarily translated."

60. Crassos, *gross.* — Palustrem. I. e. *dimmed by marsh vapors*

61. Sibi, with *ingemuere.* (Con.) — **Relictam** = *ante actam.*

63 sq. Cultor introduces the metaphor which is carried on in *purgatas, inseris,* and *fruge.* **Purgatas,** *cleared of weeds.* **Insere aures
fruge,** a variety for *inserere auribus fruges.* **Fruge,** here of grain
for seed. (Conington.)

64. Fruge Cleanthea, *the grain of Cleanthes,* i. e. the pure doc-
trines of the Stoics.

65. Finem certum, *a definite aim.*

66. Idem cras fiet. I. e. "to-morrow will tell the same tale as to-
day."

66 sq. Quid ? quasi magnum nempe diem donas ? *What? do you
mean to say that it is as if it were a great present that you give me a
day?*

69. Egerit hos annos, *is baling out these years of ours.*

1. Cantum, *the tire;* here put for the wheel itself.

72. Cum, *seeing that.*

73 sqq. With this verse the real argument of the satire begins,
after the address to Cornutus. The theme is *libertate opus est.* —
Velina, sc. *tribu.* — "The name of a man's tribe is put in the ablative as a *whence* case." — **Non hac, ut** . . . . possidet, *not after the
prevalent fashion, by which each man that has worked his way up to
a Publius in the Veline tribe is owner of a ticket for a ration of
musty spelt.* (Gildersleeve.) — **Publius.** When a slave was given his
liberty he took his master's *praenomen* and gentile name. — **Tesserula.** A contemptuous diminutive. **Cf. Juv. vii.** 174, note.

75. Veri. Genitive.

76. Vertigo, *twirl.* "The reference is to the *manumissio per vin-
dictam,* which made a slave a full citizen, the lictor touching him
with the *vindicta,* the master *turning him round* and 'dismissing him
from his hand' with the words *hunc hominem liberum esse volo.*" —
Non tressis, *not worth three coppers.*

77. In, *in the matter of.* — Farragine, *a feed of corn.*

78. Momento turbinis exit, literally *by the motion of the twirl he
comes out* with a praenomen. Almost = "by the mere act of twirl-
ing."

79. Papae, *prodigious!* "Wondrous change!"

79-81. Marco . . . . tabellas. "After *this,* can anybody think of
his antecedents — hesitate about lending money on his security —

feel qualms when he is on the bench ? Impossible! he is a Roman—
his word is good for anything — so is his signature." (Conington.)

81. **Adsigna tabellas,** *put your seal to this document,* as a witness.

82. **Pillea** (pilea), *liberty caps,* which were put on the heads of
slaves when they were manumitted.

83–85. **An . . . Bruto.** So speaks the stable-boy, just become a
citizen.

84. With the second licet supply *mihi.*

85. **Bruto.** Than the very founder of Roman liberty. — **Mendose
colligis,** *your syllogism is faulty.*

86. **Stoicus hic,** *our stoic friend,* is Persius's way of describing
himself, like the common expression *hic homo,* ἀνὴρ ὅδε. (Conington.)
— **Aurem mordaci lotus aceto,** *his ear well rinsed with good sharp
vinegar.* Vinegar was used in cases of deafness.

87. **Licet . . . . tolle.** I deny your minor. " I deny both that you
have a *will,* and that you are *free* to follow it." -- **Pretor** makes the
stoic's admission (**reliqua accipio**) less comprehensive than the major,
and confined to the word *vivere:* " The mere fact that you are a living creature I admit ; the inference contained in *licet* and *ut volo* I
altogether deny."

88. **Vindicta.** Instrumental ablative.   Cf. verse 76, note. — **Meus,**
my own man.

90. **Masuri rubrica,** *the canon of Masurius.*   The allusion is to
Masurius Sabinus, an eminent lawyer in the reigns of Tiberius and
Nero, who wrote a work in three books entitled **Jus Civile.** — **Rubrica.** Because the titles and first few words of the laws were commonly picked out with vermilion.   Cf. **Juv. xiv.** 192, note. — **Vetavit** for *vetuit* is found nowhere else, except in a note of Servius on
Verg. Aen. ii. 201.   Gildersleeve compares Kirke White's " rudely
blow'd."

92. " *While I pull your old grandmother out of the heart of you.*"
Veteres avias, " old grandmothers' notions ;" " as we say, prejudices
which you imbibed with your mother's milk."

Non erat, it was not, *as you thought.*   Gildersleeve.

93 sq. **Tenuia** (trisyllable, as in **Verg.** *Georg.* i. 397, ii. 121, iv. 38)
rerum officia, *the delicate distinctions of practical duty.* — **Usum
rapidae vitae,** " *the right management of the rapid course of life.*"

95. **Sambucam,** *dulcimer ;* " a translation not *strictly* correct, although ' dulcimer ' suggests the exotic refinement of the *sambuca,* a
four-stringed instrument of Eastern origin, synonymous with culti-
vated luxury." — **Citius aptaveris,** "θᾶττον ἂν ἁρμόσαιας· written out,

citius aptaveris quam praetor det, but it is better not written out.
Notice the Perfect Subjunctive. 'You would sooner *succeed in
making* a dulcimer fit, sooner *get* a dulcimer *to fit* [the hand of] a
hulking camp-porter.'" (Gildersleeve.)

96. Stat contra, *confronts you.* Cf. Juv. iii. 290.

97. "*That no one be allowed to do what he will spoil in the doing.*"

98 sq. Publica **lex**, "the general code," "the universal law."—
Continet hoc fas, ut teneat vetitos inscitia debilis actus, *withholds
from* **weak ignorance** *the right of reaching* heights *of action forbidden it* (i. e. above its **capacity**). **Teneo**, *to attain, reach*, as in
teneo collem, teneo portum. Here, = to compass. So J. E. Yonge
(Journal of Philology, 1873), according to whom the argument of
verses 96–99 is as follows: Reason takes away that "*licet.*" 'You
may not do,' she says, 'what you will only spoil.' 'You *cannot* do,'
adds Nature herself, 'what is above your powers.' The ordinary
interpretation is very different: thus Conington translates, "It is a
statute contained in the general code of humanity and nature, that
ignorance and imbecility operate as an embargo on a forbidden action." Jahn takes *teneat* in the sense of *pursue*, instead of either
refrain from or *attain.*

100. Certo conpescere puncto examen, *to bring the index* of the
steel-yard *to rest at a certain point;* i. e. to weigh accurately. The
examen is the tongue or index of the *statera* (steel-yard).

102. Navem poscat sibi, *should ask for the command of a ship.*

103. Melicerta, a name for Palaemon, son of Leucothoe, identified
with Portunus, a protecting god of harbors.

104. Frontem, *modesty.* — De rebus, *from the world.*—Recto **talo**
= *uprightly.*

105. Veri speciem dinoscere, *to distinguish the semblance of truth*
(from its reality).

106. Ne qua (*species*) . . . auro, "*that no* seeming truth *give a
faulty ring, due to the copper underneath the gold.*"

107. Vicissim, *on the other hand.*

109. Presso lare, "*your establishment within your income?*"

111. Cf. Hor. *Epp.* i. 16, 63 sq.

112. *Without greedily gulping down the water of treasure-trove in
your mouth?* (Conington.) So Gifford: "Without finding like a
greedy glutton that your mouth waters at the sight of such a prize."

113. Haec mea sunt, teneo, *these qualities are mine, I possess them.*

114. Praetoribus ac Jove dextro, *by the favor of the praetors and
Jove as well.*

115. Nostre farinae, of our grain; "one of our batch;" i. e. of the Stoic school.

117. Relego, *I take back.* The word is used in Valerius Flaccus vi. 237 of drawing back a spear. — **Vapido in pectore,** in the musty cellar of your bosom.

118. Funem reduco, *I draw in the rope.* — The sum of the four verses 115–118 is thus given by Gildersleeve: If, despite your fair seeming, your smooth regal brow, you retain your old nature, and the old Reynard — the old rascal that swindled his master for a feed of corn — is still in your heart, I take back all that I have granted; you're a slave still.

119 sq. Nil . . . . est? *Reason has given you no power over anything; put out your finger, and you make a wrong move; and yet* (et = et tamen) *what action so trivial?*

120. Litabis, "taken in connection with the next line, has virtually the force of *impetrabis*."

122. Haec. I. e. stultum et rectum.

123. "You cannot dance in time even three steps of Bathyllus's satyr." — **Ad numeros moveri** is to take steps in time. — **Moveare** = *moveri potes.* — **Satyrum** is a kind of cognate accusative. — Bathyllus was a comic dancer in the time of Augustus. "The mention of him here is an instance of Persius's habit of looking rather to books than to life."

124. Unde datum hoc sentis, "who gave you leave to think so?" — Subdite, vocative. The thought is, *cum subditus sis.*

126. The strigiles (cf. Juv. iii. 263) would be carried to the bath, that the master might use them after bathing. Of course he would want *his own.* — Crispinus seems to be the name of the bath-keeper.

127. Servitium acre, *the goad of bondage.*

129. Quod nervos agitet, *to jerk your wires.*

130. Qui, *how.*

131. Atque = *quam.*

132. Heia, *come!*

133. Negas, *No,* say you.

134. Ponto, *from* Pontus.

135. Lubrica Coa. Probably, *gleaming Coan garments,* the gossamer-like silks of Cos. Others, "the oily (or laxative) Coan wines."

136. Recens, *"just in."* — **Primus,** *be the first to;* "forestall the market." — **Sitiente,** "thirsty from its journey over the desert, before the driver has had time to attend to its wants."

137. Verte, turn *something* over; your money or your stock. The scholiast interprets it, *negotiare, et speciem pro specie commuta.* — Eheu, *whew!*

138 sq. **Baro** (varo) *you lout* (Conington), "Querkopf," "Tölpel." — Regustatum ... *perages*, "you will go on to the end of the chapter satisfied with drilling a hole with your thumb in the salt-cellar that you've had so many a taste out of." Rubbing the salt-cellar into holes to get the last grain of salt expresses, as says Macleane, the extremity of poverty. — **Cum**, "*on good terms with*."

140. **Pueris aptas**, you are thrusting on the slaves; you are loading the slaves with. — **Pellem**, *a skin*, used perhaps as a packing-cloth. Others, "a peasant's coat of untanned hide, βαίτη."

142. **Rapias**, *scour.* — **Sollers**, *artful.*

143. **Seductum moneat**, *takes you aside for a warning.*

144. **Mascula** = *robusta.* — **Bilis** here implies madness.

146. **Tun** = *tu-ne.* — **Fulto** agrees with *tibi.*

147 sq. **Veientanumque** .... obba, *and shall a squab jug exhale the fumes of reddish Veientan spoilt by the fusty pitch?* — Casks and jars were pitched in order to preserve the wine.

149 sq. **Ut nummi** .... deunces, *that your money you had been nursing here at a modest five per cent., may go on to sweat out a greedy eleven per cent.?*

151 sq. **Nostrum** ... vivis, *your life is ours*, belongs to you and me: all we have now is that you live. Two other explanations are, only that part of life which you bestow on me is life; and, It is all in our favor that you are alive.

153. **Hoc quod loquor inde est**, *this very speech of mine is so much taken off from it.*

154. Cf. Verg. *Aen.* ii. 39: scinditur incertum studia in contraria vulgus. — **Duplici hamo**, *a couple of hooks.*

155 and 156. **Alternus**, *by turns.* — **Oberres**, *go at large.*

159. **Nodum**, "the knot, by which the chair is fastened to the bar of the door (*sera*). Cf. Prop. iv. 11, 26."

161–174. A dialogue between a confidential slave, *Davus*, and his young master, *Chaerestratus*, imitated from the *Eunuchus* of Menander.

163. **An** .... cognatis, *what! shall I be a standing disgrace in the way of my sober relations?*

165. **Udas**, *dripping.* Variously explained, as "with unguents," "with wine," "with tears," "with rain" (cf. Hor. *Carm.* iii. 10, 19 sq.: non hoc semper erit liminis aut *aquae caelestis* patiens latus).

169. **Puer**, *my boy.*

170. Trepidare, *to be restive.*

174. Hic, adverb. "If a man can make such a resolution and keep it, *he* is the free man, — not the lictor's whirligig."

175. Festuca, *straw,* stubble. "Plutarch, *de S. N. Vind.,* p. 550, says that one of the lictors threw stubble on the manumitted slave. The word appears to be technical, not used in a contemptuous sense. *Exfestucare* occurs in the laws of the Alemanni and Saxons, and elsewhere in mediaeval Latinity. Palgrave (Hist. of Normandy and England, vol. ii., q. v.) says, 'No symbol was of such universal application among ancient nations as the *stipula,* the *festuca,* the *culm,* the *hawm.*'" (Conington.)

176. Palpo, "*maker of smooth speeches.*"

177 sq. Cretata ambitio, "*the white-washed goddess of canvassing.*" (Conington.) The toga of candidates for office (*candidati*) was rubbed with chalk to make it whiter. — Vigila, "be up early;" "look alive."—Cicer ... populo."ply the scrambling rabble well with peas." (Pretor.) Cicer, *vetches,* a cheap article of food. — Nostra. I. e. celebrated in our aedileship. — Floralia. At the festival of Flora (28th April to 3d May) plays and brilliant games were exhibited, whose handsome preparation was one of the most important duties of a curule aedile. Among other customs of the festival, beans and vetches, the customary food of the lower classes, were thrown among the people, who scrambled for them to fill their bosoms. Cf. Hor. *Sat.* ii. 3, 182; Mart. viii. 78, 8.

179. Aprici = *apricantes.* — Quid pulchrius? Best taken as the comment of the old men upon the remembered splendors of the entertainment: *Was ever anything finer?* Jahn thinks it an ironical comment of Persius.

180. Herodis dies. According to the scholiast, the birthday of Herod the Great, which would naturally be celebrated by the Herodians. "Horace, in his various mentions of Judaism,evidently implies that it was spreading, talked of, if not favored by the higher orders."

180 sqq. Unctaque .... violas, *and the lamps, arranged in the greasy windows, supporting violet-wreaths, send up their unctuous clouds.* — The violae may have been either our violets or pansies.

182. Rubrum, "the common color of pottery." —Amplexa, *coiled round.*

183. Tumet, *bulges.*

184. Sabbata. "Persius seems to mix up feasts and fasts rather strangely, apparently with the notion that all the Jewish observances were gloomy."—Palles. Cf. Hor. *Carm.* iii. 27, 28.

185. Tum, *next.* — **Lemares,** *hobgoblins.* — **Ovo pericula rupto.** The scholiast says priests used to put eggs on the fire and observe whether the moisture came out from the side or the top, the bursting of the egg being considered a very dangerous sign. This observation was called ὠοσκοπική. (Conington and Jahn.)

186. Two kinds of superstition are indicated : the old one of Cybele, and the later one of Isis. — **Lusca.** " Blindness was a special visitation of Isis. The priestess is supposed to be called *lusca,* as having herself felt the wrath of the goddess." **187. Incussere deos inflantis corpora,** *strike into you the gods that have a way of swelling out men's bodies,* i. e. that send various diseases. — **Incussere.** Gnomic aorist.

188. Praedictum, *prescribed.*

189 sq. Dixeris .. ridet = *si dixeris, ridet.* — **Varricosos,** *i. e.* qui varices habent, qualibus laborare solent qui diu multumque stant vel pedibus eunt. (Jahn.) " *With the large calves,*" Conington. Others, *straddling.*

190. Crassum ridet, "*breaks into a horse-laugh.*"—**Fulfennius.** The name is written various ways in the MSS., as *Vulfenius, Pulfennius* (" Jahn's last "). Fulfennius was preferred by Jahn in his first edition, both as found in two MSS. *summae auctoritatis* and in an ancient inscription (Murat. p. 816, 7). But the question is one on the shadow of an ass. — **Ingens,** " huge;" " great, overgrown." " Persius hates the military cordially as the most perfect specimens of developed animalism, and consequently most antipathetic to a philosopher." (Conington, on Pers. Sat. iii. 77–87.)

191. *And bids " a clipped dollar" for a hundred Greek philosophers.*

·FINIS·